STRIKING INSIDE
ANGOLA WITH

32

BATTALION

Co-published in 2012 by:

Helion & Company Limited
26 Willow Road
Solihull
West Midlands
B91 1UE
England
Tel. 0121 705 3393
Fax 0121 711 4075
email: info@helion.co.uk
website: www.helion.co.uk

and

30° South Publishers (Pty) Ltd.
16 Ivy Road
Pinetown 3610
South Africa
email: info@30degreessouth.co.za
website: www.30degreessouth.co.za

Designed and typeset by 30° Kerrin Cocks
Cover design by 30° South Publishers (Pty) Ltd., South Africa
Printed in the UK by Henry Ling Ltd, Dorchester, Dorset
and in South Africa by Pinetown Printers (Pty) Ltd, Pinetown, KwaZulu-Natal

Front cover: 'David meets Goliath': An original photograph depicting the inferior SADF armoured vehicle, a Ratel 90mm, capturing and destroying the more superior Soviet T-54/55 tank (100mm) during Operation *Askari* in early 1984 inside Angola. This photograph epitomizes the conflict. Many more such encounters followed later at Cuito Cuanavale. *South African Department of Defence Documentation Centre*

ISBN 978-1-920143-67-1 (South Africa)
ISBN 978-1-907677-77-9 (UK)

British Library Cataloguing-in-Publication Data

A catalogue record for this book is available from the British Library

STRIKING INSIDE ANGOLA WITH

32

BATTALION

MARIUS SCHEEPERS

30° South Publishers (Pty) Ltd

Helion & Company Ltd

Map of South West Africa and Angola showing important place names in 1983 during the Angolan bush war.

COLONEL JAN D BREYTENBACH DVR, SD, SM, MMM

[handwritten signature]

"Without the aid of signallers, we would have gone nowhere"
—Colonel Jan Breytenbach, founder of 32 Battalion

*With much appreciation for the support received when writing this book
from my beloved wife, Caren
and my two wonderful children, Darius and Clarisse
and for sharing an exciting but peaceful life.*

And Jesus answering them began to say ... "And when ye shall hear of wars and rumors of wars, be ye not troubled: for such things must needs be; but the end shall not be yet. For nation shall rise against nation and kingdom against kingdom ... And then shall they see the Son of man coming in the clouds with great power and glory."[1]

---

[1] *The Bible*, Matthew 24:6-30

CONTENTS

List of maps and illustrations

INTRODUCTION

The Angolan bush war fascinates many people. This book provides eye-witness accounts from a signals officer while undertaking national service with arguably the most formidable battle unit that ever existed in the history of the South African Defence Force: 32 Battalion. It describes how members of 32 Battalion lived and acted during the Angolan bush war during 1983 under the most difficult conditions.

The events described in this book took place during a period of southern African history when the South African Defence Force (SADF) made the most advances and achieved the greatest successes in battle. At the time the SADF had almost free reign in the southern region of Angola. This period could probably be best described as the year when the SADF reached its peak in the bush war.

Being the Signals Officer of 32 Battalion, the author observed 32 Battalion's manoeuvres and was present when commanders took decisions during operations. The unit established several military bases inside Angola from where clandestine operations were mounted. The reader is taken on a journey with 32 Battalion during these operations.

This book presents interesting reading but it is never its aim to give comprehensive accounts of all the unit's military actions during this period. Many records were unfortunately destroyed. Some documents included in this book were generated under extremely difficult conditions. Documents were, perhaps, drafted in the shade of a mopane tree deep in Angola while under enemy fire. It is mind-boggling how several thousand important records have been preserved over all these years.

The writer does not claim to be a military expert; he is a civilian, currently running a law practice. He does not use precise military terminology to describe events, but he qualifies to present this account because he is able to interpret information as he was present when these events took place. He also gives a brief summary of other major battles that followed and preceded this important year, to complete the story.

Many precious young lives were sacrificed during the Angolan bush war. If anything described herein appears to come across as insensitive, the writer apologizes. It is not his intention to cause distress.

The writer also restricts this story to operations inside Angola during 1983 by 32 Battalion only. The hundreds of records available involving soldiers who served under similar harsh conditions inside South West Africa cannot be discredited just because these accounts are not covered herein. The writer decided not include such records as others are more qualified to do so.

In all, the reader should be able to judge for himself what happened in Angola during this period. This story was rarely told by returning SADF members for various reasons, mostly personal, but primarily because of the strict restrictions of confidentially imposed on the media. The Angolan bush war was a secret war. At the same time, life in South Africa continued almost unhindered. Relatives and friends had no idea what their loved ones were going through while serving on 'The Border'.

After all these years, the original source documents have now been declassified (on my request) and information covered in this book is now in the public domain.

I dedicate this book to all those who served and, particularly, all those who suffered and paid the ultimate price for their country. God bless them and their loved ones.

—Marius Scheepers, Pretoria, April 2012

PROLOGUE

Right at the beginning, on this bright new Sunday morning, I wish to reaffirm our view that not only this one, but every Sunday is special, if we remember that it was on a Sunday that our Saviour rose from the grave. However, on this Sunday we are also here with the purpose of commemorating our fallen comrades.

As an introduction to our main event, I would like to hold up to you a short sketch from our mutual past. Although it is of course in time and place bound to a certain period in the bush war, I am sure that every veteran here will be able to recognize elements with which he can really identify.

Do you remember the broad, flowing waters of the Kavango river as it turns south past Buffalo towards the training area and Botswana? The tall, cool trees on its sandy banks with the assortment of buildings scattered underneath; the messes, stores, troop lines and the Kimbo near the graveyard, that for many made out our home away from home?

Can you, in your mind's eye, see the platoons marching through the early morning freshness to morning parade? Do you hear their vibrant singing? Do you feel their pulsing life?

Can you still feel the sudden entry of quiet excitement, and methodical preparation when a new operation is in the air?

Can you ever forget the long drive on an open Kwêvoël, sitting in the glaring sun while the swirling white dust settles over everything? Or the perpetual clinging to a swaying, bundu-bashing Buffel, while sticks and leaves and all sorts of flora shower down your neck?

Do you remember how, initially, three days' rat packs were actually enough for the first five days in the bush, and you could afford to discard stuff like dog biscuits and mixed veg? Do you remember filling your water bottles with welcome rainwater caught from your bivvy, or in *shona* marshes smelling of cow dung?

Can you still smell the sweetish, oily vapour of avtur and hear the high-pitched whining of an Alouette slowly swinging its sweeping rotor blades into action, the black muzzle of the 20 mill canon thrusting from its side?

Can anyone forget the incredible weight of a *mushila* freshly packed for days of action, which you had to carry through that soft sand of southern Angola? Can you still feel the close, personal sanctuary of your foxhole in the night? Seeing the pensive moon, and the same Southern Cross that was also shining over your loved ones down in 'the States'?

Will you ever forget the sudden eruption of a contact, the tightness in the throat and the intense focus during the firefight? The sharp, somehow muffled reports of rifle and machine-gun fire in the bush, the hollow, sucking thumps from mortar tubes, and the subsequent crash of their bombs exploding in the sand around you? Do you hear "*Avança!*"? And afterwards the dry, smoky smell of battle, the excited, often sobering, stock-taking of casualties—on both sides?

Can you recall the heart-warming clapping beat of a Puma's rotor blades as it banks in the air towards the smoke that marks your position, bringing fresh ammo, rats and life-giving water in plastic bags—or to lift out a casualty ... a young friend, a comrade?

Can you still experience that feeling of tired fulfilment that flows through you at the end of a mission, settling yourself on the floor of an overloaded Puma, looking at the black, sweaty faces of the others in their dirty camo, to be lifted out of the ops area to Eenhana, Elundu or wherever? For the first wash in weeks and that indescribable taste of the first two gulps of cold Castle [beer]?

Do you remember the return to Buffalo, weary but contented, smiling and greeting but inwardly reflective? Gathering in the mess that evening for robust celebration of life ... acutely aware of death?

Do you remember knocking out the bottoms of tankards of those comrades whose lips would never touch them again, have forever fallen silent, while outside the setting sun turns the flowing waters of the river the colour of blood?

Do you remember? Do you remember them ... ?

Those comrades, still silently waiting for the Bright Morning Star
to herald that great last Sunday
That will dispel
the black velvet of death
To reveal
the serenely flowing River of Eternal Life.[1]

---

[1] An address delivered by the Chairperson of 32 Battalion VA, Colonel Stefanus van der Walt, on 23 May 2010 commemorating Savate Day.

PART 1:

ENTERING INTO AND THE SCENE INSIDE ANGOLA

INTRODUCTION

This is an account of a South African Defence Force national serviceman's experiences while serving his beloved country, South Africa. During the Angola bush war, during the years 1982 and 1983, I had the privilege of joining the notorious 32 Battalion while on covert operations in Angola. During my 13 months' stay inside southern Angola, I saw much action and witnessed the running of all 32 Battalion's operations. I was present at the Tactical Headquarters while operations took place, as Signals Officer of this unit. It was my responsibility to establish and maintain all signals communications during these operations; this was a daunting task.

It begins in the office of the Commander in Chief of the Army Gymnasium at Heidelberg, Transvaal (now Gauteng). I had not yet turned 19 and I had already completed my first year's military training. The Gym's intake for that year was approximately 1,100 recruits from all walks of life. The training consisted of three months' basic training, four months' leadership training and a four-month officer's course. The mental, physical and theoretical training which we received at the Gym were invaluable and thoroughly prepared us for what lay ahead. We were now proper signallers, eager to meet all challenges that would be thrown at us. I was promoted to the rank of second lieutenant in the Signal Corps of the South African Army after I completed my training.

Physical training at the Army Gymnasium, Heidelberg. Major de Wet is on the left.

Approximately 60 newly commissioned officers were gathered in the Commanding Officer's office during late November 1982. Among this group were approximately 20 officers who had matriculated the previous year. The remainder of the group consisted of Electronic Engineering graduates. Colonel Smit called out the names, one by one, of those who were designated to serve somewhere on the South West African (now Namibian) border with Angola. I realized the significance of the occasion when only three people remained present awaiting their assignment. The tension was tangible. The colonel said that each of us had been selected for special duty. First, he named the person designated for the Bushman 201 Battalion which was based in the Caprivi Strip, South West Africa. He then named the person to serve at 61 Mechanized Battalion at Omuthiya, near Oshivello in South West Africa. I was the last person in the room. He told me that I was required to serve in 32 Battalion.

I believe that I accepted this challenge for a number of reasons but mainly because I had been raised in a family where my father and two elder brothers were already commissioned as officers in the South African Defence Force.

Another motivation was an incident that took place on 12 August 1981 at the Secondary School Voortrekkerhoogte which I had attended in Pretoria. I was the headboy of the school that year. This incident left a lasting impression on me. We arrived at the school that day to discover that members of an Umkhonto we Sizwe (MK) group, the African National Congress's military wing, had launched a number of rocket attacks in the area, and two had exploded at our school during the night. The school had to be evacuated for a while to clear the area where the rockets had exploded, but fortunately no damage was caused. The attack took place under cover of darkness; MK launched the attack from about seven kilometres away, from Laudium, an Asian suburb, with six 122mm rockets. Little damage was caused but one domestic worker was slightly wounded. In their rush to flee the scene of the launching, the terrorists shot and wounded a 17-year-old youth named Zahed Patel. They then hurried to their Mooiplaas hideout, where they remained while a massive manhunt was launched. After four days they left the country and made their way back to a military training camp in Mozambique. Agents from Canada, Great Britain, Belgium and Mozambique were all involved in the execution of this attack.[1]

This flawed attack was regarded as a cowardly act as a school was the target. Similar incidents, I thought, should be avoided at all costs, and I saw myself as part of this effort.

In early December 1982 I departed from Waterkloof air force base, Pretoria in a C-130 Hercules aircraft, generally referred to as a 'Flossie'. I arrived at Rundu Sector 20 Headquarters in South West Africa. This was the headquarters of 32 Battalion where I received my military kit, including an AK-47 automatic assault rifle of Soviet origin, special camouflage uniform and Special Forces boots which were unique to 32 Battalion. The next leg of my journey was in a DC-3 'Dakota' aircraft to Ondangwa air force base situated in Ovamboland, near Oshakati, the Sector 10 Headquarters. From here I was airlifted by Puma helicopter to a temporary base at the Tactical HQ Operation Dolfyn at Ongiva airport in southern Angola.

Colonel Eddie Viljoen was 32 Battalion's Officer in Command (1OIC) and Captain, later Major, Jan Hougaard was the 32 Battalion Operations Commander at the Tactical HQ Operation Dolfyn at Ongiva at that time.

I also reported to Major C.H. Kruger, the Signals Corps commander at Sector 10 at Oshakati, as our command for our operations in Angola was situated at Oshakati.

32 Battalion's operational HQ was based at Ongiva airport, approximately five kilometres from Ongiva town. Ongiva is situated 40 kilometres from the border, called the *kaplyn*, or cut-line. I remained there for seven months.

Thereafter, 32 Battalion relocated its headquarters to Tactical HQ Ionde, which was situated farther northeast into Angola. I remained at Ionde for the next six months. At that time, the area south of Cuvelai and east of Xangongo was under SADF control.

The year 1983 can generally be regarded as the pivotal year of the Angolan bush war. Dur-

The cut-line, or *kaplyn*, which formed the border between Angola and South West Africa. (Photo Riaan Cloete)

ing this period the war zone in southern Angola was firmly secured and dominated by our SADF forces. Operation Askari was to follow at the end of the year and thereafter a Joint Military Monitoring Team was established between the opposing forces. This led to the voluntary and partial withdrawal of our forces from Angola.

Ondangwa airport near Oshakati in South West Africa.

Oshakati in Ovamboland, South West Africa. Sector 10 HQ was at Oshakati.

Commanding Officers in South West Africa (Windhoek)

General Officer Commanding South West Africa (SADF and South West Africa Territory Force): Major-General Charles Lloyd
Commanding Officer SAAF (South West Africa): Brigadier Bossie Huyser

Military units at Sectors 10 and 20 in South West Africa

Sector 10 (Kaokoland and Ovambo)
Sector 10 Officer Commanding: Brigadier A.J.M. 'Joep' Joubert (SADF)
Officer Commanding 310 AFCP: Colonel Dick Lord (SAAF)
Signals Corps Commander: Captain C.H. Kruger

HQ Oshakati
4 modular battalions: 51 at Ruacana, 52 at Oshakati, 53 at Ondangwa and 54 at Eenhana
SWATF 101 Battalion at Ondangwa and 102 Battalion at Opuwa, 61 Mechanized Battalion at Omuthiya, 25 Engineering Squadron at Oshakati, 5 Maintenance Unit at Ondangwa and a training unit at Oshivelo

Sector 20 (Kavango and Western Caprivi)
Sector 20 Officer Commanding: Colonel Deon Ferreira (SADF)
Sector 20 Signal Corps Commander: Captain Roos

HQ Rundu
55 Battalion at Nepara, 32 Battalion at Buffalo, SWATF 201 or 31 Battalion at Omega base, 202 Battalion at Rundu and 203 Battalion at Mangeti

THE CONFLICT IN ANGOLA

Temporary helicopter administration area (HAA) at Mupa.

During 1983 the South African Defence Force was in control of the southern part of Angola, an area which stretches roughly from the Calueque dam and Xangongo (120 kilometres from Ongiva) in the west, just south of Cuvelai and Vinticete in the north, Ionde (120 kilometres from the border) in the east and to the South West African border with Angola to the south. During this period 32 Battalion concentrated its operations mainly in the Nehone, Dova and Mulola areas and more to the north, the Mupa area (130 kilometres from the border) and south of Cuvelai.[3] 32 Battalion's boundaries for these operations were set as follows:

- North: 8400WN–1106XN–6000XN
- West: 8400WN–Road to Evale
- South: Evale direct line to Nehone–1050XM–6050XM
- East: 6050XM–6000XN

No 32 Battalion activities were allowed north of the 30 northern measures (WN). Also, 1 Parachute Battalion, the 'Parabats', was positioned at Xangongo to the west. The Parabats and 32 Battalion were not included in the same operations after an incident during 1982 when 32 Battalion's Sergeant J. Conroy was unfortunately killed by members of the Parabats. The two platoons had crossed paths and the Parabats opened fire on the 32 Battalion platoon. I have been told from many sources that Sergeant Conroy attempted to show himself to the Parabats by ripping open his shirt to display his white skin in an attempt to stop their firing on his platoon, but was instantly killed by shrapnel. Numerous inquiries were made into the incident. Normally, it is expected of commanders to avoid incidents of friendly fire at all costs.[4]

The DISA force (UNITA) operated at Anhanca and Ionde to the east and in a very large chunk of territory in the eastern and southeastern regions of Angola.

During the Angolan bush war, which continued from 1974 until 1989, the SADF engaged in mainly counter-guerrilla warfare against PLAN (People's Liberation Army of Namibia), the military wing of SWAPO (South West African People's Organization). SWAPO was assisted by the military wing of the MPLA party in Angola, FAPLA, the People's Armed Forces for the Liberation of Angola, or *Forças Armadas Populares de Libertação de Angola*, as well as Soviet and Cuban advisers. During 1983 alone, approximately 25,000 Cuban soldiers served and aided the ruling party in Angola, the MPLA.[5]

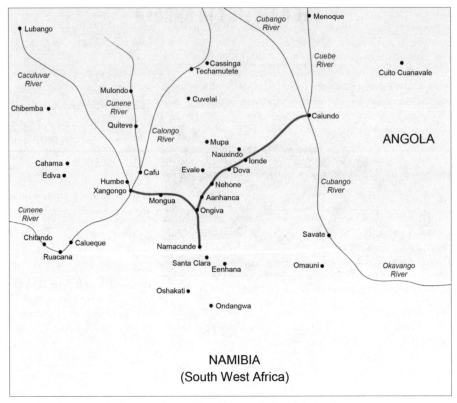

Map of southern Angola showing where 32 Battalion was deployed during 1983.

The MPLA is the People's Movement for the Liberation of Angola—Labour Party or *Movimento Popular de Libertação de Angola—Partido do Trabalho*, with *Partido do Trabalho*, or Labour Party, being appended in 1983. The MPLA declared Angola's independence on 11 November 1975, the day the Portuguese abandoned the capital Luanda. In 1976 MPLA overtly adopted Marxism-Leninism as the party ideology. It maintained close ties with the Soviet Union and the Communist bloc, establishing socialist economic policies and a one-party state. Poet and freedom fighter Agostinho Neto became the first president upon independence, succeeded by José Eduardo dos Santos in 1979.[6]

The events of 1983 were preceded by several large military operations inside Angola. I will deal briefly with a few of these larger operations.

The first military confrontation with SWAPO took place on 26 August 1966 at Ongulumbashe during Operation *Blou Wildebees* when a SWAPO base was attacked by 30 South African policemen (SAP) in eight helicopters. Twenty to 30 SWAPO cadres were in the base and two were killed. This was the only SWAPO base that ever existed inside South West Africa during the Angolan bush war. One of the force members who participated in the attack was Colonel Jan Breytenbach who later founded 32 Battalion.[7]

The South African government became involved in the Angolan conflict after certain African heads of state, supported by the CIA, asked for support to counter the communist

Chinese presence. There were fears that the localized conflicts would escalate into a superpower theatre of the Cold War. South African Prime Minister B.J. Vorster, anxious to be seen as a reliable African partner consistent with his Détente initiative, concurred. Operation Savannah was the result.[8]

This operation was instigated by the need to protect engineers constructing the Calueque dam near Ruacana. Unruly UNITA soldiers had taken over the protection of the dam, putting the construction at risk. In response, an armoured task force was dispatched to secure Calueque and from this Operation Savannah evolved. By the end of September 1975, the South African government had approved a four-phase plan to assist the FNLA and UNITA liberation movements in Angola against the communist MPLA.

Phase 4 had as its objective the capture of Luanda. This was almost achieved with SADF arriving at the outskirts of the city, before being turned back at the behest of the CIA who had got cold feet.

During May 1978 Operation Reindeer was launched, the first of a series of incursions into Angola which were to extend over the next decade. This first pre-emptive strike over the border included an attack on SWAPO's training camp at Cassinga (approximately 250 kilometres north of the border),and an attack on the SWAPO base at Chetaquera (approximately 30 kilometres north of the border). The training camp at Cassinga was initially bombarded by SAAF jet aircraft and then attacked by Parabats. More than 600 SWAPO members were killed, while the South Africans lost six men.[9]

During 1980 32 Battalion, commanded by Colonel Ferreira, conducted its most memorable operation, Operation Tiro-a-Tiro at Savate. Savate, situated on the Cubango River, 75 kilometres north of the South West African–Angolan border, served as a base for a FAPLA brigade. Piet Nortjé describes the operation in his book, *32 Battalion: The Inside Story of South Africa's Elite Fighting Unit*.[10] Two 32 Battalion companies, a mortar group, and 32 Battalion Recce Wing took part in the operation with little helicopter air support. After poor intelligence was received from a secret source, the Recce Wing, led by Captain Willem Ratte, discovered that Savate housed an under-strength FAPLA brigade and that 14.5mm AAA (anti-aircraft artillery) guns were also present. With the attack due to commence, the force was still misguided as to the exact location of the base and its strength. Captain Ratte was by this time unable to relate this information due to communication problems. On 21 May 1980 the attack commenced and the FAPLA force fled after numerous contacts with 32 Battalion who managed to capture Savate, which was subsequently occupied by UNITA. However, 15 32 Battalion members were killed and 22 wounded during the attack. FAPLA lost 558 men. The base consisted of 1,060 FAPLA troops; the strength of 32 Battalion force was only 300 men. (The 32 Battalion Veterans' Association annually commemorates Savate Day.)

Between 1981 and 1986 the Soviet Union supplied vast amounts of military aid to the MPLA, supplying the Angolan government with more than US$2 billion in aid in 1984 alone.[11]

In 1981, under the newly elected United States President Ronald Reagan's administration, Assistant Secretary of State for African Affairs, Chester Crocker, developed a 'linkage' policy tying Namibian independence to a Cuban withdrawal and subsequent peace in Angola.[12] The United States now showed its hand in the conflict, escalating its military aid to UNITA and working to expand recognition of UNITA's Jonas Savimbi as a key US ally in an important Cold War struggle. In January 1986 Reagan invited Savimbi for talks at the White House. Following this meeting, Reagan spoke of UNITA winning a victory that "electrifies the world". Two months later Reagan announced the delivery of Stinger surface-to-air missiles as part of a US$25-million aid package to UNITA,[13] bizarrely with strict instructions to UNITA that their southern African ally, the SADF, was under no circumstances allowed access to the Stingers.

In August 1981 Operation Protea was launched, described as the biggest mechanized offensive by South Africa since the Second World War. During the campaign 4,000 tons of weapons were seized, including ten Soviet T-34 tanks, four PT76 amphibian tanks and two 'Stalin Organ' rocket launchers. A few months later, in November 1981, Operation Daisy followed, thrusting 240 kilometres into Angolan territory. SWAPO lost 1,493 men in 1981, while the South African losses amounted to 54 troops.[14]

During 1983 SWAPO's pressure in northern South West Africa increased. In addition to landmine detonations, political murders and kidnapping, which continued unabated, 14 SWAPO units, each consisting of 50 men, invaded Ovamboland and Kavango in February 1983.[15] The South African Defence Force announced in May 1983 that 309 of these SWAPO members had been killed, but that some had succeeded in penetrating into the white farming districts of Tsumeb, Otavi and Grootfontein.[16]

I was part of Operation Meebos, Operation Snoek and Operation Dolfyn (or Sevta), which took place during 1982 and 1983, when mainly 32 Battalion units were operating inside Angola to prevent SWAPO from reaching South West Africa from their Angolan bases.

Operation Askari was launched in December 1983 to prevent similar infiltrations. Approximately 2,000 SADF troops invaded Angola and advanced to Cuvelai, 200 kilometres north of the border, without any notable resistance. The SWAPO headquarters were situated in the area and when the SADF attacked the 11th FAPLA Brigade, two Cuban battalions rushed to the fray to assist. It took a fierce three-day battle before the SADF was able to occupy Cuvelai. SWAPO and the FAPLA lost 324 men between them, with the South Africans officially reporting that their losses amounted to 21 dead, more than in any previous battle.

A few months later, after the battle of Cuvelai, South Africa and Angola negotiated a ceasefire.[17]

Casualty figures (KIA) for SWAPO and the SADF for this three-year period are shown at right. Sector 10 operational statistics also provide the number of incidents that took place in Ovamboland, South West Africa as per the table below:

Year	SWAPO	SADF
1981	1,494	61
1982	1,280	77
1983	913	96

SWAPO and SADF personnel losses. Source: Brig-Gen R.S. Lord, OC Air Force Command Post[18]

Period	EF Killed	EF Captured	OF Killed	OF Wounded
7–31 March 1983	49	7	7	46
1–4 April 1983	25	3	2	23
9–27 April 1983	33	6	3	24
1–16 May 1983	30	1	2	24
19–28 May 1983	8	2	5	0
1–30 June 1983	64	7	2	0
1–31 July 1983	32	10	2	15

EF = enemy forces;
OF = own forces

Source: SANDF Military Archives.[19]

By the end of the war, FAPLA and SWAPO had lost 11,291 soldiers; however, this is most likely understated as FAPLA and SWAPO records are notoriously minimalist. The official number of SADF members who lost their lives is 715.[20] This is a ratio of almost 16:1 enemy to

SADF losses. The official number of number of South West African civilians killed is 1,087. A SWAPO source, Horace Campbell provides his own interpretation of the situation:[21]

> From 1981–1988 the racist army occupied the Angolan provinces of Cunene and Cuando Cubango. FAPLA, the Angolan army, was not prepared for this massive invasion of over 11,000 SADF troops with the most sophisticated artillery pieces. The SADF was seeking to perfect a form of air-land battle, where the air force carried out operations in conjunction with the army. The provincial capital of Cunene at Ngiva was sacked. Over 100,000 peasants fled their homes. The South African army stole cattle, which it carried off to Namibia to feed its troops.

This is a form of cheap propaganda and totally devoid of the truth and should be rejected as such.

During 1983 various operations were launched against SWAPO which preceded the major offensive, Operation Askari, at the end of the year. One such offensive that took place during the middle of the year was the deployment of the largest contingent of South African troops on foreign soil since the Second World War. The force was named Task Force Oscar, consisting of Combat Group Bravo, with Combat Groups Alpha and Charlie in reserve. However, the operation was put on hold for political reasons. I was part of the planning and the supplying of all radio communications during these initial stages of what was to later become Operation Askari. In 1983 32 Battalion was responsible for holding ground in the area between Xangongo and Ionde, roughly 200 kilometres wide and stretching approximately 120 kilometres into Angola north of the border. 32 Battalion was deployed to serve as a buffer to prevent and monitor all attempted SWAPO infiltrations into Ovamboland in South West Africa.

Various tactics were used against the SWAPO insurgents, including laying ambushes, launching surprise attacks on enemy bases and searching for and destroying enemy caches containing supplies and ammunition. A comprehensive network of observation posts was established to detect the enemy.

32 Battalion's operations were directed only against SWAPO to prevent SWAPO from launching terrorist attacks against the local population of South West Africa who were ostensibly neutral in the conflict. It was the aim of SWAPO's 'liberation struggle' to win the 'hearts and minds' of the local people through Maoist-Stalinist-type terror in order to acquire independence for South West Africa from South African rule, and to introduce a marxist government with close ties to the Soviet Union. Independence was later achieved in the early 1990s, but only after the collapse of global communism, South Africa's s withdrawal from the territory and free and fair democratic elections.

UNITA's forces

UNITA, sometimes referred to as DISA or 'Silver Force', under the leadership of the charismatic Dr Jonas Savimbi, generally operated in the east of Angola. UNITA's ethnic and regional support base was in the Ovimbundu heartland of central Angola. UNITA was closely allied to South Africa and the USA and was one of the three liberation movements during the Angolan civil war. UNITA officially declared war against the MPLA on 21 August 1975. 32 Battalion and UNITA, however, tended to avoid one and another, not being on the friendliest of terms, as many 32 Battalion members were ex-FNLA, with little love lost between the two liberation movements.

During April 1983 UNITA directly assisted the SADF and acted actively against SWAPO. They were deployed in the south of Angola, with their Brigade HQ in the Namaiaca/Naema area controlling two companies situated northeast of Anhanca, and with another one and a half companies at Chitando.[22] At each position UNITA was issued with B22 HF radios to communicate. (Details of UNITA–SWAPO clashes are described later in this book.) SWAPO saw UNITA as a threat in these areas, as UNITA was able to successfully indoctrinate the local population against SWAPO. Little needs to be said about the UNITA forces located in southern Angola, save that they were essentially a rough group of bandits who basically lived off the land and the local peasantry. 32 Battalion, on numerous occasions, did their 'dirty' work by secretly attacking FAPLA targets and giving UNITA the credit. This was all part and parcel of the clandestine war that raged inside Angola.

In the latter part of the 1980s, UNITA was forced to become more actively involved in the conflict when FAPLA and Cuban forces were driven out of the Mavinga region by the SADF during 1986, and again during the major offensive at Cuito Cuanavale during 1987/88. During this battle, countless UNITA soldiers died. It is said that the tracks of the SADF Olifant tanks had to be cleared after each attack of corpses and body parts of fallen UNITA soldiers entangled in the wheels.[23]

32 BATTALION'S OPERATIONS INSIDE ANGOLA PRECEEDING ASKARI

December 1982 was, as usual, with the onset of the rainy season, the start of SWAPO's annual infiltration into South West Africa.[24]

On 4 December a group of SWAPO attacked a settlement south of Xangongo, killing one civilian and wounding four. Another civilian later died from his wounds at Ongiva.

32 Battalion was operating in the Mupa area at the time and on 6 December a platoon contacted a small group of four SWAPO, but the group immediately fled north to the protection of their Angolan bases.

Two more contacts were made with SWAPO on 11 and 20 December respectively by call sign 72 of Golf Company.

On 10 January 1983 a 32 Battalion armoured personnel carrier detonated a landmine, injuring eight members.

Two days later another landmine was detonated by a Buffalo, carrying Platoon 4 of 1 Parachute Battalion, injuring the platoon leader.

During January A, D, and E companies of 32 Battalion were deployed inside Angola. Three platoons of 1 Parachute Battalion were also present.

Several units served as protection for the Ongiva Tactical HQ, consisting of:

- 3 SA Infantry Battalion 81mm mortar group
- 32 Battalion 81mm mortar group
- 61 Mechanized Battalion armoured vehicles
- 103 Battery 10 LAA

- 1 x platoon from C Company 1 Parachute Battalion
- 1 x platoon from C Company 32 Battalion
- Maintenance, sappers, signallers and LTW personnel

Serving as protection units at Xangongo were one platoon from E Company 32 Battalion and one 81mm mortar team from 3 SA Infantry Battalion.

On 13 January a double TMA3 landmine was detonated but this time limited damage was caused to the vehicle involved. Platoon 4 of Alpha Company 32 Battalion made contact with 20 FAPLA members, 15 kilometres east of Mupa and one enemy soldier was wounded and captured. The same platoon again made contact the next day, this time 15 kilometres north of Mupa, with eight enemy force members.

On 4 February Platoon 3 Alpha Company 32 Battalion had a contact with 40 SWAPOs, killing between six and eleven and capturing four. 32 Battalion sustained four casualties. Lance-Corporal Mario Oliviera was hit by an M60 rifle grenade in his chest. A more detailed description of this incident follows later. Platoon 2 Alpha Company 32 Battalion was deployed north of Mupa.

From 8 February 32 Battalion's B, C, and F companies began relieving the units operating inside Angola. An RPG-7 was fired at a Puma helicopter during these troopings but missed its target.

Two days later Platoon 3 Alpha Company made contact with 40 SWAPOs, killing six and wounding four. A 32 Battalion member sustained injuries from his own MOI grenade launcher.

On 12 February Platoon 3 C Company and a platoon of F Company made contact with 20 and 60 SWAPOs respectively. One terrorist was wounded.

On 15 February the first signs of high numbers of SWAPOs infiltrating South West Africa were detected east of Dova, consisting of tracks of groups of 30, 40 and 60 carrying heavy loads.

On 16 February call sign 71 of 32 Battalion made contact with 60 SWAPOs and wounded one. The same day call sign 73 and call sign 61 made contact with 14 and 60 terrorists respectively.

On 18 February 100 SWAPOs attacked a UNITA base, killing one and wounding three UNITA members.

On 22 February 32 Battalion companies conducted searches in the Nehone and Dova areas, while Platoon 24 F Company 32 Battalion killed one terrorist and wounded a civilian woman caught in the crossfire.

Companies received their fortnightly resupplies by two Puma helicopters on 24 February. They were provided with ration packs, as well as water, ammunition, medical supplies and extra radio battery packs.

On 28 February Corporal W.J. Schoeman from Platoon 4 C Company 32 Battalion sustained a stomach wound.

On 3 March three terrorists were wounded during a contact.

On 6 March Platoon 2 F Company 32 Battalion, while moving into position to form a temporary base, saw a group of terrorists. They set up an ambush and killed one terrorist. The next day another terrorist was killed when a group of six was encountered.

On 8 March 200 SWAPOs vacated their base when they detected a Puma helicopter passing overhead in close proximity to their base. During a follow-up operation, one terrorist was killed.

Two days later a group of 150 SWAPO members walked into an ambush. The terrorists initiated the attack, but were pinned down for more than 15 minutes before they managed to withdraw in packets of 25 terorists. Three terrorists were killed and three wounded.

On 12 March Second Lieutenant J. Swart's Platoon 6 Bravo Company 32 Battalion made contact with SWAPO at Mulola.

32 Battalion now began operating in an area between Cuvelai and Vinticete, where four terrorists were killed during a contact with ten terrorists.

On 17 March Bravo and Charlie companies made contact with a group of 16 terrorists, killing all but one. The fortunate terrorist was later captured.

The next day Second Lieutenant van Dyk's Platoon 8 B Company 32 Battalion made contact with SWAPO near Bambi. On the same day Bravo and Charlie companies encountered a SWAPO group unloading a vehicle carrying bags of maize meal.

On 23 March 600 UNITA members were redeployed on six Kwêvoël transport vehicles from Mongua to Anhanca.

Two days later 32 Battalion Recce Wing and one company of 32 Battalion were also transported on six Urals, vehicles of Soviet origin, to a specific location after a six-hour drive. Thereafter, they walked for four days to reach the UNITA HQ at Sequendiva. However, the alleged facts of this deployment cannot be verified by the author.

The airfield at Evale was cleared and a Hercules aircraft dropped off fuel at the mini-HAA (Helicopter Administration Area) that had been established.

32 Battalion was now deployed in the following areas:

- Call sign 51 at Ionde, southwest to Chitando
- Call sign 52 between Chitando and Ionde
- Call sign 53 between Evale and Acmela
- Call sign 54 between Dova and Ionde
- Call sign 55 at Xangongo
- Call sign 56 at Xangongo
- Call sign 57 between Acmela and Nehone
- Call signs V31 and V33 (1 Parachute Battalion) north of Anhanca
- Call sign V43 south of Anhanca

Three 32 Battalion companies generally operated in the area east of Mupa.

On 27 March call sign 72 of Platoon 2 Golf Company 32 Battalion made contact with 40 SWAPOs, killing six. Two days later another contact was made.

On 31 March call sign 70 of Golf Company 32 Battalion made contact, killing two terrorists.

During April the Tactical HQ Operation Dolfyn at Ongiva consisted of the following elements:

- 1 x troop 10 LLA anti-aircraft guns
- 1 x 81mm mortar platoon
- 2 x platoons, call signs 30 and 31, from 32 Battalion

At Xangongo was situated one 81mm mortar platoon. The HAA consisted of one 81mm mortar platoon and 32 Battalion call signs 51, 53 and 54 (three platoons). A platoon from 1 Parachute Battalion was deployed at Ionde to serve as protection for the airfield.

On 3 April Sergeant A. Mande and Rifleman J.D. Kativa from call signs 11 and 14, Platoons 1 and 2 of Alpha Company 32 Battalion respectively were killed, and Second Lieutenant G.W. Roos and another two soldiers were wounded at Vinticete while laying an ambush. One terrorist was killed and three wounded.

The next day, while a Puma helicopter was unloading its cargo, SWAPO walked into the landing zone. Six terrorists were killed and many more were reported to have been wounded.

On 18 April a platoon of UNITA, consisting of 18 members, contacted SWAPO in a firefight that lasted 15 minutes in the Namaiaca/Naema area. All the UNITA members were wounded save two.

On 25 April the initial planning for Operation Dolfyn was completed. D-Day was set for 1 May. Colonel Eddie Viljoen joined 32 Battalion on the ground at a landing zone north of Ionde where equipment and medics were being ferried in for the operation.

On 13 May 32 Battalion was deployed near Jalula, northeast of Techamutete, for Operation Dolfyn. In a contiguous area, six members of 1 Parachute Battalion were wounded when they made contact with 20 SWAPOs. One terrorist was killed.

Operation Dolfyn

An operation was planned against SWAPO to confirm the location of a SWAPO base 80 kilometres north of Mupa by means reconnaissance. On 5 May 1983, once the location was confirmed, an attack was launched against the base by two infantry companies and one 81mm mortar group, with cut-off groups positioned next to the Cuvelai–Techamutete road.

On 30 April three companies, one 81mm mortar group and three recce teams departed from the HAA situated south of the Calonga River.

On 1 May the HAA moved north of the river, followed by the main force. At the same time one recce team reconnoitred the high ground and the weir in the immediate area. The main force joined the recce team on the high ground the following day.

On 3 May one recce team reconnoitred east and north of the Camene River to establish cut-off positions next to the road. Another recce team established an observation post on the Camene hill. A third team was sent ahead to secure a safe crossing over the river and to reconnoitre the area southeast of the position of the suspected SWAPO base.

On 031730B the first recce team reported noises that sounded like crates being packed onto vehicles and talking in the immediate vicinity. More noise was reported the next day.

At 041130B the recce team on Camene hill made contact with nine enemy soldiers who were also taking up observation positions on the hill. One enemy soldier was wounded during the firefight and the others fled. This captive confirmed the presence of the SWAPO base in the area and its location north of the Camene River. He also advised that the fleeing SWAPO would alert the base of the SADF presence. Three more SWAPO members were observed fleeing in a northeasterly direction at 1230B.

It was decided that H-Hour would be brought forward to 041600B and not wait for the next day in order to prevent any SWAPO from leaving the area. At 041530B the recce team reported that enemy vehicles were leaving the area in an easterly direction.

Two companies from 32 Battalion commenced pursuit at 041445B without deploying cut-off groups first. A reserve troop from 1 Parachute Battalion was lifted by Puma helicopter to the HAA to stand by in reserve. No Pumas would fly east of the Camene hill, ruling out their deployment as a cut-off group.

At 041600B higher command from Sector 10 HQ prohibited any Offensive Force movement to the target area, as no gunship support was available during the pursuit of the enemy.

At 041625B, two companies advanced to between 200 and 380 metres southwest of the SWAPO base

The companies commenced the attack, with small-arms and 14.5mm AAA fire being received from the EF.

At 041755B the gunship helicopters arrived at the scene of the battle and immediately participated by providing air cover to the OF.

One gunship helicopter was hit by 14.5mm and was grounded close to a recce team.

The 14.5mm AAA positions were silenced, and the attack continued until last light. Thereafter the companies withdrew and took up cut-off positions and set ambushes.

At first light on 5 May the SWAPO base was cleared until 051430B. SWAPO documents, equipment and weapons were captured and removed by Puma helicopters; SWAPO bodies were buried at the site.

Operation Dolfyn continued as planned.

Operation Dolfyn now replaced Operation Snoek. The aim of this latter operation had been to find and attack SWAPO's Eastern Area Headquarters. The SADF units consisted of 32 Battalion, with 4 SA Infantry Battalion and 61 Mechanized Battalion participating during the initial stages of the operation.

Between 10 May and 18 June 1983, mechanized infantry mounted on Ratel armoured vehicles were deployed across a large area of southern Angola out of Ongiva, where 32 Battalion's senior officers were stationed; Ongiva also served as the Tactical HQ for the operation. Task Force Oscar, comprising combat groups Alpha, Bravo and Charlie, was constituted using equipment supplied by 61 Mechanized Battalion. 32 Battalion, continuing with its operations inside Angola, remained separate and was not under the command of Task Force Oscar. This was the start of Operation Dolfyn.

The aims of Operation Dolfyn were outlined as follows:[25]

- To isolate SWAPO from the local community
- To maintain good communication with DISA (UNITA) forces to the east
- To lay ambushes on all identified SWAPO logistical routes, and to lay claymore mines in uninhabited areas
- To monitor all SWAPO activities at waterholes
- Not to be involved in any violence against the local communities

Operation Dolfyn consisted of five phases:

Phase 1: Air-storm operation against SWAPO command position, west of the road between Techamutete and Cuvelai, as well as SWAPO's logistical platoon east of this road.

Phase 2: Area operation east and west of the Cunene River in the area covered by Operation Robyn.

Phase 3: Area operation west of the road between Ongiva–Evale–Mupa–Cuvelai, as far north as Vintecete, including the road.

Phase 4: Area operation east of the road between Ongiva–Evale–Mupa–Cuvelai, in cooperation with UNITA, as far north as Vintecete.

Phase 5: The isolation of FAPLA forces at Cuvelai and possible action against this target if shown to be necessary, but only after prior authorization hag been granted by the Head SADF.

The offensive should only include positively identified SWAPO targets, except in instances of self defence. OF losses should be avoided at all costs and no OF should be exposed to enemy capture. The SAAF was not allowed to perform any offensive air operations north of the 150-kilometre line north of the border.

On 12 May elements from Task Force Oscar engaged SWAPO, and returned heavy fire from small arms and 82mm mortars at two locations. This engagement lasted for almost an hour. One SADF member was killed and 17 wounded, while 23 terrorists were killed. The SADF lost some equipment, including four R-4 semi-automatic rifles, and an A52 VHF radio due to the chaos that prevailed during the firefight.

On 13 May approximately 60 SWAPOs attacked a platoon of 1 Parachute Battalion, wounding six Parabats. The Parabats managed to kill one SWAPO member who was the commander of SWAPO's Special Forces group; three SWAPOs were wounded. The follow-up operation was ended when the SWAPO tracks were lost after crossing a stream.

Several Ratels detonated landmines on 29 May and 6, 14 and 15 June. More vehicles detonated landmines, including a Samil 100 on 5 June, a Samil 20 on 6 June, a Samil 50 on 7 June and an Eland on 13 June.

On 15 May elements of Task Force Oscar engaged in a contact with five members of SWAPO at 345662XM, killing one terrorist.

On 17 May, Task Force Bravo had a contact, wounding two naked terrorists while they were busy bathing at a waterhole.

On 18 May three civilian women and two civilian men were abducted by SWAPO, ten kilometres southwest of Xangongo.

On 19 May Corporal Kindness was killed in a shooting accident.

Captain H.J. Boshoff certified that the Ionde airfield had now been cleared of any landmines. However, later, several landmines were detonated by SADF vehicles.

On 20 May a vehicle of Task Force Bravo's Samil detachment detonated a landmine. One member of the SADF was killed during a contact and another wounded. Also, two SWAPOs were killed and one was wounded.

On this day a powerful car bomb was detonated in front of the SAAF HQ in Church Street, Pretoria, killing and injuring many civilians.

On 24 May three SWAPOs were killed and two were wounded during a contact with 13 terrorists. Another SWAPO was wounded when a security patrol was engaged by six terrorists.

During June companies of 32 Battalion patrolled inside Angola, set up observation posts and laid several ambushes. 32 Battalion was operating mainly in the Nehone, Dova and Mulola areas. Platoons of 1 Parachute Battalion were positioned at Xangongo; UNITA was deployed at Anhanca.

The D-Day for the Operation Dolfyn assault was moved to 1 June.

An attack was launched on a SWAPO base at RV 4679XN. Unfortunately tracks of a 32 Battalion platoon were discovered by SWAPO members, which alerted the group to the SADF presence in the area. SWAPO's base was thus already evacuated prior to the attack.

Earlier, an HAA had been established to be used during the attack at XN360285.

Brigadier Joep Joubert, Colonel R.S. Lord, Brigadier van Niekerk, and Brigadier Huyser were stationed at the HAA. The attack was under the command of Commandant Eddie Viljoen of 32 Battalion.

The plan of attack consisted of:[26]

Phase 1:

Recce teams to move into position on 1 June to serve as stopper groups north of the SWAPO base.

Two companies of 32 Battalion to attack the SWAPO base from the south.

Phase 2:

H-Hour set for 10:00 on 2 June.

Impala fighter planes commence the attack, dropping napalm bombs east of the target. SWAPO members expected to flee in a westerly direction.

At H-Hour + 3 minutes: a mortar group to be flown in from the mini-HAA.

1 Parachute Battalion platoons to be flown in as stopper groups.

At H-Hour + 5 minutes: gunships to provide air support to the ground forces.

Phase 3:

Attack to commence by two companies of 32 Battalion and a mortar group, moving from south to north.

Other forces on stand-by:

- 148 paratrooper soldiers at the HAA
- 3 Puma helicopters
- 4 gunship helicopters
- 1 Telstar fixed-wing spotter aircraft
- 1 trooping fixed-wing aircraft
- 12 Impala fighter aircraft
- Medical support provided at Ongiva

A platoon from 1 Parachute Battalion was stationed at Ionde airfield to provide protection.

On 5 June Combat Group Bravo killed one terrorist, wounded two and captured another. The next day elements of Task Force Oscar killed a terrorist at Shatotwa and wounded another when they engaged with six terrorists. Four days later they had another contact at Vintecete. The next day Task Force Bravo killed two and captured one terrorist; while laying an ambush, five SWAPOs were encountered. Also, Combat Group Bravo (call sign 30) unexpectedly came across a forward FAPLA position, situated ten kilometres north of Cuvelai, while they were deploying to serve as stopper groups, causing a brief exchange of fire. FAPLA responded with inaccurate 82mm mortar and 122mm rocket fire. The combat group captured documents, ammunition and destroyed radio equipment. Combat Group Bravo's commander moved his force east across the Cuvelai River, and then turned north to search the area from north to south. The combat group commander was reprimanded for engaging a FAPLA position before being ordered south towards Vintecete.

On 120715B Combat Team 1 (call sign 10), with two platoons, disembarked their vehicles and moved through dense bush next to the river. At 0800B they heard loud noises west of the river. It was ruled out that call sign 20 was present, as their location was two kilometres to their south. The platoons crossed the river and position themselves in combat formation. One soldier overheard someone saying: "Here they come, captain," and observed an EF mortar group which was then eliminated with an RPG-7 rocket.

Heavy fighting commenced with EF small arms fire, RPGs, mortars, 14.5mm AAA and a 23mm AAA gun, which ceased firing almost immediately, being directed at the OF, who were pinned down but returned fire with small arms, RPGs, M79s and 60mm mortars.

Within 15 minutes, the OF received support from 81mm mortars, with 300 mortar bombs exploding inside the EF tactical base. Within 20 minutes, OF artillery provided fire support and fired nine rounds per piece. They stopped firing as soon as the OF members were in close proximity to the target area.

Call sign 20 was ordered to swing in a northeasterly direction and to use call sign 10's vehicles to provide supporting fire. Their Ratels moved south along the eastern side of the river, but were unable to provide 20mm fire due to the dense bush. They delivered fire with mounted machine guns, but the presence of call sign 10 in the area resulted in a cease-fire situation. They were, however, unfortunately unable to cross the river with these Ratels.

The battle continued until 0920B, while the platoons were evacuated from the area to positions east of the river, where they boarded their vehicles.

While crossing the river, an EF mortar explosion wounded 14 OF members and killed Staff Sergeant D. Coleby, a platoon commander.

At 0845B two platoons of call sign 20 received EF mortar fire southeast of the EF tactical base. They disengaged the contact. The EF mortar fire was actually directed towards call sign 10 but was way off target and exploded in close proximity of these two platoons.

At the same time an OF platoon protecting their overnight location, made contact with EF members who had fled in their direction. Heavy fire was exchanged for a period of between 15 and 20 minutes. The EF suffered a large number of casualties during this firefight. The EF withdrawal from their tactical base was a well coordinated attempt to escape from the accurate OF mortar fire.

At 0900B an OF platoon cleared the target and discovered 20 EF bodies, but their equipment had already been carried off by their comrades. Due to further mortar fire in the area, the clearing of the EF target was abandoned. Four OF members were wounded at the target zone.

Call sign 20 of Combat Team 2 regrouped south of the target at 0910B.

Combat Team 3 was ordered to join the other combat teams and cross the river to the west before moving south in support of the other combat teams southwest of the target. Due to the dense bush, they made a wide turn and only joined Combat Team 2 south of the target after Combat Team 2 had already been ordered to withdraw.

Between 0920B and 1108B, OF delivered mortar fire and also engaged from their Ratels. The EF also fired from Cuvelai, to the northeast, but were way off target. It was concluded that the EF consisted of 400-man-strong PLAN Typhoon Brigade (crack SWAPO troops) after documents had been evaluated. Twenty-three SWAPO members were killed during the battle. The SWAPO strength was estimated by taking into account signs left on the ground, including the number of EF tracks, marks left from their sleeping areas and fire positions. The EF mortars were positioned northwest of the tactical base and utilized at maximum range, hence the reason for their inaccurate fire. One OF member was killed and 17 OF members were wounded during the attack.

After the target was finally cleared by Combat Group Bravo, Combat Group Charlie and a company from 44 Parachute Battalion, the force withdrew to Ongiva on 1 June 1983.

The official operational map overleaf is provided to explain the battle in more detail, with the target shown as the large circle left of the river, and the advance of call signs 20 and 30 above the target, moving left of the target, and call sign 10's movement right of the target, and crossing the river at the bottom.

On 13 June the author began establishing the radio communication at the new Tactical HQ at Ionde.

On 14 June Parabats attacked a SWAPO base in the Vinticete area that a group of the

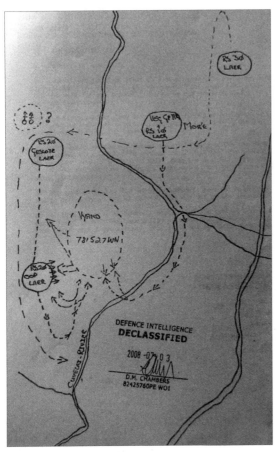

Map of the Task Force Bravo battle of 12 June 1983.
(Military Archives)

51 Reconnaissance Commando reported to have existed in the area. However, this attack was described as "a lemon" or "cock-up", as the army blamed the air force for dropping the stopper group at the wrong landing zone, allowing all the terrorists to escape.

On 17, 29 and 30 June a number of landmines were detonated by vehicles carrying cargo at Ionde. The author was wounded during one such explosion.

On 17 June task forces Charlie and Bravo withdrew from the operational theatre.

After the unofficial termination of Task Force Oscar's involvement inside Angola, it was reported that a total of 14 incidents took place where the SADF engaged with SWAPO, only two of which were initiated by SWAPO. The head count was 34 SWAPO killed and three captured, while the SADF lost two members.

The next day 300 members of 32 Battalion's A, B and G companies were deployed inside Angola to relieve the companies on the ground. It took the Puma helicopters 23 and a half hours' flying time, doing 30 trips, to complete the trooping, a massive effort on behalf of the SAAF helicopter pilots.

On 20 June a 32 Battalion member sustained a shoulder wound when call sign 72 of Golf Company had a contact with eight SWAPOs.

Over the next four days contact was made with SWAPO on a daily basis.

On 25 June all 32 Battalion platoons were resupplied by Puma helicopters.

32 Battalion was now operating mainly in the Evale, Nehone, Anhanca and Cataue areas.

On 1 July Second Lieutenant G.H. du Randt, and Rifleman E. Cassera were killed at Oshendje in an unfortunate incident, while Second Lieutenant G.W. Roos, Corporal P.G. Slabbert and Riflemen P. Tgoetao and M. Moango were wounded during a SWAPO attack. The incident is fully described later in this book. Two members were reported missing but were later found unscathed.

On 2 July Operation Neptune was launched, with 32 Battalion operating in the Vintecete and Mupa areas. On the same day a SWAPO member was killed and another wounded during an attack by 32 Battalion.

32 Battalion contacted the same 30-strong SWAPO group that had attacked their platoon on 1 July, killing one terrorist.

On 4 July two Impala aircraft were called to fire at a suspected target northwest of Ionde. Suspicious lights were observed at night moving towards Ionde, but it transpired to have been bushfires burning at a distance.

On 9 July it was reported that SWAPO had received equipment and reinforcements from Cuvelai. It was expected that SWAPO would infiltrate through the Nehone, Mulola, Dova and Oshendje areas and lay ambushes against SADF forces.

Between 11 and 16 July, SWAPO tracks were spotted daily.

On 18 July a terrorist was killed during a contact with SWAPO. On 21 July Rifleman A. Inossencio was wounded during a contact with eight SWAPOs. One terrorist was killed and another wounded.

On 22 July 30 SWAPOs were captured at a village while they were partaking in a festivity.

32 Battalion was operating in the Mulola area. It was reported that SWAPO's 8th Battalion, consisting of two companies, together with the Red Square Company, were operating to the south. 32 Battalion was deployed south and east of Dova and north of Nehone.

At the end of July, the first trooping between Buffalo base and Ionde took place, using Buffalo vehicles. As the 32 Battalion base was situated at Buffalo in eastern Kavango, the troopings were routed from Buffalo to Rundu and Omauni, from where they crossed the border into Angola to Ionde. The convoy consisted of 70 vehicles as follows:[27]

- 36 x Buffalo vehicles to transport the members of the three companies
- 3 x Buffalo vehicles to transport the mortar group
- 1 x Buffalo vehicle to serve as a command vehicle
- 2 x Buffalo vehicles used as a 'tiffy' vehicle by the mechanics
- 2 x reserve Buffalo vehicles
- (44 x Buffalo vehicles in total)
- 3 x Kwêvoël vehicles to carry members' equipment, one each per company
- 2 x Kwêvoël vehicles to carry ammunition
- 2 x Kwêvoël vehicles to carry rations
- 3 x Kwêvoël vehicles to carry general provisions
- 4 x Kwêvoël vehicles to carry diesel
- 6 x Kwêvoël vehicles to carry avtur aircraft fuel
- 2 x Kwêvoël vehicles to carry canteen provisions: sweets, canned sodas and a few beers
- 1 x Kwêvoël vehicle with extra water
- 2 x Kwêvoël vehicles with vehicle spares
- 1 x recovery vehicle
- (26 x Kwêvoël vehicles in total)

On 2 August one terrorist was killed, and another wounded during a contact with 32 Battalion.

On 8 August reports were received that SWAPO was preparing to celebrate Namibia Day on 26 August. This would coincide with parades in Luanda, Cuanza and Lubango. They would target SADF forces at Ondangwa air force base and were expected to lay ambushes at Ondangwa and Oshivello, and to sabotage installations at Walvis Bay, Tsumeb Mine and the Ruacana power line. *Wegstaan bestokings* (remote fire) of bases was anticipated. They also had orderes to capture an SADF soldier. The response by the SADF was to conduct roadblocks and to sharpen border control. It emerged that SWAPO had withdrawn 700 members from the field for action against the SADF and was to utilize 200 of its members to attack Ondangwa on 22 August.

On 9, 10, 11 and 12 August SWAPO tracks were spotted daily.

On 13 August it was reported that 300 local civilians were attended to at Ionde, being provided with food and medical treatment.

On 14 August Rifleman Augusto sustained a wound from a bullet that was fired from his own rifle.

On 19 August four SWAPOs were located in a village. One terrorist was captured.

On 28 August Second Lieutenant A.D. McCallum sustained an eye injury and was relocated to Ionde. Rifleman J. Nambi was killed during a contact with SWAPO.

Another vehicle-borne trooping between Baffalo and Ionde took place.

On 4 September 1,250 members from SA Infantry School were deployed in the Dova, Nehone, Mupa, and Chiede areas as part of Operation Dolfyn.

On 8 and 16 September two SWAPO bases were reported to be at locations 18 kilometres east of Mupa and in the Vintecete area.

On 29 September Brigadier Joup Joubert (Sector 20 commander), Commandant Preston-Thomas (SAAF) and Captain Jan Hougaard (32 Battalion operational commander) commenced with planning of the next operation at Ongiva. On 2 October a strike force was formed consisting of two companies of 32 Battalion, 32 Battalion mortar platoon, 32 Battalion Recce Wing, 2nd Regiment AA, six gunship helicopters, six Puma helicopters and six Impala fighter aircraft which were on stand-by at Ondangwa.

On 6 October a Puma helicopter was forced to do an emergency landing. This incident is described later in this book.

On 8 October an airborne assault was conducted in the Jaula area deep inside Angola. The author was at the HAA that was established for the attack, responsible for establishing communications at the HAA and to provide all radio communication needed during the operational attack phase.

One company (call sign 10) and the Recce Wing infiltrated the area north of the target to serve as a stopper group. The assault was conducted by a second company and an 81mm mortar section. Medical support was provided at the Ionde Tactical HQ.

An air-storm operation was launched at 11:00. Seventy SWAPO members withdrew from the area just three hours before H-Hour in northerly and northwesterly directions.

The SADF dress code was camouflage, with dayglows displayed on bush hats to aerially distinguish them from SWAPO. Based at Ionde, the overall commander of the operation was Commandant Preston-Thomas, with Captain Hougaard, 32 Battalion operational commander, at the HAA. The radio frequencies for A72 handheld radios with air support was channel 11, and with ground forces channel 8. After the operation was completed, the SADF forces withdrew from the area.

On 22 October a trooping commenced between Buffalo base and Ionde; thereafter the platoons were deployed to their locations by Puma helicopters.

During November, December and January 1984, Operation Askari commenced, which is more fully described later.

SWAPO'S FORCES

SWAPO's headquarters was situated at Luanda, from where they directed their camps primarily based in southern Angola. From such camps, SWAPO guerrillas could infiltrate into Namibia in small units. SWAPO's military wing, PLAN, had main command centres in Luanda and Lubango, and training camps in the Huíla, Benguela, and Cuanza Sul provinces. Most of its camps were mobile to avoid identification, infiltration and attack by the SADF. SWAPO recruits were trained at Angolan and Cuban military facilities, from where they were dispatched to SWAPO camps and formally organized into battalions of 400 to 800 troops each. PLAN's strength in 1988 was estimated at 9,000 troops.

SADF operations in Angola during 1983 were aimed at SWAPO's 8th Battalion headquarters at Mulola (XP2711), 20 kilometres southeast of Techamutete. It was established that five companies were active in the area, of which two companies were present in the Mulola area (XM 2584) and three companies in the Dova (XM3466) and Nehone (XM1060) areas. SWAPO OG HQ was at Campulo (XP2518), 12 kilometres northeast of Techamutete and their OGVBP at Lumbambula.[28]

SWAPO's Battalion headquarters consisted of 35 members, while 40 to 50 members served with each company. The total strength of SWAPO's 8th Battalion was approximately 220 members.

People's Liberation Army of Namibia (PLAN) training in Angola during 1983.

The SWAPO leadership structure consisted of the following:[29]

Battalion Commander: Ernos
CDE: Kadhila (Ben Amoomo)
Political Commissar: Manique (Elago)
COOP: Choice (Kasheta)
EC: Shitikukutu (Kambula)

Company Commanders:
Kaongo, Kongode, Lotty, Malomino, Matrosva, Namwulowambi, Plan, Situation, Shilonga, Tommy and Namwandi

SWAPO had the following companies on the battalion strength:

- Greenwill Matongo
- Kremlin
- Sofia
- Satiago
- Red Square
- Black Sea

SWAPO members were armed with[30] SKS and AK-47 rifles, PKM machine guns, RPG-7s 60mm and 82mm mortars and SAM-7 missiles (which were used during a contact on 1 July 1983 near Shendje).

SWAPO used the following infiltration routes through the south of Angola to reach South West Africa:[31]

- Cuvelai–Vinticete–Mupa–Nehone–Catale
- Gluma–Puturhanga–Culemo–Chifufua–Mulola–Oshendje–Catale. This route was no longer used due to 32 Battalion's involvement in the area
- Cuvelai–Vinticete–Mupa–Jamba–Itai–Egavi–Anhanca–Chitumbo

SWAPO's modus operandi

SWAPO's major insurgency usually commenced with the onset of the rainy season in late January every year, and continued until May. The rains gave mobility to SWAPO members and supplied them with the water they required for their deployment; it washed away their tracks, and the foliage of the trees provided cover. During the following dry season, SWAPO withdrew its forces to bases inside Angola to rehearse for the next insurgency with the following rainy season.

The security forces generally launched offensive operations into Angola during the dry winter months. During these periods SADF vehicles were more mobile, as the region was more accessible due to the dry conditions.

SWAPO sometimes used donkeys to carry provisions and equipment, and they mainly travelled at night.

SWAPO members were issued with arms and ammunition, but they had to provide their own food, mainly bought from local communities. Food was stored in underground caches or bunkers, and anti-personnel mines were set to serve as protection.

SWAPO's 8th Battalion consisted mainly of conventional elements because it was observed that they used poor anti-tracking techniques.

SWAPO members often laid landmines. They were sometimes laid in a boosted combination of three mines at one location to cause maximum destruction.

SWAPO's tactics consisted of L-shaped ambushes, with one section on the short leg and three sections on the long leg. They used small-arms and mortar fire during contacts, but quickly retreated after 20–30 seconds to their flanks, from which they disbursed, referred to as 'bombshelling', to later reconvene at a safe pre-designated rendezvous.

The SADF held a conference where SWAPO's tactics were analyzed.[32] It was described how SWAPO directed their efforts, once inside South West Africa, against local infrastructure and the local community. SWAPO used force against the local community to persuade the locals to support them. For SWAPO, the local community was the main source of information regarding all SADF movement, which was used very effectively.

On 6 May 1983, during a single incident, seven SADF members were massacred with bayonets, and only one escaped to provide his testimony of the carnage.[33] SWAPO had a reputation for brutality and extreme aggression against its opponents, perceived or not. The worst imaginable atrocities were committed by SWAPO.

During SWAPO's infiltration into South West Africa, their members carried weapons that could be used effectively against SADF vehicles and to destroy buildings.

SWAPO's movements were difficult to trace, as they took measures to ensure that their tracks were not clearly identifiable. They used vehicles commandeered from the local population. It was even reported that ambulances were used to transport them rapidly through an area.

The size and density of the region dicated that SWAPO members could easily vanish whenever they so chose. They wore civilian clothes and appeared inconspicuous to the SADF. Food and supplies could easily be obtained from the local population throughout the region.

They absolutely avoided any contact with SADF members. They had easy access to infrastructure, such as power lines and telephone lines, which were often targeted.

When confronted, SWAPO members immediately fired 60mm mortars in defence against the SADF. When they were followed by the SADF, they laid landmines and set POMZ mines to cause distraction.

The local population inside Angola was regarded as neutral to pro-SWAPO, but their loyalty often changed when new forces entered the area. The leaders of the local population in South West Africa were required to police the situation, and to act against their people who were found to have assisted SWAPO members.

With a dusk-to-dawn curfew in place, no vehicle movements by local people were allowed after dark. Their cattle had to remain in their shelters until 10 a.m. which meant that SWAPO's tracks could easily be discovered. The SADF used dogs and specialized trackers, such as Bushmen, to track SWAPO movements. When SWAPO's presence was recorded, quick action was taken against them, referred to as a 'fire force'. This was achieved with the aid of Alouette gunship helicopters to provide rapid fire and mobilty from the sky. SWAPO members were not to be given an opportunity to regroup once the SADF presence was established.

SWAPO's Angolan base conditions

After Namibian independence in 1990, 41,787 refugees who had fled South West Africa returned to the country.[34] Among those who returned were 153 prisoners[35] who had been released from the several SWAPO death camps.[36] They gave the most horrific accounts of their most inhuman treatment and the extended torture they had suffered at the hands of their SWAPO captors. An International Red Cross report of 30 April 1993 found that of 2,161 cases of people who had apparently died in these camps, 1,605 simply vanished.[37] In and around these detention camps in southern Angola, unmarked mass graves bear the remains of countless people tortured to death and which are unlikely to ever be repatriated.

At the time of this report, it could not be officially confirmed if there were more SWAPO detainees still held inside such camps. These practices were always vehemently denied by SWAPO to avoid further damage to its already poor reputation in regards to human rights.

Siegfried Groth, a pastor of the German Lutheran Church, describes conditions that prevailed in these SWAPO death camps in his book, *Namibia, The Wall of Silence: The Dark Days of the Liberation Struggle*. He spent 16 years in exile but was not in favour with SWAPO, mainly due to his Christian convictions that were not in line with SWAPO's Marxist-Leninist-Maoist philosophies.

Prior to South West Africa's independence, many citizens left the country through its northern borders to pursue SWAPO's promises, a dream of a better life and supposed opportunities. Many of these people's dreams were shattered when they were rudely awoken to the real conditions that prevailed on the other side of the border. Many of these exiles were made up of whole families consisting of husbands, wives and children. They settled in camps near Lusaka in Zambia. Some received basic military training from Chinese instructors of barely a few weeks before being deployed to infiltrate Ovamboland in South West Africa.

Although Christianity was permitted by the SWAPO leaders in the earlier days, during 1976 a crisis broke out in SWAPO and the Christian ministry in exile collapsed.

The SADF and Koevoet, the South West African police force unit, used various means to interrogate SWAPO prisoners to solicit important information regarding the location and strengths of SWAPO military bases in Angola. The Appeal Court in Bloemfontein, South Africa, confirmed a High Court ruling that was issued on 24 February 1975 to abolish flogging as a form of punishment or coercion.[38]

During 1976 one such SWAPO exile, Tangeni Nuukuuawo, returned to Zambia after he had spent some time in Europe. He was immediately arrested and taken to the Nampundwe camp.[39] With Nuukuuawo, ten other supposed opponents of SWAPO were found not guilty during their trial, but after Sam Nujoma, the SWAPO leader, personally intervened, they were all imprisoned in the Ukonga prison in Dar es Salaam, Tanzania, where they were kept in appalling conditions for two years.

In Zambia, the refugees were living in shocking conditions in the bush, suffering from malnutrition, while SWAPO leaders were living in comfort in Lusaka. The SWAPO 'old guard' owned properties and businesses, such as hotels and bars and avoided the front and the fighting as much as possible. There were ongoing reports of deficiencies and mismanagement of SWAPO's affairs due to corruption.[40]

The young Turks were increasingly calling for an immediate SWAPO Party Congress, normally held only once every five years, to discuss and remedy the situation. During May 1976 over a thousand "insubordinate" freedom fighters were arrested and taken to the Mboroma prison camp in the mountains near Kabwe, Zambia. One such prisoner, Cornelius Motinga, described conditions and how they competed with the monkeys for food.[41] They ate leaves to avoid starvation because the soldiers cut off their food supplies. Ben Shipinga's personal accounts at Mboroma are described in a report of over 200 pages. After successful appeals were made to be transferred to Angola, finally, on 5 August 1976, the prisoners were allowed to peacefully "march out of the concentration camp", under armed guard, of course. After reaching a shallow valley, the commanding officer ordered the guards to commence shooting. The guards danced and laughed as they slaughtered the prisoners. Many prisoners died on the spot and others later died of their wounds, including a pregnant woman. The incident was reported by the BBC.[42] During the 1976 Mozambican independence celebrations, Sam Nujoma announced that a military tribunal would be launched to investigate the incident and that those found guilty would be executed. No such tribunal or investigation materialized[43].

Meheba was a refugee camp in northern Zambia, run by the United Nations High Commissioner for Refugees. Two hundred refugees, all ex-SWAPO members from South West Africa, had sought shelter in this camp. During this period, Zambia was housing 100,000 refugees, including over 10,000 from South West Africa.[44]

During 1983 a new SWAPO Security Service was formed. The head was Solomon Hawala, formally trained by the Soviet security service, the KGB. His special Security Service of 250 men was stationed at Lubango in southwest Angola. Hawala referred to himself as 'Jesus' but was nicknamed 'The Butcher of Lubango'. On 23 October 1990, seven months after Namibia's independence, Hawala became the first commander-in-chief of the Namibian army, and the third most powerful[45] person in the military hierarchy.[46]

The SWAPO leadership, all mainly Ovambo, had conducted a tribal 'cleansing' of the party, separating the Ovambos from the so-called inferior southern tribes, the Nama, Damara and Herero.[47]

SWAPO set up a number of death camps around its various bases. Prisoners accused of being South African spies were first taken to Luanda, and then transported to the Karl Marx Reception Centre near Lubango where they were interrogated.[48] The centre consisted of underground accommodation for the guards and the interrogators. The torture chambers were situated in several buildings. The underground 'dungeons', as they were known, consisted of a network of dark underground caves of various sizes. Each 'room' was six feet high; toilets consisted of open buckets. Prisoners were fed twice a day in wooden bowls, with meals of cornflower or rice, and a pot of soup to share. Sometimes they received no food for several days. All the guards were Ovambos but the prisoners were forced to speak English. These dungeons, or caves, were always overcrowded, with often more than a hundred prisoners sharing a space fit only for a dozen. They were usually always locked and sealed, so fresh air was at a premium.[49]

Victor Nekondo was banished to once such cave at the Ominya prison, ten feet underground, with a pole in the middle. He was fastened to the pole by a steel chain fitted with a padlock and chained up like a dog for four months. He had to tear off his clothes because he was totally infected with lice.[50]

These dungeons had only a single hole in the middle of the roof that served as a door, with a ladder going up to it. It was locked at three in the afternoon, with prisoners left in total darkness. There was not enough air with only a few holes to provide ventilation for the fifty or more prisoners. Sick prisoners were never treated. The appalling conditions resulted in untold deaths. Many accounts exist of ill and starving prisoners dying in the arms of their cellmates. Many prisoners spent years in these dungeons until their release after the implementation of United Nations Resolution 435.

On 21 April 1986 Sam Nujoma visited Victor Nekondo's prison and made the following speech: "I greet you in the name of our great forefathers and all the great leaders who gave their lives in the cause of freedom. I don't know why you love money so much, and why you have put your hearts on beautiful things. You were prepared to betray the Namibian Revolution for the sake of beautiful cars, money and the white man's farms. Your mothers gave birth to spies and traitors of the Namibian Revolution. You will be kept in the dungeons until Namibia is independent. Then you will be shown to the people of Namibia, and your heads will be cut off by Namibians as punishment for your evil deeds." Nujoma also visited other prisons, spreading his sick gospel wherever he went.[51]

Women prisoners were forced to perform different tasks, such as cooking, gardening, construction work and carrying water. Emma Kambangula was arrested in October 1986. She was incarcerated in the Karl Marx Reception Centre, where she was stripped naked and beaten for several days. They put her in a big bag, carried her to a hole and threw her in, telling her that she was to be buried alive. They then tied her to the back of a car and dragged her over the ground. She was fortunate to receive treatment for her injuries, and spent seven months in a wheelchair. Thereafter, she was returned to the same centre, where the torture continued for a further two weeks. She was compelled to incriminate herself as an "enemy agent". She had earlier studied Marxism in Moscow which had such a profound influence on her that she abandoned her faith in God.[52]

Cornelius Haikali was arrested in Romania. He arrived at the Lubango Reception Centre and was given a blood-soaked blanket to lie on in his cell. He was forced to tell the interrogating officers his life story, but was repeatedly told that he was telling lies. He was whipped with freshly cut saplings but still did not admit to being a South African spy. He was taken to the torture room where he was suspended from a crossbeam and while suspended, was beaten repeatedly. The beatings continued non-stop for several days, after which he was bundled into a large bag and towed behind a car over rocky terrain. He was then taken into the bush where he was ordered to dig his own grave. He was told to lie down with his arms in the air. They began to bury him alive but after a few minutes pulled him out. At the end of his tether, he 'confessed' that he had been recruited as a spy by a white South African. Many other prisoners also made such 'confessions' which resulted in their convictions. The brutality with which these deeds of torture were committed was as a result of a mixture of causes: Namibian tribalism, communist ideology, guerrilla mentality, megalomania and anti-intellectualism.[53]

Gaomab was arrested on 26 March 1984 while on his way to SWAPO's Typhoon Headquarters. He was then taken to the Kilimanjaro prison where he was tortured for six months. He was suspended between the branches of two trees and beaten. Thereafter he was made to sit on burning coals.[54]

The same methods of torture were used in the cells of Soviet prisons. The torturers were trained by Russians and Russians were present during these torture sessions, often participating in the interrogations.

Former SWAPO political prisoners later formed a Political Consultative Committee (PCC) and produced *A Report to the Namibian People: Historical Account of the SWAPO Spy Drama*.[55] Therein they describe 24 different methods of torture used at the death camps. Other reports suggest that these SWAPO interrogators were clearly sadistic. Many more accounts of extreme cases of torture and prisoners being beaten to death are contained in this report.

Sam Nujoma addressed an International Namibian Conference in Brussels in May 1986. He tried to placate the clergymen when pressed for clarification on the arrests and maltreatment of the alleged spies. When they mentioned torture, he replied that it was all South African propaganda, that there were no human rights violations within SWAPO.[56]

Refugees in Angola were told not to pray at meetings and funerals, as it was against the principles taught by their Chinese instructors. Only liberation songs were permitted at funerals. Marxism is openly atheist and anti-Christian. Once, before two church leaders visited a college where SWAPO students were studying, the students were instructed by the principal to behave like Christians and to listen attentively to the prayers. A Christian show was put on to create the impression that Christianity played an important role at the college. SWAPO leaders are adept at putting on two faces: acting in a Christian manner for the West, and displaying revolutionary fervour for the East.[57]

After the war, SWAPO could not account for 1,605 of its own imprisoned members.[58] To put this figure into perspective, it means that SWAPO butchered and murdered more of its own people in these death camps than the number of South African security force members they managed to kill over more than 22 years.

During the period of these acts of human rights violations, I was, at times, stationed at locations a mere 250 kilometres from these death camps. We were totally unaware that murder was taking place. I have no doubt that if SWAPO had managed to capture more members of the South African security forces, they certainly would have suffered a similar fate.

ANC Angolan base conditions
The African National Congress (ANC), while banned in South Africa, operated mainly from Angola under the protection and control of Luanda. At least seven major training camps were established inside Angola, for an estimated 1,000 to 1,400 members of the ANC's military wing, *Umkhonto we Sizwe* (Zulu, meaning 'Spear of the Nation'). Most ANC personnel

were organized into three battalions, with their encampment at Viana, outside Luanda. This location in northern Angola provided security from South African attacks, but restricted the ANC's ability to infiltrate and mount attacks in South Africa. Cleverly manipulated by the MPLA, ANC militants, like PLAN, were, in 1984, integrated into FAPLA units fighting UNITA. Such joint operations facilitated the ANC's access to weapons and supplies which came from the Soviet Union and its allies.

Sanctuary in Angola became all the more important after the March 1984 Mozambique-South Africa non-aggression and mutual security pact, the Nkomati Accord, which obliged Maputo to monitor and restrict ANC activities.

As with SWAPO, the ANC also had training camps for its military wing, Umkhonto we Sizwe (informally 'MK', an abbreviation of the first syllable) inside Angola. These camps were Quatro, Camp 13, Pango Quibaxe, Viana Transit Camp and Caculama.[59] The large camp at Novo Katenga was destroyed by the SAAF on 14 March 1979.[60]

The appalling conditions that existed inside these camps are described in *Umkhonto we Sizwe, Fighting for a Divided People* by Thula Bobela and Daluxolo Luthuli. As previously mentioned, similar conditions prevailed in the SWAPO camps, where it was well reported that civilians, mostly children and women, were held in virtual captivity, having been abducted from South West Africa. The adminstrators running these camps were often nothing more than sadistic tryrants, with unlimited powers.

South Africa dispatched agents to these camps to infiltrate the ANC and MK. The *Mbokodo* (a Xhosa word meaning 'grindstone'), the ANC security department, was often able to identify these spies from among the rank-and-file cadres. With absolute power and total control, Mbokodo used counter-intelligence agents to serve as spy-catchers. They resorted to torture to extract information from suspects. If pronounced guilty, a suspect, innocent or not, could expect execution, or a length prison sentence at best. Life in the camps, described as a nightmare, ultimately led to a revolt by cadres, but it was ruthlessly and brutally put down.[61]

This resulted in the formation of an ANC working committee, the Stuart Commission, to investiogate the explosive situation that had developed. The conveners were James Stuart, Sizakele Sigxashe, Mtu Jwili, Antony Mongalo and Aziz Pahad.[62] A picture emerged from these reports that filled the commission with horror and revulsion. When shortages had developed at the Novo Katenga camp, the administrators continued to enjoy good fare, including a variety of meat which the common folk never had access to. The administrators and senior staff enjoyed separate housing and cooking and dining facilities, with ample supplies of cigarettes, liquor and other luxuries. They threw regular parties to which female cadres were invited, with the administrators using their senior positions to seduce them. There were several cases of husbands or boyfriends being transferred to other camps to make their partners more sexually available. Women who granted sexual favours to the administrators were given preferential treatment. This began to affect discipline as these women began to reject the authority of their immediate superiors. Attractive women became sex objects rather than soldiers under training. Many female cadres were nothing more than slaves, being forced to perform household chores, such as fetching bath water, cleaning rooms and washing and ironing for the senior staff.

Mbokodo was an army within an army, feared, unaccountable and immune from punishment. Much like the Gestapo, they achieved lofty status. The National Commissar called the security comrades, "his boys, the red ants". The result was that the ANC policemen became the organization's judge, jury and executioner.

The Stuart Commission found in its report of 14 March 1984 that the methods used to enforce discipline made it "the most notorious and infamous department in the camps, and perhaps in the whole movement".[63] The commission received evidence that security comrades had tortured and killed many cadres; flogging scars were found on the backs of cadres at the Caculama camp. Yet the Mbokodo perpetrators responsible for such atrocities were never brought to book.[64]

In his book, *The Making of an MK Cadre*, Wonga Welile Bottoman describes the conditions that prevailed at ANC camps inside Angola. During 1982 he arrived at the Viana Transit Camp, a few hours' drive from Luanda, having been transferred from Mozambique. Thereafter his training commenced at the Camalundi Training Centre (or Hoji Ya Henda Training Camp) in the eastern province of Malange.[65] His six months' training consisted of political education (given great attention), as well as physical exercise, firearms handling, tactics, military engineering, topography and martial drill. Military engineering focused on the strengths of various construction materials, and the strengths of different explosive charges which were important to assess in sabotage operations.[66] Recruits needed to be knowledgeable in physics and mathematics, before selection for more advanced training such as the communications course.[67]

Thereafter, he was transferred to the training town of Teterov, near East Berlin, where he received more specialized training in subjects such as information gathering, setting meeting points, surveillance, hand to hand combat and personal protection.[68] He returned, trained as a "fully fledged guerrilla", to Viana in January 1982, whereafter he was deployed to the Quibaxe camp, codename Camp 13.[70]

Situated next to Quibaxe was an ANC security prison, Camp 32 (where alleged enemy agents were held captive), where he performed duties as a prison guard. He also experienced combat experience for the first time when the guards' military truck was ambushed and looted by UNITA solders near the camp. Eight MK cadres were killed in the action. UNITA was on the offensive against MK and FAPLA in the Malanje province in eastern Angola at the time.[71]

At Camp 32 were five cells holding different categories of prisoner; the fourth cell was occupied by female prisoners, including "a tall white woman".[72] The fifth cell held prisoners, disgruntled with the organization. who wished to leave the ANC and return home. These prisoners were punished by "the notorious slap in the face on inflated cheeks, or a frenzy of kicks to the body and buttocks, punches or whipping with coffee- or guava-tree sticks".[73] At times, executions occurred outside the camp.[74]

As mentioned, in 1984, MK forces were split up and incorporated into FAPLA units, to fight UNITA more cohesively.[75] Thereafter, the first in a series of rebellions and mutinies occurred due to complaints against the ANC leadership living in the lap of luxury in Lusaka and London, where their children were being educated at expensive private schools, while the cadres compalined that it seemed that they had "taken AKs for wives".[76] At the top of the list was Joe Modise, who later became the Minister of Defence in the democratic South African government. The cadres formed a Committee of Ten to serve as their mouthpiece to voice their grievances.[77] However, they were woken one morning by the sounds of gunfire: FAPLA soldiers were on the rampage with the cadre guard, Babsy, killed in the initial volley.

The cadres were then rounded up by the FAPLA troops before Chris Hani, Andrew Masondo and Joe Modise addressed them. A list of names was read out and the troublemakers were forcibly removed on FAPLA trucks to look forward to incarceration as guests of the Angolan government.[78]

On 13 May another mutiny occurred at Pungo, another MK camp in the region. The cadres disarmed and shot the guards, armed themselves and launched an attack on the administration building. During the battle eight loyal and six rebel cadres were killed. The camp was then surrounded by loyal MK forces and a further 13 rebels were killed. The remaining rebels were captured and immediately brought before a military tribunal. Seven were found guilty of murder and promptly executed by a firing squad. Large numbers of remaining rebels were imprisoned at Camp 32.[79]

In September 1985 Bottoman attended a ten-month course in Marxist philosophy and The Theory of Class Struggle at the Lenin International College in Moscow,[80] before being transferred to the ANC refugee camp in Morogoro, 200 kilometres from Dar es Salaam. By 1987, like Mozambique, Tanzania had been declared an ANC/MK 'demilitarized zone' where only *bona fide* South African refugees were permitted to reside. After the Tripartite Accord between South Africa, Angola and Cuba (after the battle at Cuito Cuanavale), all foreign military forces, including MK, were forced to withdraw from Angola as well.

One of the final acts of mutiny occurred when an MK cadre attempted to hijack a Soviet passenger aircraft transferring MK cadres out of Angola. Producing a hand grenade, he ordered that the plane to change course to South Africa. The cadre was overpowered and the plane landed safley at Dar es Salaam.[81]

COMMUNICATIONS AT 32 BATTALION

Ongiva serves as the capital of the Cunene province, the most southerly province in Angola. Ongiva occupied a very strategic position due to its airport. Its runway has a tarred surface, convenient for use by almost all aircraft. The airport's terminal building housed the Operation Dolfyn Tactical HQ operations and signals room. Here, the commanding officer mapped all our forces' and enemy movements, planned operations and issued orders to our forces.

A more recent aerial photograph of Ongiva airport.

It was essential to maintain permanent communication at all times with 32 Battalion's platoons on the ground during operations. Three companies, consisting of four platoons each, were deployed in Angola during 1983. Each platoon had 28 to 32 members, comprising 'sticks' of 14 soldiers each. (A stick was the number of troops capable of being airlifted by a Puma helicopter at one time.)

I was primarily responsible for providing all the means at Operation Dolfyn Tactical HQ for communicating with our forces in the field. This included communications with the SAAF and with our higher command at both Sector 10 HQ in Oshakati and 32 Battalion HQ, Sector 20 at Rundu. I was also responsible for supplying power to our base. I maintained and managed the distribution of batteries and all other radio equipment to all concerned. Radio transmissions were the only means of communication as later systems such as GPS, cellular and satellite communication, and the internet were unavailable then.

At the Tactical HQ Operation Dolfyn we utilized a stationary TR15 Hopper HF radio, delivering 100 watts of power, and which was connected to an inverted V-antenna. (A complete description of the signals equipment used at 32 Battalion's Tactical HQ Operation Dolfyn, at Ionde, follows later in this book.)

Each 32 Battalion platoon was issued with either a B22 HF or a B22 HF Hopper radio, and four or five battery packs. B22 HF radios only delivered 20 watts of power output and used a vertical-sloping or fish-reel antenna. We were fortunate to have been the only battalion in the SADF issued with this special operations equipment. The B22 radio required very little power input, as frequencies were selected manually. The B25 HF radio used by other units selects its frequencies automatically. It uses a lot of power which drains the batteries. Using less power, the B22 radio obviated the extra weight of battery packs. Batteries could also be disposed of after power was depleted.

Platoons were also issued with A72 VHF ground-to-air radios, and at times A52 VHF or A53 VHF radios. These radios have a short range of not more than five kilometres and deliver less than six watts of power output. Regular reports, such as sitreps, minereps, trackreps, inforeps and other messages such as requests for resupplies from our higher command, were managed by typing messages with an encrypting teleprinter. A teleprinter was connected to a TR15 Hopper HF radio, which was used as the means to send the message. (Pictures of radio equipment used by 32 Battalion are included in the appendices.)

During the preparatory stages of Operation Askari, I installed a powerful B81 UHF radio system at Ongiva. The B81 is heavy piece of equipment and uses a very high directional-disk antenna. This radio was connected to another B81 that served as a repeat station at Eenhana, 40 kilometres south of Ongiva. Eenhana was in turn connected by a third B81 radio, with a fourth B81 installed at Oshakati. This was a duplex system, which means that signals could be sent and received at the same time, providing an easy form of communicating, similar to using a normal fixed telephone line. This form of communication was secure from the interception due to its directional line-of-sight communication that allowed for broadcasting the signal on a very narrow path. This B81 radio was the only one of its kind to have seen service during the Angolan bush war.

Teleprinter used to type coded messages for electronic warfare in Ongiva. (Photo B. Koch)

Save for the convenience provided by the B81 radio, it was always an extremely daunting task to maintain communications at Ongiva. We frequently experienced sunspots, resulting in no communication between sunrise and sunset on a particular day. During the winter months, maintaining communications at night was difficult and not always guaranteed. The almost diminished ionosphere (the thin layer around the earth which

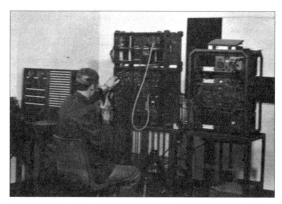

B80 TXRX radio and telephone line switchboard.

A 32 Battalion platoon leader making communications.

reflects radio-waves back to the earth), vast distances, sandy soil conditions and the limited power output of our equipment, contributed to this situation.

No operation can be managed without proper command and control. If the commander is unable to talk to his forces, no orders will be issued and no coordinated movement is possible. Simply stated, if you can't talk you can't make war. During earlier operations various fatal incidents occurred and tactical mistakes were made due to poor coordination and poor or no communications, such as during the battles of Savate and Cassinga. Lives depended on good communications

ELECTRONIC WARFARE

During 1983 the SADF made use of its electronic warfare (EW) capability. It was the responsibility of the South African Signals Corps to provide the means to listen to SWAPO's and FAPLA's communications. Their radio frequencies were regularly monitored. When radio equipment was captured from the enemy, the settings provided reliable information on the frequencies they were using. EW signalers were fluent in Portuguese and when enemy communications were intercepted, the message was instantly translated. These messages were then prioritized and sent to the Sector 10 HQ at Oshakati for interpretation. FAPLA used five-digit codes for every letter they broadcast. Their messages were decoded from codes captured during operations.

One incident occurred when a signaller, Corporal Bertie Koch,[82] was serving in EW at the Tactical HQ at Ongiva. He had just noticed two Impala fighter jets overhead, flying north, and intercepted a message that enemy MiG-21 fighter aircraft were scrambling to intercept them. As a fighter, the Impala was vastly inferior to the MiG-21. Corporal Koch quickly relayed the message as the highest priority to HQ. Within minutes, he heard the welcoming sound of the Impalas returning, having been forewarned of the waiting MiGs in the nick of time.

SWAPO's communications were easily recognizable. They began each broadcast with a whistling sound and used Morse code to send messages, which we promptly intercepted, decoded by EW before relaying the information to HQ.

Morse code served as a secure method to communicate. Morse was also used by SADF Special Forces. Very little battery power was used, requiring fewer batteries to carry around and therefore less weight. (A Morse code list and the other codes used by 32 Battalion is provided in the appendices.)

32 Battalion platoons used speech to communicate on the radio. It was always important to encode messages when referring to place names, people's identities and ranks, unit's identities and strengths, weapons, frequencies, radio hopping settings, supplies and directions. Our forces' positions, referred to as RVs, were encoded before they could be transmitted. These codes were changed regularly.

The B22 Hopper radio is capable of jumping through various frequencies while broadcasting a message. It was manually synchronized with the Tactical HQ's TR15 Hopper radio. Both radios followed the same jumping pattern, providing uninterrupted speech. Messages were therefore not being broadcast on one single frequency only, as both radios were able to jump through various frequencies while remaining synchronized. This provided a safe way to communicate as it was impossible to intercept such messages.

SWAPO's very outdated radio equipment, captured after an operation.

Notes

1   Personal recollections of Paul Els
2   Lord, Dick, *From Fledgling to Eagle: The South African Airforce during the Border War,* (Johannesburg: 30° South, 2008) p. 224
3   From original sources contained in signals at the South African Department of Defence Documentation Centre
4   Bothma, Louis Johannes, *Die Buffel Struikel: 'n Storie van 32 Battalion en sy Mense,* (Bloemfontein: L.J. Bothma, 2007) p. 302
5   Wikipedia, *Armed Forces for the Liberation of Angola,* http://en.wikipedia.org/wiki/ Armed_Forces_for_the_Liberation_of_Angola (Accessed February 2012)
6   *ibid*
7   *ibid*

8 *ibid*
9 Steenkamp, Willem, *Suid-Afrika se Grensoorlog, 1966-1989,* (Rivonia: Ashanti, 1990)
10 Nortjé, Piet, *32 Battalion: The Inside Story of South Africa's Elite Fighting Unit*, (Cape Town: Zebra, 2003) pp. 147-152
11 Bridgland, Fred, *The War for Africa: Twelve Months that Transformed a Continent,* (Gibraltar: Ashanti, 1990)
12 Steenkamp, Willem, *op.cit.*, p. 110
13 Wikipedia, *Jonas Savimbi*, http://en.wikipedia.org/wiki/Jonas_Savimbi (Accessed February 2012)
14 Steenkamp, Willem, *op.cit.*, p. 97
15 *ibid*, p. 108
16 *ibid*, p. 109
17 *ibid*, p. 115
18 Lord, Dick, *op.cit.*, p. 288
19 South African Department of Defence Documentation Centre, original sources
20 Steenkamp, Willem, *op.cit.*, p. 184
21 Internet
22 South African Department of Defence Documentation Centre, original sources
23 Bridgland, pp, 282 & 386
24 South African Department of Defence Documentation Centre, original sources
25 *ibid*
26 *ibid*
27 *ibid*
28 *ibid*
29 *ibid*
30 *ibid*
31 *ibid*
32 *ibid*
33 *ibid*
34 *ibid*, p. 172
35 *ibid*, p. 194
36 Groth, Siegfried, *Namibia, The Wall of Silence: the Dark Days of the Liberation Struggle*, (Wuppertal: P. Hammer, 1995) p. 37
37 *ibid*, p. 180
38 *ibid*, p. 47
39 *ibid*, p. 49
40 *ibid*, p. 55
41 *ibid*, p. 57
42 *ibid*, p. 60
43 *ibid*, p. 60
44 *ibid*, p. 67
45 *ibid*, p. 182
46 *ibid*, p. 100
47 *ibid*, p. 105
48 *ibid*, p 121
49 *ibid*, p. 106
50 *ibid*, p. 124
51 *ibid*, p. 125
52 *ibid*, p. 116
53 *ibid*, p. 117
54 *ibid*, p. 120
55 *ibid*, p. 119
56 *ibid*, p. 160
57 *ibid*, p. 156
58 *ibid*, p. 180
59 *ibid*, p. 174
60 Bopela, Thula, *Umkhonto we Sizwe: Fighting for a Divided People,* (Alberton: Galago, 2005) p. 173
61 *ibid*, p. 173
62 *ibid*, p. 174
63 *ibid*, p. 176
64 *ibid*, p. 177
65 Bottoman, Wonga Welile, *The Making of an MK Cadre*, (LiNc Publishers, 2010) p. 65
66 *ibid*, p. 77
67 *ibid*, p. 75
68 *ibid*, pp. 80 & 82
69 *ibid*, p. 87
70 *ibid*, p. 91
71 *ibid*, p.121
72 *ibid*, p. 131
73 *ibid*, p. 133
74 *ibid*, p. 137
75 *ibid*, p. 139
76 *ibid*, p. 141
77 *ibid*, p. 144
78 *ibid*, p. 147
79 *ibid*, p. 153
80 *ibid*, p. 159
81 *ibid*, p. 185
82 Personal consultation with Mr Koch

PART 2:

TACTICAL HQ AT ONGIVA

ONGIVA BASE

Above: Pumas and an Alouette helicopter at Ongiva airport.

SADF soldiers awaiting deployment on the runway at Ongiva.

Pumas departing from Ongiva airport, 1983. (Photo B. Koch)

Pumas at Ongiva, 1983.
(Photo B. Koch)

Ongiva airport at sunset, 1983. The guard tower was positioned on top of the terminal building housing the operations room. (Photo B. Koch)

The electronic warfare (EW) tent and vehicle at Ongiva, 1983. (Photo B. Koch)

20mm AA installation and the mobile radar at Ongiva, 1983. (Photo B. Koch)

Earlier scenes from Ongiva airport.

Although it boasted a long runway, the airport at Ongiva was small, the terminal buildings and the base area only measuring 100 x 200 metres or so. The base housed the operations leader group, a signals troop and the Intelligence Officer. An infantry rifle platoon, mortar group and an AAA battery supplied protection for the base. Other support came in the form of sappers, a logistics group running stores and Air Force Command. SAAF helicopter pilots were also based here from time to time.

The SADF had earlier captured Ongiva during Operation Protea two years previously. On 27 August 1981 air strikes were put in on FAPLA AAA sites that ringed the town by Mirage III, Mirage F-1, Buccaneers and Canberra aircraft.[1] An enemy convoy had fled in a northeasterly direction in an attempt to escape but was stopped by C Company 32 Battalion,

Ongiva town and airport were captured by the SADF during Operation Protea in 1981.

Warrant Officer N.F. Pestretsov (Starshina), the first and most senior Russian captured by the SADF. He was captured during Operation Protea near Ongiva.

serving as a stopper group. Two Soviet T-34 tanks and several BTR armoured personnel carriers were captured. During the battle, four Russians were killed. Warrant Officer N.F. Pestretsov (Starshina) was the first and most senior Russian to be captured by the SADF during the war, serving as irrefutable proof of the Soviet Union's active involvement in the Angolan war.[2]

On 28 August 1981 Ongiva airport was taken by the SADF, and radar installations were destroyed at Chibemba and Cahama. The SADF occupied Xangongo (formerly Forte Roçadas), Ongiva (also referred to as Ondjiva or Ngiva and previously Vila Pereira d'Eça), Peu-Peu and Humbe. By occupying a 50-kilometre swath north of the border between South West Africa and Angola, the Cunene Province of Angola was thus cleared of all SWAPO and FAPLA forces. This area remained under the SADF control until 1984 when the SADF voluntarily withdrew during the peace talks with SWAPO and the MPLA.

In January 1983 Ongiva Tactical HQ consisted of the following units:

- 1 x 3 SA Infantry Battalion 81mm mortar group
- 1 x 32 Battalion 81 mm mortar group
- 61 Mechanized Battalion armoured vehicles
- 1 x 103 Bty 10 LAA
- 1 x platoon from C Company 1 Parachute Battalion
- 1 x platoon from C Company 32 Battalion
- Maintenance, Sappers, Signallers and LTW

Elements were also deployed to protect Xangongo on the Cunene River crossing northwest of Ongiva, consisting of:

- 1 x platoon from 32 Battalion
- 1 x 3 SA Infantry Battalion 81mm mortar group

During initial operations, a company of 1 Parachute Battalion was also situated at Ongiva. They were later relocated to Xangongo and Ionde to relieve 32 Battalion platoons on the ground. During this period I also supplied communications to this Parabat unit.

An air force contingent with four to six Alouette gunship helicopters and two larger Puma helicopters (nicknamed 'Giants') was occasionally stationed at Ongiva. Fighter aircraft, including Impalas, Mirage F1s and Mirage Mark IIIs, were stationed at Ondangwa air base

The bridge over the Cunene River at Xangongo, destroyed during Operation Protea.

approximately 150 kilometres south of Ongiva.

32 Battalion platoons performed operational duties 'in the bush' for six weeks at a time, whereafter they returned to Buffalo, 32 Battalion's base inside South West Africa. At Buffalo they would take a few days to rest and recover, before embarking on a six-week retraining programme. I was responsible for collecting and maintaining all radio equipment, and for re-issuing the fresh platoons with serviced radios.

Survival in the bush was arduous. 32 Battalion members carried heavy backpacks, referred to as *mashillas*, containing at least two weeks' rations, several two-litre water bottles, weapons, ammunition and radio equipment. They were able to move swiftly, covering vast distances on foot without any motorized or vehicle support. They did not bath or clean on deployment and wore the same clothes without changing in order to merge with the environment and become part of the bush.

Once a fortnight platoons on operations in the bush were resupplied with water, dry rations ('rat packs'), ammunition and fresh radio battery packs, delivered by two Puma helicopters, to the respective platoon positions. Later, resupplies were delivered by Dakota fixed-wing aircraft by parachute drop at night. Apart from the Dakota being a far cheaper method, the Puma helicopters were not always available. Before the night air drop, the platoon cleared an area in the bush; candles were placed in a straight line on the ground to indicate the location and direction of the drop zone and were then lit just before the aircraft arrived overhead. However, supplies were frequently damaged on impact with the ground. As such, sensitive radio equipment was only ever supplied by helicopter.

My daily routine at the 32 Battalion Tactical HQ Operation Dolfyn, Ongiva, and later at Ionde, consisted of servicing radio equipment, recharging batteries and changing the radio frequencies: just after sunrise and before sunset frequencies were changed to allow for the difference in the ionosphere caused by fluctuating temperatures.

Platoon leaders made radio contact with Tactical HQ four to six times a day, when they were required to report their positions and provide information to the operations commander. The various platoon positions were plotted on a large map, with new reference points, or RVs, issued as and when the situation on the ground changed. When contact was made with the enemy, radio communication was immediately established with the Tactical HQ to en-

32 Battalion members boarding a Puma.

sure that any casualties could be quickly evacuated. Each incident was recorded in the operations logbook; situation reports (sitreps) and operational reports were relayed daily to the Sector 10 HQ. I was present when most orders were received and issued during operations.

The signaller who operated the radio needed to be highly skilled. I found that even well-trained signallers sometimes struggled to master the intricacies of operational communications. A good signaller could pick up the faintest sound on the radio and accurately record what was being said. When reception was poor because of static interference, for example, the signaller needed to interpret what was being said and make assumptions that fitted the situation. Such assumptions were then repeated back to the sender to confirm that what he was saying was being correctly received. The message was again repeated by the signaller, with the platoon leader verifying the accuracy with a simple "positive" or "negative". The signaller was thus expected to record every detail to a high degree of accuracy. Soldiers' lives depended on his skills so there was absolutely no room for error. Requests for lists of resupplies were received, accurately recorded and directed to logistics. Signallers were a crucial cog in all operations and performed critical service for the troops in the field. They worked long shifts, night and day, and had to perform at their peak and maintain a high standard of alertness at all times. Situations were always tense during firefights: correct tactical decisions had to be made quickly, on the spot, based on accurate communications and information.

I am indebted to the countless signallers at 32 Battalion who assisted me. Some of their names I cannot recall but I should mention Sergeant Quintus and Lance-Corporal de Goede. Second Lieutenant Kenny remained at Sector 20, where he performed invaluable service in establishing and maintaining the radio network between Buffalo, Rundu and Omauni, while I was involved with 32 Battalion operations inside Angola for over a year.

A typical radio conversation went something like this:

> "*One-zero, one-zero, this is Echo Victor, do you copy?*"
> "Echo Victor, I copy you … I read you three out of five, how do you read me?"
> "*I read you fives.*" [confirming the signal strength and clarity of the sound]
> "You set and I sync."
> "*Setting …*"
> "Syncing ..." [a purring sound follows when synchronized frequency hopping between the two radios is achieved]
> "Echo Victor, do you copy?
> "*Copy.*"
> "Echo Victor, what is your Romeo-Victor?"
> "*It is mike seven and juliet five, ext.* [coded] Copy?"
> "Roger copied, one-zero, your new Romeo-Victor is alpha three, mike six, ext. Copy?"
> "I copy, Echo Victor. Out."
> "Copy, roger out."

An old photograph of FNLA soldiers.

ON PATROL WITH 32 BATTALION

32 Battalion became renowned for killing the most enemy soldiers during the Angolan bush war. They were always at the forefront of hostilities and the often the first to engage the enemy. The battalion was formed in the mid 1970s, consisting mainly of Portuguese-speaking ex-FNLA soldiers, and based at Savate under the control of FNLA commanders. Bravo Group was divided into three rifle companies, and each was put under control of a 2 Recconnaisance Commando operator. Following Operation Savannah in 1975, Jan Breytrenbach withdrew Bravo Group to South West Africa, and so it was that 32 Battalion established itself at Buffalo base. Starting out as a Special Forces unit under Special Forces command, infantry leaders were later introduced, subtly changing the battalion's role.

During the bush war, 32 Battalion was rarely spoken of, and their active involvement during many battles was barely mentioned. Even today, accounts of the bush war tend to gloss over 32 Battalion's involvement, primarily due to the unit's clandestine existence and mode of operation.

Founded in 1962, the FNLA under Holden Roberto, along with the MPLA and UNITA liberation movements, was one of the primary guerrilla movements in the fight against the Portuguese for Angolan independence. In 1975, when the MPLA took power, FNLA and UNITA went back to the bush to continue the struggle in what became the protracted Angolan civil war. The FNLA gradually fell by the wayside, usurped by UNITA as the primary non-communist opposition, until it collapsed completely. This left many FNLA soldiers looking for a new home and Jan Breytenbach was happy to oblige.

These ex-FNLA troops were highly effective, skilled fighters, accustomed to serving under extreme conditions. They were absolutely fearless in battle. During a firefight, through sheer guts and determination, they would relentlessly and ruthlessly close with the enemy, They were renowned for their battle cry, "*Avança!*" which instilled terror in the enemy who was either swiftly eliminated or fled. 32 Battalion were a special brand of people. Armed with Special Forces equipment, strong leadership, discipline, military skill and solid logistical and medical back-up, they became a fearsome force to be reckoned with.

I had the privilege of accompanying various platoons of 32 Battalion on patrol during operations. I recall the swift manner with which they were capable of moving through dense bush, and their ability to detect the enemy's presence with barely the slightest indication manifest. I remember on one patrol when we stopped to set up camp (a temporary base or TB) for the night just before last light. Everybody quickly dug shell-scrapes to sleep in and set boobytraps and claymore mines around the perimeter, before preparing the evening meal (open fires were strictly forbidden). By nightfall, dead silence prevailed over the entire TB: the discipline was extreme and never wavered.

The platoon commanders of 32 Battalion were normally highly respected by their troops, and their orders were followed precisely. These leaders were specially selected officers and non-commissioned officers. After completing their first year of training, they received vigorous and stringent training at Buffalo base. Only the best were recruited to become leaders at 32 Battalion.

On one occasion, while I accompanied a 32 Battalion rifle platoon on patrol, we ran out of drinking water. The front section was heading towards an unknown water source, whilst our section had already found a drum filled with water. As a result, the two sections became separated and we were unable to catch up with the front section. I was now in command of half a platoon. Needless to say that when we were re-united with the other section, the platoon commander had little difficulty in expressing his extreme dissatisfaction over what had happened.

Being tall, I found it difficult to find my way through dense bush. I could hardly bear those most irritating little insects, mopane bees. They crawled up one's nostrils and seemed to find a way into one's eyeballs. This continued for hours on end, with clouds of houseflies also everywhere, covering the back of one's shirt like a carpet; and when the sharp thorns of a tree got hold of you they pierced right through your flesh, causing severe pain.

32 Battalion killed large numbers of the enemy, making contact on almost a daily basis. These records are contained in the sitreps, some of which follow later in this book. It is difficult to provide an exact head count of how many SWAPO and FAPLA soldiers were killed by 32 Battalion during this period, but in relation to our own losses, which were minimal, enemy casualties at 32 Battalion's hands were staggering.

Back at operations tactical headquarters I can still recall the sounds of anxious voices on the radio reporting, "*Kontak, kontak! Staan by!*" ("Contact, contact! Stand by!") While listening to the broadcast, I could clearly hear sounds of gunfire and mortars exploding in the background. After a while, another message followed, reporting the number of enemy that had been killed, wounded or captured.

Sometimes, requests were made for gunship helicopters or 'choppers', to provide air cover during the firefight, and occasionally casualty evacuation requests for our own members who had been wounded or killed. It was a most spectacular sight when standing on the Ongiva

runway, witnessing four to six gunship helicopters passing overhead in a victorious fly-past formation, and after landing, dropping off piles of bodybags with enemy corpses: the result of yet another day's combat, another 32 Battalion victory.

32 Battalion worked closely with the SAAF gunship pilots. During attacks on the enemy, our forces were frequently offered air cover by them. (The SAAF's involvement in the Angolan bush war is well described in

32 Battalion soldiers boarding a Puma. (Photo R. Griessel)

From Fledgling to Eagle by Brigadier-General Dick Lord.)

SAAF Impala fighter aircraft were involed in Operation *Maanskyn* (Moonlight),[3] when enemy convoys were attacked at night. The Impalas were soon the dominant force in the Cunene province, except at Cahama where 57mm radar-guided AAA batteries were positioned. The logistical routes through Cahama, Mulondo and Cuvelai were targeted. The enemy generally only moved their convoys at night, for during the day armed reconnaissance flights by Impalas prevented any enemy logistical movement. If the Impalas reached the limit of their planned patrol range and had not found any enemy convoys, they delivered their weapons on pre-selected targets, using old-generation 115kg bombs known as '*Varkies*' (little pigs).[4]

During one such attack on an enemy target, Dick Lord wrote that a report was intercepted from a source at the FAPLA 2nd Brigade that "the racists had bombed 600 metres west of my position". The following night, the target was again bombed, but now the 600-metre error had been accordingly adjusted. Thereafter, no more messages were received from this source.[5] Dick Lord stated that the road from Xangongo to Cahama was scattered with the wrecks of petrol tankers, BTR-152s, Gaz and Zil logistic trucks with severe shrapnel damage sustained from these air attacks by the Impalas.[6]

The Angolan representative at the United Nations complained about the SAAF using such tactics, and so the US government applied pressure on the South African government which resulted in them ceasing. Even later, SAAF requests to continue with these attacks were denied by the politicians. It was indeed a bizarre way to fight a war: when the knock-out punch was imminent, the boxing match was stopped. The enemy used this period to bring in radars, SAM missiles and AAA systems, again gaining a measure of control over their air space.

The Alouette III gunships played a major role when a contact was made with the enemy. The firepower of the 20mm gunship cannon is a fearsome spectacle; few enemy soldiers survived its explosive power. These gunship pilots and their gunners were the bravest of the brave, with many achieving the highest honour: the award of the Honoris Crux medal for bravery. Major Arthur Walker, one such helicopter pilot, was the only South African serviceman to receive two Honoris Crux Gold medals. Similarly, Puma pilots faced frightening odds when evacuating wounded or dead soldiers, often under intense hostile fire, and many were decorated for their acts of heroism. One such incident is described later in this book.

On 6 October 1983 a Puma helicopter crash-landed in dense bush during an operation because of overloading, a result of the confusion that followed while soldiers were being evacuated from an operational area. Too many soldiers boarded the Puma which was already heavily laden with supplies. While attempting to lift off, the Puma crashed. A further operation had to be mounted to salvage the damaged aircraft to prevent the wreck from falling into enemy hands, the kind of trophy that communists relish.

PEOPLE SERVING IN 32 BATTALION

Many interesting personalities served in 32 Battalion during this period. Sergeant-Major Koos 'Krokodil' Kruger was renowned for surviving an attack by a crocodile; not many people are alive to share their story after such an incident. He also single-handedly wiped out an enemy platoon being transported in the back of a truck. He fired a well-directed RPG-7 rocket which found its target.

Commandant Eddy Viljoen (during my stay he was promoted to colonel), known as 'Big Daddy', went by the famous codename of 'Echo Victor'. He was promoted to Commanding Officer 32 Battalion during 1982, following in the footsteps of Colonel Jan Breytenbach,

Brigadier Gert Nel and Colonel Deon Ferreira. He received the Honoris Crux medal for bravery during a contact with SWAPO in 1978. He enforced discipline in 32 Battalion, he did not tolerate failure or cowardice and he was authoritarian but only had the well-being of all at 32 Battalion at heart.

He once severely punished a group of soldiers who, after returning from 1 Military Hospital, brought with them bags of crockery, knives and forks, stolen from a kitchen. He once suspected a few officers of consuming alcohol while returning from an operation inside Angola. His suspicion was confirmed after we boarded a Dakota aircraft; while airborne all those who had had too much to drink the previous night became airsick and started vomiting. The old 'Kotskoets' ('vomit coach'), as the Dakota was referred to, had implicated the culprits. The guilty platoon leaders were severely punished, as Colonel Viljoen instructed them to return to the Angolan bush for a further six weeks without any rest period.

Captain Jan Hougaard (during my stay he was first promoted to major, then commandant, and later holding the rank of brigadier-general before retiring from the SANDF) was a professional soldier who had only one interest: to engage with the enemy and to succeed in everything he did. He was very dedicated to this task; he spent long periods running operations in the bush without any relief or taking leave. He was in charge of all 32 Battalion operations inside Angola during this period. He had previously been decorated with the Honoris Crux, together with two other officers, for brave conduct on 9 December 1976 during an incident at Eenhana base when he rescued two wounded 3 South African Infantry Battalion soldiers when ammunition was set alight and exploded among the troops. He was also almost killed when an enemy SA-6 missile exploded close to his Bosbok fixed-wing aircraft and the pilot had to perform an emergency landing inside Angola.[7]

After the war, Captain Willem Ratte (later promoted to commandant) gained right-wing infamy in the post-democratic-election period for his occupation of an old Anglo-Boer war fort in Pretoria, and has been accused of being in possession of illegal military arms and ammunition on several occasions. He was in command of the 32 Battalion Reconnaissance Wing. They had been stationed at a base at Omsuai (established in 1976), west of Rundu, but vacated the base at the end of 1983. He was a tough man, capable of surviving under extreme conditions for extended periods without support. Much was expected of the Reconnaissance Wing: they had to seek and locate enemy positions, at which the next operation was aimed. (I didn't deal with him directly, but was told that he severely punished signallers who made mistakes!)

Sergeant-Major Gary Wright was a former soldier in the Australian army before he joined 32 Battalion. He made certain that the preparation of our food was always of a high standard. Frequently, I witnessed cooks flipping tractor tyres down the road as punishment for not preparing a decent meal.

Among some of the soldiers that I served with at 32 Battalion was Lieutenant Johan Swart, the grandson of a former State President of South Africa, C.R. Swart. He later was my roommate at university and we became good friends.

I cannot single out other individuals at 32 Battalion, as everyone played an important role in the unit. The following list outlines the leadership element at 32 Battalion, who participated in operations in Angola in mid 1983:[8]

32 Battalion Commander: Col Eddie Viljoen
Operations Commander: Capt Jan Hougaard
Signals Officer: 2Lt M. Scheepers
Intelligence Officer: 2Lt Rudman
Engineer Officer: 2Lt A.J. Theron

A Company
Commander — Lt B.G. Olivier

A1 (c/s 11) — 2Lt A. du Plessis
Cpl C.J. Moolman

A2 (c/s 12) — 2Lt M. Lourence
Cpl J.P.A. Marais

A3 (c/s 13) — 2Lt F.C. Olivier replaced
by 2Lt M.D. Claasen
2Lt A.J. Nel
Sgt G.H. du Randt
(KIA 1/7/83)
Cpl D. Lucus

A4 (c/s 14) — 2Lt G.W. Roos (WIA 3/4/83)
Cpl C.F. Meyer
Cpl P.G. Slabbert

B Company
Commander — vacant & Capt B. Swanepoel

B5 (c/s 21) — Lt B.J. Bosch
Cpl J.P. Botha

B6 (c/s 22) — 2Lt J. Swart
Sgt M.W. Henning
Cpl Coetzee

B7 (c/s 23) — 2Lt Evans
Cpl H.A. Hesse

B8 (c/s 24) — 2Lt B. van Dyk
Cpl van Rooyen

C Company
Commander — Capt J.T. Barron

C9 (c/s 31) — 2Lt D. Willows
Cpl P. Stein

C10 (c/s 32) — 2Lt K. Mackenzie
Cpl J.H. Parreira

C11 (c/s 33) — 2Lt B.C. Rankin

C12 (c/s 44) — 2Lt H.J. Kruger
Cpl Schoeman

D Company
Commander — Lt M.A. Store

D13 (c/s 41) — 2Lt P.J. Louw
Sgt Z.A. de Beer

D14 (c/s 42) — 2Lt P.C .Hoffman
Cpl J.W.J. Joubert

D15 (c/s 43) — 2Lt AM Rodgers
Cpl L Kotze

D16 (c/s 44) — 2Lt Slabbert
or S.C.J. Alberts
Cpl D. Morrison

E Company
Commander — Lt D. van der Merwe

E17 (c/s 51) — Cpl P. Jordaan
or Lt J.D.V. Oberholzer
Cpl M. Marlor

E18 (c/s 52) — 2Lt P.G. Leach
Cpl S. Smith

E19 (c/s 53) — 2Lt A.D. McCallum
Cpl P. du Plooy
Cpl R. Vincent

E20 (c/s 54) — 2Lt P.J. de Wet
Cpl J. Meise

F Company
Commander — Lt F.H. Heyns

F21 (c/s 61) — 2Lt P. Louw
Cpl J. Smith
Cpl I. Tomson

F22 (c/s 62) — 2Lt J. Hamman
Cpl A. van Niekerk
Cpl S. Engelbrecht

F23 (c/s 63) — 2Lt L. du Toit
Cpl J. Strauss

F24 (c/s 64) — 2Lt S. Notelovitz
Cpl P. Jates

G Company
Commander — Capt M. Bastin

G25 (c/s 71) — 2Lt E. Hendricks
Cpl J.W. Mallon
Cpl P. Bothma
Cpl J. Petzer

G Company continued ...		**Mortar Group**	
G26 (c/s 72)	2Lt J. Human	M1	2Lt R.K. Olsen
	Cpl P. Burley		Cpl J.J. Brand
G27 (c/s 73)	2Lt R.D. Marais	M2	2Lt H.B Pretorius
	Cpl G. Scheepers		Cpl S.M. du Plessis
	Cpl M.S. Parreira	M3	Lt F. Erasmus
G28 (c/s 74)	Lt W.A. Eichorn		2Lt F. von Soloms
	Cpl M. du Plessis		
	Cpl E.H. Rheeder	M4	2Lt D.J. Rossouw
			Cpl C. Charter

KILLED IN ACTION

On 1 July 1983 Sergeant G.H. 'Salty' du Randt (78226370PE) and Rifleman E. Cassera (83708339SP) were fatally wounded at Oshendje (XM 2560 or 210670XM), southwest of Dova, during a contact with SWAPO.[9] The incident reports are included later in this book. At 010735B July 1983 a section of Platoon 3 A Company left their TB on patrol. Sergeant du Randt and the rest of his platoon stayed behind at the TB. A group of between 30 and 50 SWAPO members, in single file, then walked right into the TB. The SWAPOs were caught totally by surprise but in the ensuing confusion, managed to fire off several 82mm mortars onto the platoon. A report even suggests that an SA-7 missile was fired as well. During the chaos, a number of 32 Battalion soldiers uncharateristically panicked and fled, leaving behind their dead and wounded, as it was apparent that their position was about to be overrun. The wounded soldiers played dead as the SWAPO members hastily looted their equipment, including a B22 and an A72 radio. Thereafter, they left and bombshelled in all directions. Second Lieutenant Roos, Corporal P.G. Slabbert, Rifleman P. Tgoetao and Rifleman M. Moango were wounded during the attack. Du Randt and Cassera were killed.

An official signal, OPS/246/01 JUL 83, from Sector 10, reported the incident, stating erroneously that four EF members had been killed. The contact was a huge moral victory for SWAPO as a 32 Battalion platoon had panicked and fled, something that rarely occurred. It was, however, a sad day, an isolated incident caused by lack of discipline in one platoon. Days later some of the equipment, including the A72 radio, was discovered, scattered over a wide area. Members of 32 Battalion were also reported missing after the attack but were later found some distance away from the contact area. (On 3 July another platoon of 32 Battalion contacted the same SWAPO group but no reports of casualties were received.)

The wounded were casevaced by Buffalo personnel carriers to a secure location, whereafter they were airlifted out on 9 July by Puma helicopter. Sergeant Salty du Randt was a very tall man, with a very warm personality. I still have a pair of his size 13 Special Forces boots in my possession, issued to me due to us sharing the same shoe size.

Following is the list of 32 Battalion members killed in action in 1983:[10]

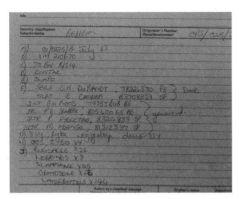

- Mande, A.
- du Randt, G.H.
- Kativa, J.D.
- Nambi, J.
- Kasera, E.
- Manganhes, T.

Signal written by Major Hougaard, reporting that Seargeant G.H. du Randt and Rifleman E. Cassera had been killed in action.

INCIDENTS AT 32 BATTALION'S TACTICAL HQS

It comes as no surprise that unusual conditions lead to unusual circumstances. During a conflict such as the one outlined above, unusual circumstances were often experienced. Some will regard it as part of the adventure, while others contribute the unusual nature of warfare as the reason. Here, I describe a number of the personal experiences still I cherish while I was serving inside Angola. I probably was the only person in the SADF to serve the longest uninterrupted period inside Angola during 1982 and 1983, lasting almost 13 months.[11]

The UFO and the gunship
One morning, on 29 January 1983, to our surprise and amazement we were awakened to witness a large, round, shiny disc-like object that remained in a steady position above our base at Ongiva. Of course, anything that could not be identified qualified immediately as the enemy about to launch a military operation. After healthy debate, our commander, Captain Jan Hougaard, ordered an airstrike against the object. Because we did not have fighter planes to provide us with air cover at that time, Captain Hougaard decided to take it upon himself to dispatch a gunship helicopter, one being available at Ongiva.

After the attack was ordered, we discovered that this object was positioned at such an extreme height, that even when the gunship reached its highest altitude and using all its firepower, it still could not manage to find its target. To date, no one knows for certain what this object really was. One explanation is that it was a wayward weather balloon, drifting over our base at a very high altitude.

Runaway aeroplane
One quiet Sunday afternoon, while I was sitting in front of my tent at Ongiva, a slight breeze

was blowing across the runway. At the one end of the runway was parked a Dakota aircraft. But not for long. The next thing, the plane started to move in our direction as if taking off. The only problem was that the plane was moving backwards, and not towards the runway, but rather towards a tent where a number of electronic warfare troops were sleeping. A gust of wind had propelled the plane into motion and nothing but the tent was going to stop it. Gracefully the plane came to a standstill right in the middle of the tent. Miraculously, nobody was hurt The plane was subsequently grounded for a couple of weeks, and only after it had been properly inspected by air force tiffies, was it declared airworthy again.

Foul-tasting water

We obtained our drinking water at Operation Dolfyn Tactical HQ, Ongiva from a nearby pond. It was purified until it reached an acceptable level to be regarded as safe for human consumption. The extreme temperatures during summer regularly exceeded 50°C inside the tent; consumption of water was therefore, among other forms of liquid, very important.

We made a plan to keep the water cool, putting the water in large plastic bottles which we covered with material that was kept wet, the same material used for sandbags. If the fabric was kept moist the water inside stayed cool.

Later, everybody began complaining about the bad smell and taste of our drinking water. The engineers were instructed to resolve the crisis immediately, but after various attempts were made, failed miserably. More and more pressure was put on them to improve their purification process. Morale was by now was severely affected due to the bad taste and smell of our drinking water.

After lengthy deliberation, it was decided to remove all the fabric from the water bottles, emerging that the problem came from inside the bottles. At night, mice had found their way inside the bottles, drowned and decomposed in the water. This problem was quickly resolved and everybody had pure water to drink again, but now only available at a warmer temperature.

Casevac

Casevac, or casualty evacuation, is the term used when an wounded soldier is evacuated and transported to a medical facility for treatment. At one stage, it became more and more difficult to obtain air support to evacuate wounded soldiers, especially at night.

One of our troops, enjoying an energy bar, an item in the ration packs, was left in severe pain as he had broken his upper and lower front teeth while biting into this particular treat.

It took several days to arrange for a helicopter to evacuate him.

At the time, the son of a well-known general was slightly wounded in a landmine explosion while driving a Buffalo vehicle. Not only was he driving on a gravel road (which was forbidden because of the frequent occurrence of landmine explosions), but it also occurred after dark (when driving was strictly prohibited). The general's son was immediately airlifted and evacuated. Perhaps the

Sappers retrieving water from a *shona* near Ongiva base, 1983. (Photo B. Koch)

An SADF soldier being casevaced by a Puma. (SADF Archives)

message came across to our members that not all received equal treatment.

The rifle grenade

During one of our operations, on 4 February 1983, I was present when a 32 Battalion member, Lance-Corporal Mario Oliviera was casevaced due to a painful wound. His platoon had engaged with approximately 40 SWAPO members in the Mupa area, between six and eleven terrorists were killed, four were wounded and 32 Battalion sustained four casualties. Oliviera was struck by an enemy M60 rifle grenade which pierced his shoulder and remained completely buried inside his chest. The grenade was not initially discovered when he was first attended to by medics. This grenade-type projectile is approximately 15 inches long and two inches in diameter, with small plastic fins at the back for guidance. A report later described the incident: "A human bomb that could have gone off with the slightest jolt was transported on a helicopter for more than an hour without anybody knowing of the danger."

Lance-Corporal Mario Oliviera, was injured (now his third wound sustained in action) on the border on 4 February. Within ten minutes a helicopter was on the scene to evacuate him, while medical orderlies provided a drip and antibiotics. He was taken to our base at Ongiva, where a medical officer examined him. The doctor inserted a drain to withdraw blood from his chest.

At that stage nobody knew that the wound had been caused by an M60 rifle grenade and that it was still inside his chest.

Oliviera was then flown to Oshakati, where the doctors prepared him for surgery. It was only after the first insertion had been made by the surgeon, Captain Paul Eloff, that the plastic fins of the M60 rifle grenade were uncovered. An explosives expert was called in and the fins were identified as those of an M60 grenade.

X-Rays confirmed the fact and the theatre was evacuated. Captain Paul Eloff and Captain Koos Reyneke, the anesthetist, stayed behind and attended to the patient. A barrier of sandbags and armoured plates from the sides of a Buffalo personnel carrier was erected in the operating theatre to protect the operating team. Major de Villiers and Staff Sergeant Lubbe also participated during the operation. Captain H. van Vuuren from 25 Field Regiment, an explosives expert, immediately evacuated the operating theatre and the vicinity thereof. Major de Villiers later received the Honoris Crux for bravery for his role during the medical procedure. Captain Eloff and Captain Reineke, both Citizen Force (territorial) members, received the Southern Cross medal for exceptional and meritorious service and devotion to duty.

A hole was burned through the plastic fin and a cable from a pulley in the roof of the theatre was fastened to the grenade. The operating team took cover behind the steel plates as the bomb was slowly pulled out of Lance-Corporal Oliviera's torso.

Oliviera later told *The Citizen* newspaper that he was conscious from the time of the shooting until taken inside the operating theatre. Captain Eloff said that Oliviera was fully

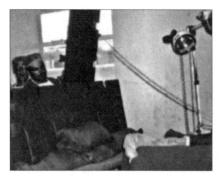

The scene in the Ondangwa operating theatre where this unusual surgery was performed.

Lance-Corporal Oliviera with Major de Villiers, showing the position of the M60 rifle grenade.

aware of what was going on and that he was scared that he was going to die. The projectile had penetrated the left shoulder and then both lungs without touching the ribs, and had come to rest against the ribcage on the right-hand side. Eloff said that if the bomb had touched the ribs on entry, it would have certainly exploded. He said that the soft tissue it went through was not sufficient to depress the striking pin, adding that when they removed the grenade, they found that the striking pin was depressed but not enough to explode the grenade.

The M60 rifle grenade can kill up to a distance of 50 metres from point of impact and maim up to a distance of 100 metres.

Another explosives expert, Captain A. Fourie, told *The Citizen*[12] that all the safety mechanisms had been taken out of the grenade and that it could have exploded any time after entering Corporal Oliviera's body.

It is an irony that, 21 years after this incident, the same surgeon, Captain Paul Eloff, who performed the operation and survived the incident, had retired, but at the age of 75 was killed in a tragic accident at his home in Polokwane by a blast caused by an oxygen cylinder which exploded.[13]

Medical doctors performed a major role during operations and saved numerous lives, with both SADF soldiers and local civilians benefitting from their expert care. At the time, when fresh doctors were introduced to relieve the doctors returning home, the Puma helicopter pilots played an amusing prank on them. The 'new' doctors were all invited to fly in a Puma helicopter for their first time in their lives, with everybody present at the base still unknown to the new doctors. The 'old' doctors were wearing pilot overalls, acting as the pilots, and the pilots were wearing white doctors' jackets, acting as the doctors. Before boarding the Pumas, the pilots and the old doctors quickly swapped uniforms in front of the new doctors, suggesting that the old doctors were actually flying the aircraft. The real pilots then flew the Pumas, causing the new doctors much anxiety. Back on *terra firma*, the new doctors appeared quite confused and very ill. After the true identities of the pilots were revealed, it caused much mirth for all present except, of course, the new doctors.

Medical support was always of a very high standard. I once had a tooth examined and filled by a dentist who carried all his equipment, including his field dentist's chair and drills in a bag. The whole procedure took place inside Angola under a mopane tree.

Christmas 1982

At the commencement of my service during December 1982, my elder brother, Johan, a

Lance-Corporal Mario Oliviera and the position of the M60 rifle grenade inside his chest. (Photo *The Citizen*)

The surgeon, Captain Paul Eloff, displays the rifle grenade. (Photo *The Citizen*)

SADF soldiers being transported by Puma into Angola.

Citizen Force member and also an officer in the Signals Corps, was called up for duty on a six-week military camp. We met at a briefing session at Oshakati in the office of the Sector 10 Signals Commander, Major Chris Kruger. Johan was assigned to accompany me while he performed his duties at the Operation Dolfyn Tactical HQ, Ongiva.

About a week before Christmas, to our surprise, we located our eldest brother at Oshakati. Dawie was also a Citizen Force member and an officer, and also underatking a military camp at the time.

As things turned out, we all travelled to Ongiva together. The trip was quite unique, as all three brothers boarded the same helicopter and were airlifted under operational circumstances and flown into Angola. Only by the grace of God did nothing happen and we arrived safely at Ongiva. Dawie later conducted the church service at Ongiva on Christmas Day.

Later, I was often reminded of this most dangerous period of my life, serving inside Angola, how I felt spiritually removed from God. I was still young then and I had a great appetite for adventure. Any kind of war is clearly wrong as it encourages hatred and anger; these conditions unfortunately prevailed at 32 Battalion, which was probably why I was not able to seek spiritual communion with anyone at 32 Battalion. A pastor, who once visited our base, did not find any need to share the gospel with us. I made an attempt to form a small prayer group with some 32 Battalion members. I still have notes for a reading from Psalm 91 from my small military Bible, but unfortunately this did not appeal to anybody else as they were all too occupied with other things. I believe war should be avoided at all costs; war does not serve as a solution for a problem.

New Year in Angola

We all decided that New Year's Eve at Ongiva should be a special occasion. We planned to throw a party to celebrate the event. As Signals Officer, I was also required to provide the power supply on the base. Soon, everyone started connecting up cables, using bare electric wires which had been scavenged from Ongiva town. The annual rainy season normally started in December, and this year, on New Year's Eve, while

Standing from left: Lt Dawie Scheepers, Lt Johan Scheepers, 2Lt Marius Scheepers; seated: Chaplain Dawid Scheepers and Mrs. M. Scheepers.

everybody was enjoying the party, we experienced the first severe rainstorm of the season. Everywhere, small electric explosions were occurring on wet surfaces, the water short-circuiting the electric cabling. That night, I was kept occupied running around to restore the power supply. I was therefore unable to enjoy the party.

Fortunately, the signallers and members of the anti-aircraft battery were all good friends. At the time, the AAA commander, Captain Hendrik du Toit (later to hold a senior position at Investec Bank), invited my brother Johan and me to attend a 'formal' dinner, Ongiva style. We were treated to a delicious, well-prepared three-course meal, which included drinks and, especially, lots of Bailey's, a very popular cream liqueur unheard of in Angola.

After enjoying an excellent meal, we were then surprised by an entertaining night-firing exercise with their 20mm AA guns. We were then each presented with a fully loaded anti-aircraft gun. After a few flares were fired, we began target practice, aiming and shooting at the flares as they looped up into the night sky. It was a most memorable experience: we created our own light show, lighting up the Angolan night sky with thousands of tracer rounds. For me, the New Year's party came late that year, or early the next, but it was very special.

The anti-aircraft gunners practised their firing skills in this manner as part of their training. Previously, they practicsed by directing their gunsights at approaching SAAF Puma helicopters coming in to land at Ongiva. This practice ended when it bacame clear that the helicopter pilots did not appreciate the unwelcoming sight of looking down the barrel of an anti-aircraft gun when landing at Ongiva.

Minor accidents

I recall that, due to human error, a few accidents happened at Ongiva. My brother was once loading a three-ton generator onto the back of a truck. Somehow the generator slipped and fell off the side of the truck, causing severe damage.

I was also responsible for providing the equipment used for surveillance at night. One of the larger pieces was placed in a makeshift tower on the roof of the airport terminal building, to observe the area at night. A severe wind took hold of the equipment and blew it off the roof, causing severe damage to the very sensitive piece of equipment. A high-level inquiry investigated the cause of the accident, however the true cause was never established.

During one of our operations, the brakes of a big Samil 100 transport truck failed while approaching our base. The vehicle came to a sudden standstill right in the middle of my tent, leaving my telegraph printer and radio equipment in a state of total disrepair. Fortunately, nobody was hurt.

A Kwêvoël truck spontaneously caught fire while transporting supplies. The findings of the inquiry that followed the incident were that the fire must have been caused by a radio battery pack which had ignited.

Visiting Ongiva town

Visits to the nearby towns in Angola always caused a lot of excitement. Ongiva was a town complete with sporting facilities, churches, government buildings and a huge town square. But in 1983 not a single person resided in Ongiva, as the years of war had turned the town into a state of total disrepair. Following the road past our base, it ran northwest through several small villages until it reached the village of Xangongo, situated on the Cunene. Our road ended here as it was impossible to cross the river. The bridge had previously been demolished at Xangongo during Operation Protea in 1981.

Ongiva town.   Ongiva town.

Notes

[1] Lord, Dick, *op.cit.*, p. 174
[2] National Museum of Military History, Johannesburg, archives
[3] Lord, Dick, *op.cit.*, p. 248
[4] *ibid*, p. 232
[5] *ibid*, p. 232
[6] *ibid*, p. 233
[7] Van Wyk, A.T., *Honoris Crux,* (Kaapstad: Saayman & Weber, 1985)
[8] SANDF Archives original sources.
[9] *ibid*
[10] Bothma, L.J., *Die Buffel Struikel: 'n Storie van 32 Battalion en sy Mense*, (Bloemfontein: L.J. Bothma, 2007) p. 379
[11] Author's personal documents
[12] *The Citizen*, 5 February 1983
[13] *Die Beeld*, 2 February 2004

PART 3:

TACTICAL HQ AT IONDE

MUCH DEEPER INSIDE ANGOLA

During July 1983 Operation Dolfyn Tactical HQ at Ongiva became a hive of activity. During the early 1980s several similar operations had been conducted from this base, such as Operations Meebos, Snoek, Tralies and, most noteworthy and recently, Operation Dolfyn. However, such high-profile activity did not suit 32 Battalion's style of operating.

Ongiva was stacked with rations, ammunition and spare parts with more and more convoys arriving with war matériel every day. This was a sign that something big was about to happen. In actuality, this was the early stages of Operation Askari, which was to follow at the end of 1983.

During July 1983, a large number of South African troops, fully mechanized, were deployed inside Angola, the largest contingent of South African troops ever to have been simultaneously present in a foreign country. I was responsible for establishing and maintaining communications with the task forces deployed over a vast area of southern Angola.

I recall numerous times when our base received visits by dignitaries, such as General Constand Viljoen, General Jannie Geldenhuys and, at one stage, by the then Minister of Defence, General Magnus Malan. We had huge respect for these generals, as they were often seen at the forefront of operations.

One morning at Ionde, while servicing radio batteries, I noticed a very tall person standing next to me. It was General George Meiring who was visiting Ionde on an inspection of SADF bases at the front. Also a signaller, he was shortly to become the new commander of Sector 10. He later became the last head of the SADF.

Prior to one of these high-level visits, one of our base commandants (not a member of 32 Battalion) at Ongiva ordered that the base be properly cleaned. The thought of sweeping the base, planting flowers and making roads was totally ridiculous, considering that Ongiva was an operational base inside a foreign, hostile country. This commandant had us complete the task just in time for the arrival of one of the generals, but was duly admonished for his ill judgment in turning an operational base into a showcase.

Later, severe pressure got to this same commandant as he was frequently overheard shouting in a high-pitched voice: "Scheepers, Scheepers and Scheepers!" He would curse both my brother and me in a similar high-pitched tone, clearly showing his dislike for something we were blissfully unaware of. At one time my brother was servicing our radio equipment and needed to take down the main radio antenna. When the commandant inquired why there were no communications at the time, we discovered that he was actually busy with a secret operation, but unfortunately, did not consider it necessary to inform his signals officers about it. Needless to say, the operation was not a success without any form of proper communication.

It was then decided that Ongiva had become too 'crowded' for 32 Battalion, as it was now fashionable for senior SADF members to visit to Ongiva and issue all kinds of random orders to battalion members. In May 1983 Captain Willem Ratte, commander of the 32 Battalion Recce Wing, compiled a report after he had investigated feasibilty of deployment of a mobile task force to a place called Ionde. His report follows:

Viability study for the Mobile Task Force at 32 Battalion Tactical HQ, Ionde:[1]
1. 32 Battalion is responsible for operations against SWAPO in the 'Deep Area', above the line Evale/Nehone with a fixed base at Ionde, from which operations could be controlled.
2. Within this framework, there is scope for more operations to be conducted.
3. A small contingent of a mobile task force consisting of vehicles has already been put on trial in previous operations and information is available to take this matter further.

The purpose to establish Ionde:
4. To investigate the future application of a mobile task force.

Discussion:
5. The following factors support the implementation of a mobile task force:
    a. Availability of Ionde to serve as fixed base.
    b. Own force air control that expands north of Cuvelai.
    c. Restriction of FAPLA to the greater central area, e.g., Cuvelai and Techamutete.
    d. Relatively light armed SWAPO members are in the area, with the biggest threat being 14.5mm cannons at front headquarters.
    e. Existence of broad, easily accessible and open river valleys without obstacles that stretch to the Calonga River.
    f. Accessibility of bush areas for own vehicles.
    g. Ability to carry fuel for helicopters on vehicles, a sort of mini Helicopter Admin Area that is mobile.
    h. Resupply by air with parachutes that could be recycled for other uses.

Disadvantages:
6. The following factors restrict the implementation of a mobile task force:
    a. Vehicles make a lot of noise.
    b. Vehicle tracks that are left in the area that cannot be erased.

A mobile task force could fulfil the following requirements:
7. Deployment and redeployment of smaller units.
8. Advanced mini-HAA for special operations.
9. Day and night support as reaction force in case of emergencies.
10. Mobile supply of helicopters and refuelling facilities.
11. Raids against enemy bases and routes.
12. More firepower and support for companies and recce teams if needed.
13. Misleading the enemy to divert attention away from other operations.

14. Its advantages are obvious.

Disadvantages could be overcome by:
15. Slow movement of vehicles close to enemy lines.
16. Avoiding normal routes
17. Movement through UNITA areas from the north.

The following are already available for a mobile task force:
18. Three Buffalo APCs with mounted weapons.
19. Three commanders to serve as vehicle commanders and weapon instructors.
20. Weapons to fit six more vehicles.
21. Vehicle drivers.
22. Radio equipment.

Conclusion:
23. The principle of a mobile task force could promote the efficiency of conduct against the enemy.
24. Commanders could avoid stereotypical conduct and thus surprise the enemy.

The following is required to implement this successfully:
25. Three Buffalo and two Moffel vehicles should be dedicated to this task force.
26. Five leaders and ten troops required to man vehicles and to give protection.
27. Eight avtur bladders and four drums avtur to be loaded on Moffel vehicles.
28. One capable mechanic with tools.
29. A channel to provide urgent requirements for the task force.
30. All of these pre-requirements could be achieved. Various role players should be prepared to make it available.
31. More personnel could be provided by parts of companies, Mortar Group and Recce Wing to fill in the gaps.

Apart from the above, a high level of training, practice and good control over the mobile task force could make its application almost unlimited.

The result of this report was that no new mobile task force was established at Ionde, but rather, the manner of conducting operations at Ongiva was reviewed, and the Tactical HQ was

then relocated to Ionde. The difference was that at Ionde, very little logistical support was provided by helicopter, the trooping of 32 Battalion's members and their resupply was done by vehicles and no longer by Puma helicopter. Troopings were done with Buffalo personnel carriers and fortnightly resupplies were done by fixed-wing Dakota aircraft.

32 Battalion being resupplied with ammunition by a Puma.

OPERATION DOLFYN TACTICAL HQ AT IONDE

32 Battalion's commanding officer, Colonel Eddie Viljoen, took it upon himself to order 32 Battalion's evacuation from the Tactical HQ at Ongiva. I believe this was done against the wishes of some of the members of the higher command. We relocated our Tactical HQ to a very remote site at Ionde.

Ionde is situated approximately 120 kilometres north of the Angolan border with South West Africa, and 172 kilometres from Omauni, a 32 Battalion base in South West Africa. Ionde had been captured from the enemy by Task Force Bravo on 25 August 1981, on the same day that Ongiva fell into SADF hands.

Ionde was a valuable site; it later served as the Tactical HQ for Operation Daisy on 3 November 1981. During this operation, the attack was commenced at Embundo, six kilometres south west of Ionde, by 32 Battalion, 61 Mechanized Battalion, 201 Battalion and 1 Parachute Battalion. One SWAPO base was destroyed, with two others already deserted by the time of the attack.

During Operation Daisy, on 6 November 1981, SAAF Lieutenant Johan du Plessis in a Mirage F1CZ shot down an Angolan MiG-21, the first enemy aircraft destroyed in a dogfight by the SAAF since the Korean War of the early 1950s. Later, on 5 October 1982, a second Angolan MiG-21 was shot down by the SAAFs Major Rankin, also flying a Mirage F1CZ.[2]

Ionde consisted of three buildings next to a gravel airstrip. We used one building for our operations and radio room, another served as a store and the third as a kitchen. Ionde was established as a fully constituted operational base inside Angola, and matched any scene from

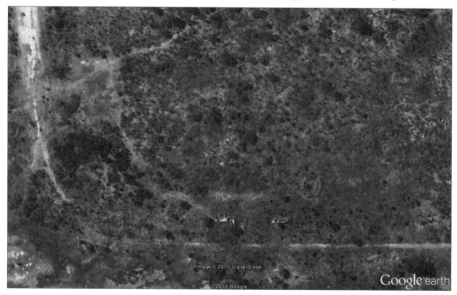

A more recent aerial photograph of Ionde base

The operations room at Ionde. (Photo M. Scheepers)

The operations room at Ionde from another angle. (Photo M. Scheepers)

Ionde from another perspective. (Photo M. Scheepers)

Underground ammunition storage bunkers under construction at Ionde. (Photo M. Scheepers)

Buffalo vehicle at Ionde, with the *shona* visible at rear. (Photo M. Scheepers)

Corner bunker at Ionde overlooking the *shona*. (Photo M. Scheepers)

a Hollywood action movie. It consisted of underground bunkers strengthened with huge logs and sandbags, and every building and every bunker were covered with camouflage nets; the base was barely visible from the air.

Ionde was established on 16 June 1983 to serve as the 32 Battalion Operation Dolfyn Tactical HQ. This was the location from which troopings were undertaken and ensured that 32 Battalion remained operational in Angola at all relevant times. Ionde's primary function was to serve as the hub from which to deploy companies on operations, to rotate companies and to protect the strategic airfield. From Ionde all our own forces' and enemy movements were monitored and instructions issued accordingly to members in the field.

A specific instruction was issued that the minimum of equipment was to be held at Ionde to allow for easy relocation if so required. Ionde base remained in operation for almost a year, which made it a far more permanent base than had initially been anticipated.

An extensive trench system was created for the protection of the base and observation posts were established in particularly high trees. The surrounding area was cleared of vegetation to allow for a *skootsvelde* (good view). The base was secured with daily patrols in the vicinity, and the runway swept daily for landmines.

Ionde came under the direct control of Operations Headquarters at Ongiva, Operation Dolfyn. Daily contact was made with DISA forces (UNITA) in the area.

Supplies were provided by aircraft from time to time, however, during my six-month stay at Ionde, we did not receive any fresh provisions. Meals consisted of dry rations from the ratpacks, accompanied by cooked meals prepared using soya beans and freshly baked Portuguese bread from an outside oven.

The base was quite inaccessible; for several months we were almost completely isolated from the outside world. As a result, we grew our hair and our beards, unable to have haircuts and reluctant to shave. Also, the reaction time from Ondangwa to Ionde was now considerably longer for any air support to reach us. During troopings all platoons were required to be as near as possible to Ionde to allow for lower fuel consumption and reduced flying time.

Logistics at Ionde

The following logistical provisions were maintained at Ionde:[3]

- 1 x 1,300-litre diesel bladder
- 2 x 2,200litre avtur (helicopter fuel) bladder
- 3 x avtur pumps
- 2 x diesel pumps
- 1 x avtur hand pump
- Gas cylinders as required
- Ammunition for six weeks
- 10,000 x ration packs
- Fresh food supplied by aircraft every ten days (this never materialized)
- 1 x 10,000-litre water bladder

RADIO COMMUNICATIONS AT IONDE

After the relocation of 32 Battalion to Ionde, Lieutenant von Balen became the new Tactical HQ Signals Officer at Ongiva and Second Lieutenant Marius Scheepers was transferred with 32 Battalion from Ongiva to Ionde, to continue serving as the 32 Battalion Signals Officer at the new base.

The radio communication at the Tactical HQ consisted of a rear link between Ionde and Ongiva, a front link between Ionde and the companies, and another rear link between Ionde and 32 Battalion HQ in Rundu. The operations and radio room were housed in the main building at Ionde. The signals room was supplied with one portable power supply, two Anderson battery chargers and an A-frame for charging radio batteries.

The signals room had a storeroom in a bunker next to the operations room, where all additional radio equipment and batteries were stored. Fifteen boxes of A52/53/72 radio batteries and A39 batteries (disposable batteries used to make battery packs for B22 radios) were supplied to Ongiva every two weeks. Usable radios and equipment were supplied every two weeks from Ongiva to Ionde by Dakota aircraft.

The new HF frequencies ('foxies') for radio communication assigned to Ionde Tactical HQ during winter months, as from 1 July 1983, were as follows:[4]

Between 8:00 and 9:00: 4702 MHz
Between 9:00 and 10:00: 5450 MHz
Between 10:00 and 17:00: 7679 MHz
Between 17:00 and 19:00: 5450 MHz
Between 19:00 and 20:00: 4702MHz
Between 20:00 and 8:00: 3123 MHz
Spare: 8395 MHz

The call signs were Ongiva: 72, Ionde: 87 and Xangongo: 97. The frequency used for ground-to-air communication was channel 9 (132,750 MHz) on A72 VHF portable radios. The following radio equipment was supplied to 32 Battalion's Tactical Operations HQ at Ionde:

A72 portable radios
10 per company x 3
7 per recce team
8 in reserve
Total: 45 radios

B22 HF portable radios
4 per company x 3
6 per recce team
7 in reserve
Total: 25 radios

B22 Hopper HF portable radios
1 per company x 3
3 per recce team
2 in reserve at Ionde
2 in reserve at Sector 10 HQ, Oshakati
Total: 10 radios

C23 HTX (or TR15H) hopper fixed radios
3 at Ionde

10 x T13M batteries (car batteries)
3 x 6-metre masts
1 x 3.5 KVA generator
100 metres x copper wire
8 x jumper cables
3 x dipole antennas complete

Radio security during Operation Dolfyn
Different means of communication were provided for the different levels of security that had to be maintained, which were a T1000CA teleprinter: Top Secret; a TC812 teleprinter: Secret; and C23H (or TR15H) and B22H HF radios: Confidential.

We erected two 'ape cages' at the top of very high trees to serve as observation posts. One night, on 4 July 1983, the guard reported that a number of lights were rapidly moving in our

Ionde airstrip viewed from the 'ape cage' up a tree, near where 2Lt M. Scheepers was wounded in a landmine explosion. (Photo M, Scheepers)

direction. We were convinced that a full-scale enemy attack was about be launched against the base, as a FAPLA brigade was situated at Caiundo, not far away. Notwithstanding bad communications, we managed to acquire air support from Ondangwa who immediately dispatched two Impalas. An air-to-surface missile attack was launched at this 'force'. The next day we discovered that the lights were large bush fires blazing in the distance, creating the impression of vehicle headlights moving towards us.

FULL-SCALE MILITARY ATTACK

I was part of a well-executed attack by 32 Battalion on a SWAPO base situated in the Jaula area, approximately 450 kilometres inside Angola, northeast of Cassinga. The overall commander of the operation at Ionde was Commandant Preston-Thomas, with Captain Hougaard as the commander at the Helicopter Admin Area.

It was my responsibility to supply all communications to 32 Battalion platoons, to HQ and with the air force during this operation.

32 Battalion established a Helicopter Admin Area near the target on 3 October 1983 and brought in all available military capabilities, including gunships, Puma helicopters and 32 Battalion. Impala jet fighter were also deployed to provide air cover for the Puma helicopters and initiate the action with air strikes.

An air-storm operation commenced at 11:00 on 7 October 1983. One 32 Battalion company (call sign 10) and the 32 Battalion Recce Wing infiltrated north to serve as stopper group. The assault was conducted by a second 32 Battalion company and an 81mm mortar section.

At H-Hour, with full radio silence instituted, an air-to-surface missile strike by Impala aircraft attacked SWAPO's AAA installations, followed by gunship helicopters arriving to provide air cover for the next wave of attacks, undertaken by 32 Battalion troops inserted by Puma helicopter. All actions occurred in short succession. The enemy base was totally destroyed, while 32 Battalion sustained no casualties during the attack. It was reported that 70 SWAPO members had been pulled out of the area just three hours before H-Hour, heading in a north and northwesterly direction. 32 Battalion also captured several SWAPO members. Our Commander in Chief at Sector 10, Brigadier A.J.M. 'Joep' Joubert, who was also present during the operation, complimented 32 Battalion for conducting a well-coordinated attack.

MINEFIELD AT IONDE

On 17 June 1983, a day after the official date for the 'inauguration' of Ionde, a number of transport vehicles, including Kwêvoël and Samil 100 trucks, arrived at Ionde to deliver supplies, aircraft fuel, ammunition and vehicle spares. After a number of these vehicles, heavily laden with supplies, had already entered the base, they, one by one, detonated enemy anti-tank landmines. We didn't realize it but Ionde was actually situated on an enemy minefield, littered with dozens of anti-tank mines. The sappers had missed the mines when they had swept the area earlier, obviously because of the depth at which they were buried, but the pressure from the weight of the laden heavy-duty vehicles detonated them. The sappers were ordered to do a thorough sweep of the area and clear all the remaining landmines, but, on 29 and 30 June, more vehicles were damaged in further landmine explosions.

At the time of one such explosion, I was returning to the operations room. I was walking a few feet in front of a vehicle on the stretch of road between the base and the airstrip. The front wheel of the vehicle detonated a mine and the force of the explosion swept me right off my feet. I lay next to the vehicle, covered with dust and debris, with dirt and bits of rubber blown into my face. For weeks, I experienced difficulty hearing properly, as one eardrum had been damaged, causing me severe discomfort; so much so that I was unable to perform my duties properly while monitoring communications on the radio networks.

SUPPLIES AND TROOPINGS TO IONDE

By now, our base had lost its appeal to HQ. The only means by which we could obtain fresh supplies was directly from 32 Battalion's home base at Buffalo, near the Caprivi Strip. It took four days to cover the journey from Buffalo to Ionde by vehicle, and another four days back. No roads existed in that area north of the border, with Buffalo situated more than 500 kilometres southeast of Ionde. It was a daunting journey through dense bush and over vast distances. We used Buffalo and Kwêvoël trucks to transport troops and supplies, with the vehicles driving roughshod, or 'bundu-bashing', over sandy terrain and through forests and thick bush.

A standing order was that all 32 Battalion personnel wear steal helmets during the trip. The weight of the helmet puts much strain on one's neck and back, aggravated by the swaying motion of the vehicle travelling on uneven surfaces. It is difficult to explain in words how difficult it was to reach Ionde by vehicle.

Troopings of 32 Battalion members were done every six weeks to relieve and replace the three companies operating in Angola with the same number of replacement companies.

As the 32 Battalion's home base was situated at Buffalo in eastern Kavango, we used the route from Buffalo via Rundu to Omauni, where the convoy crossed the border into Angola to reach Ionde.

On 22 October 1983 one such trooping from Ionde was performed by aircraft. Four Puma helicopters shuttled between Ongiva and Ionde and two Dakotas departed from Ondangwa to Ionde, transporting troops between Ionde and Ongiva. The Pumas and Dakotas then returned to Ondangwa with full loads of troops just relived from the field. But it was a time-consuming and cumbersome process, so we requested that a C-160 Transall aircraft be made available to land at Ongiva to conduct three trips, and to fly from Ondangwa to Omega. On such a trip, a C-160, apart from its far larger payload, would be able to significantly reduce the turnaround time: 16 hours on a Puma and six hours on a Dakota. However, the request was denided because of safety issues at Ongiva.

NEAR ACCIDENT AT IONDE AIRFIELD

On one occasion, as a Dakota was approaching the airstrip to land at Ionde, I was with the operations commanding officer, Captain Hougaard, standing next to the runway, to fire a smoke grenade to show the pilot the wind direction. As the plane touched down, it appeared that the wind suddenly changed direction; a strong tail wind suddenly drove the plane towards us. Worryingly, the rubber tanks containing highly flammable aircraft fuel were right behind us. We quickly jumped out of the way of the runaway Dakota, expecting the worst but, most skilfully, the pilot deftly executed a U-turn at the end of the runway. The plane had managed to avoid the fuel tanks by mere feet. When the pilots emerged from the aircraft, they were quite distressed by this near accident.

We frequently held training exercises at Ionde. During one such exercise, one of our soldiers members fired a 60-millimetre mortar precisely on target but, unfortunately, the wrong target: onto our only water tank, leaving us without proper drinking water for several days.

SWAPO absolutely avoided any area where 32 Battalion was operating. It seemed unnecessary, but we continued to perform our standard drills such as *klaarstaan* (stand-to) just before sunrise and sunset, demostrating our preparedness in the event of an attack on the base. We regularly spent nights sleeping in trenches, often practising our defensive drills, and were always ready to deal with an attack.

On one occasion, a group of SWAPO accidently passed by the base at Ionde. After being spotted in the middle of a *shona* (or *oshona* or *chana*, a marsh, or empty pan in the dry season), we immediately opened fire on them. However, they fled immediately, as surprised as we no doubt were and they all escaped.

Wild animals were scarce in the area. I only ever noticed a few ostriches and one small herd of blue wildebeest grazing in the vicinity. An officer once shot an ostrich for a meal and he was severely punished, as the killing of game was strictly prohibited.

We stayed fit by jogging on the runway, and we regularly played volleyball in the evenings, followed by cracking open a cold Lion Lager. At Ongiva we used to have barbeques, or *braais,* on

Sappers sweeping Ionde runway for landmines.
(Photo M. Scheepers)

32 Battalion members undergoing weapon training
at Ionde. (Photo M. Scheepers)

The dry floodplain, or *shona*, west of Ionde. (Photo
M. Scheepers)

Before an attack on a SWAPO base in the
Jaula area inside Angola. From Left: 2Lt
Marius Scheepers, 2Lt Brand van Dyk and the
Engineers officer, 2Lt A.J. Theron (Photo M.
Scheepers)

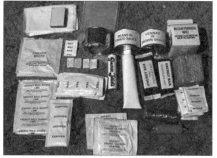

Contents of a ration pack.

2Lt Marius Scheepers at Ionde.
(Photo M. Scheepers)

Friday evenings, but without fresh meat this was not possible at Ionde. Our only shower consisted of cold water provided from a bucket hanging from a tree.

It was not possible to listen to popular music, nor did we see any movies for the 13 months I was in Angola. Many important global events that took place that year went unnoticed, such as the Church Street bombing in Pretoria, and the British–Argentine war over the Falkland Islands. Isolated from the outside world, we were totally unaware of these events. I recall the then President of South Africa, P.W. Botha, venomously denying having any military presence in Angola, while 32 Battalion was actively conducting military operations in the area.

The Operation Dolfyn Tactical HQ, Ionde was totally dismantled in early 1984, after the Joint Military Monitoring Commission was formed, and it was agreed that SADF would withdraw from the area. On 15 April 1985 South African forces withdrew even further from southern Angola during Operation Dikmelk. A military parade was staged north of the border at Santa Clara. FAPLA representatives were expected to attend this event.

FINAL PASSING-OUT FUNCTION AT 32 BATTALION, 1983

During my stay in Angola in 1983, I was only able to take leave once, and that was a few days before my period of military service expired. There had just been no opportunity to take any time off due to our situation and frenetic workloads. When I did finally go on leave, I left Ionde directly for Ondangwa, before flying to Waterkloof air force base in Pretoria in December 1983. I realized that I was still carrying my AK-47 assault rifle. On arrival, dressed in my camouflage uniform and carrying my AK-47, eyebrows were raised by the Military Police. South African soldiers did not carry weapons of Soviet origin. The situation was shortly resolved when someone remarked that I was part of Special Forces and should be treated with respect.

I handed over my duties to Second Lieutenant van der Merwe who replaced me at Ionde as the new 32 Battalion Signals Troop commander.

A week later I returned to Rundu just in time to attend our passing-out parade on 10 December 1983. The 32 Battalion leader group members were each presented with a special award, a small shield bearing the unit's coat of arms. At the end of the ceremony, I found I was the only person not to have been given an award. The reason was that the staff at Rundu could not find any records of Signals officer Second Lieutenant Marius Scheepers, blissfully unaware of my existence. Because I had served uninterruptedly in Angola for such a long period, I had become a ghost soldier.

I was later promoted to the rank of captain in the SADF after I had undergone further military training, and became a Signals commander in the Citizen Force. I received the Pro Patria, the Southern African and the General Service medals for playing my part in defending the sovereignty of South Africa.

Notes

[1] South African Department of Defence
   Documentation Centre, original sources
[2] Lord, Dick, *op.cit.*, p. 194
[3] South African Department of Defence
   Documentation Centre, original sources
[4] Author's personal notes

PART 4:

THE POLITICAL SCENE

IT'S ALL POLITICS

In 1984 President Reagan won the US presidential election by the largest margin in history. Prior to this, attempts had been made to reach a ceasefire between the opposing parties in Angola, proposing that the opposing forces begin negotiations on the Cape Verde Islands. Angolan forces were to withdraw north of the 14th degree of latitude, 150 kilometres north of the border with South West Africa, to be followed by a ceasefire on 1 February 1983.[1]

The Angolan ambassador to France denied that these negotiations ever took place.

At the end of February, a second round of negotiations took place in Cape Verde. The talks came to nothing as Angola was represented by its Minister of Foreign Affairs, Alexandre Rodrigues, but the South African delegation consisted only of officials and military personnel without any authority to cut a deal.[2]

On 26 April a conference took place in Paris during which the Algerian ambassador to the United Nations accused South Africa of having launched an attack on the Luanda oil refinery, causing R46 million of damage.[3] During the attack one South African soldier was killed in a blast. This incident is reminiscent of similar events on Operation Kerslig when a South African Recce team operator died in a blast during one such an attack.[4]

On 16 August 1983 the Angolan Angop Broadcast Corporation accused South Africa of having 10,000 SADF members deployed at Ongiva and Xangongo in preparation for an attack on Cangamba[5].

SAAF AIR STRIKE AT CANGAMBA

In August a meeting was held between Jonas Savimbi of UNITA and high-ranking officers of the SADF and the SAAF at Rundu. He asked South African forces to assist UNITA in capturing an MPLA HQ at Cangamba. After nine days of frontal assualts, UNITA forces had been unable to take Cangamba. This target was a long way from SWAPO's and South Africa's normal sphere of activity and, as FAPLA was not the main target of operations in

Angola, an attack at Cangamba would be regarded as South African aggression against the people of Angola. Rather than commit ground troops, Brigadier Bossie Huyser suggested that the SAAF bomb Cangamba.[6]

Operation Karton therefore opened, deploying two Puma helicopters and C-130 Hercules aircraft, to deliver arms and ammunition to UNITA. Captured SA-7 Strela missiles were also provided. Four Buccaneer and four Canberra bomber aircraft conducted the airstrike against Cangamba on 14 August, with Mirage F1s providing top cover. Dick Lord described this to have been the most effective airstrike ever performed by the SAAF in Angola.

Officially, it was reported that the offensive was conducted by UNITA forces, who successfully forced 100 Cuban soldiers from the area and killed 829 Angolan and Cuban soldiers during the attack. This victory placed UNITA firmly on the map as a force to be reckoned with, giving them control of 25% of Angola, while actively involved in another 50% of the country. UNITA's presence in eastern and southeastern Angola was of great value to the SADF, with UNITA preventing SWAPO from entering the Kavango and Caprivi areas of eastern South West Africa.

However, the result of UNITA's gains was that Cuba increased its troop deployments by a further 5,000, to a total of 25,000 men, during 1983. The Soviet Union sent more sophisticated T-65 tanks, attack helicopters and ground-to-air missile systems to Angola. By forcing FAPLA to form much closer ties with SWAPO, South Africa was now facing a massive conventional enemy force.

SOME NEGOTIATIONS AND MORE FIGHTING

On 26 August 1983 Perez de Cuellar, the UN Secretary-General, arrived in Luanda to meet with President dos Santos and Sam Nujoma, describing SWAPO as "the representative of the people of Namibia".[7]

South Africa insisted that Resolution 435, the United Nation's blueprint for the independence of South West Africa, had to be linked to the withdrawal of Cuban forces from Angola.[8] At the same time the Soviet Union sent a diplomatic message to South Africa, stating that the SADF presence in Angola would not be tolerated. South Africa responded that the Soviet stance was seen as a threat and perceived it in a hostile manner. Operation Askari was therefore given the go-ahead, because of and regardless of the communist superpower's threats.

The South African Minister of Foreign Affairs, Pik Botha, then met with Chester Crocker, offering to withdraw from Angola by the end of January 1984, on the proviso that SWAPO and Cuba did not exploit the situation.[9]

Operation Askari was now in full swing. On 20 December 1983, Angop accused the SADF of attacking Caiundo, killing scores of civilians and destroying schools and hospitals.

On 3 January 1984 the SADF, for the first time during the Angolan war, came face to face with T-54/55 tanks. Many such tanks encountered at Cuvelai were captured by the SADF. Piet Nortjé well describes this in his book.[10] During the night of 4 January 1984, a heavy bombardment by FAPLA forces took place. At first light the following day, a 32 Battalion platoon walked straight into the barrel of a T-54/55 tank. Fire erupted as the T-54/55 careered off the road and straight into a kraal, flattened a hut and came to a standstill in a swamp, where the crew abandoned the vehicle. All the crew were killed or captured. By then, 32 Battalion, to HQ's surprise had already captured Techamutete.[11]

On 5 January 1984 Sam Nujoma sent an urgent message to Perez de Cuellar requesting a ceasefire.[12]

On 15 January the last SADF forces were withdrawn from the area. On 8 February President P.W. Botha announced that a ceasefire had effectively been implemented in Angola.

On 13 February the Mulungushi Declaration was issued after talks in Lusaka between South African, Angolan and United States delegates. On 25 February the first Joint Military Monitoring Commission was established in southern Angola, as a means of keeping the opposing forces apart.[13]

The commission was, however, toothless, as by 13 April 1985, 142 breaches of the Lusaka treaty had been recorded, of which only four had been committed by the SADF. South Africa withdrew endorsement of the Lusaka treaty, with the SADF, in a show of strength, holding a grand parade on the border with Angola, welcoming their returning troops home.[14]

On 15 September 1985 Operation Egret was launched, the SADF's first attack into Angola since Operation Askari of January 1984. This followed numerous reported contraventions of the Lusaka treaty by SWAPO members. The peace treaty was in a shambles and further conflict loomed. The SADF avoided engaging with FAPLA at any cost, so as not to aggravate further escalation of tensions. Egret was completed by 22 September 1985.[15]

During May 1986 the SADF again crossed the border into Angola and engaged with FAPLA at Xangongo. On 5 June the South African navy launched an attack on Namibe, against oil depots and three cargo ships berthed in the harbour, to curtail the supply of weapons to Cuito Cuanavale.[16] This was followed by an attack on Cuito Cuanavale on 9 and 10 August 1986 by supposed UNITA forces but which were actually 32 Battalion. Continuing with tradition, 32 Battalion spearheaded many such attacks for which UNITA took the credit in order to avoid an international outcry against South Africa.

During August and September 1987, Operation Modular was launched to support UNITA. For the first time, SADF Olifant tanks and eight G5 guns were flown into Angola on a C-130 Hercules aircraft for deployment in the field. In November 1987 32 Battalion engaged FAPLA's 16 Brigade with three G6 guns, a mobile version of the G5, deployed for the first time. By now, 32 Battalion was fully integrated as part of a mechanized force, deployed by Ratels, debussing and advancing to the target in formation, followed by a Ratel 90 anti-tank squadron, Olifant tanks and Ratel 60s with ZT3 missile systems. This truly changed the nature of the conflict to full-blown conventional warfare.[17]

From 13 January to 23 March 1988, with the launching of Operation Modular, UNITA and South African forces attacked the FAPLA base at Cuito Cuanavale in the Cuando Cubango province. It was described as the second largest battle in the history of Africa after the Battle of El Alamein and the largest in sub-Saharan Africa since the Second World War.

Cuito Cuanavale's importance derived not from its size or its wealth but its location, where the SADF fixed the FAPLA forces in the town using the new G-5 artillery pieces. 32 Battalion operations were at this time under the command of Commandant Jan Hougaard. Both sides claimed victory in the ensuing battle. On 10 October 1988 General Geldenhuys stated that it had never been the SADF's intention to capture Cuito Cuanavale. On 5 December the SADF withdrew and Operation Modular closed.

Operation Hooper commenced on 15 December 1987, to disrupt supply lines and institute offensive operations against FAPLA's 21 Brigade. On 15 February 1988 61 Mechanized Battalion launched an attack on 59 Brigade, with 32 Battalion launching an attack on Menongue. Four SADF members were killed, five Ratels were hit and a Mirage was shot down; the pilot, Major Edward Every, was killed. During the battle of Tumpo four Olifant tanks and two Ratels were damaged. This was the last great SADF offensive in Angola. Operation Tempo III took place on 23 March 1988, resulting in three Olifant tanks being knocked out and captured by FAPLA.

Operation Packer followed, to gradually reduce SADF forces in Angola.

During the battles in the Cuito Cuanavale region, FAPLA lost 4,768 troops, 94 tanks, eight MiG-23 and four MiG-21 aircraft, and a vast array of weaponry, including SA-8 and SA-9 missile systems. The SADF lost 31 members; the cost of their ammunition was estimated at

R328.7 million.[18]

For failing to secure a Cuban/FAPLA victory at Cuito Cuanavale, President Fidel Castro of Cuba executed one of his most senior generals, General-Major Armando Ochoa Sanchez. A report on this, by the Washington correspondent of the *Cape Times*, was published on 27 January 1989.[19]

From left: Gen George Meiring (Chief SWATF), Gen Jannie Geldenhuys (Chief SA Army), Gen Constand Viljoen (Chief SADF), Brig A.J.M. 'Joep' Joubert, (Sector 10 Commander) and Dr Willie van Niekerk, Administrator General of South West Africa.

Notes

1. Steenkamp, Willem, *op.cit.,* p. 107
2. *ibid*
3. *ibid*, p. 108
4. Stiff, P., *The Silent War: South African Recce Operations, 1969-1994,* (Alberton: Galago, 1999) p. 357
5. *ibid*, p. 109
6. Lord, Dick, *op.cit.,* p.289
7. Steenkemp, Willem, *op.cit.,* pp 110
8. *ibid*
9. *bid*, p. 113
10. Nortjé, Piet, *32 Battalion: The Inside Story of South Africa's Elite Fighting Unit,* (Cape Town: Zebra, 2003) p. 197
11. Stiff, Peter, *op.cit.,* p. 365
12. Steenkemp, Wilem, *op.cit.,* p. 115
13. *ibid*, p. 117
14. *ibid*, p. 127
15. *ibid*, p. 135
16. *ibid*, p. 143
17. *ibid*
18. *ibid*
19. *ibid*

PART 5:

OPERATION ASKARI

THE COMPOSITION OF OPERATION ASKARI

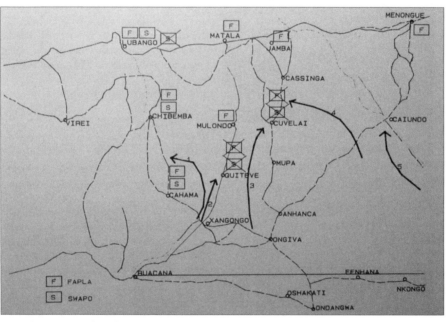

Map of Operation Askari showing SADF movements. (SADF)

Operation Askari force composition:[1]

Task Force X (61 Mech Bn Gp)
2 x 4 SAI companies

1 x 8 SAI company

1 x armoured car sqn (1SDB)

2 x troops MRL (10 Arty Bde)

1 x Arty bty (10 AAA)

2 x AAA btys (10 AAA)

1 x Recce element

1 x engineering troop (25 Field)

Task Force V (Combat Group Delta)
82 Mech Bde HQ
1 x company RGK + elements RPS and Regt De la Rey
1 x 1 SAI company
1x armoured sqn (RMR) + elements Regt Molopo
1 x Arty bty (7 Med Regt)
2 x AAA troop
1 x MRL troop (4 SAI)
1 x engineers troop (13 Field)
1 x signals troop (82 Signals)
1 x combined platoon (3 Support Unit)
1 x LWT (71 Field Work Area)
1 x med platoon (5 Medical Bn)
1 x provost section (7 Pro Coy)

Combat Group Tango
1 x 4 SAI company
1 x armoured car sqn (1 SDB/2 SDB).
1 x Arty troop (2 SAI Bn Gp)
1 x mortar section (5 SAI)
2 x engineers sections (25 Field)
1 x Recce element
1 x maintenance echelon (CMDMT Wit Maint Unit).
1 x LTW (35 Field Work Area)

Task Force EV
4 x companies 32 Battalion
Drivers (5 Support Unit)

For an SADF soldier serving inside South West Africa during 1983, the cut-line with Angola was probably the most northerly boundary, with few exceptions, that necessitated patrolling north of the border. 32 Battalion and 1 Parachute Battalion permanently operated across the border in the areas of Xangongo, Mongua, Evale, Anhanca, Nehone and Dova, and 32 Battalion as far up as Mupa, and also east of Cuvelai. For a brief period during Operation Dolfyn, other combat groups also penetrated these areas, but withdrew on completion of the operations.

The final frontier for SADF forces was the operational area deep inside southern Angola, north of the Cunene River (north of Xangongo) and north of Cuvelai/Cassinga and Caiundo. These areas were largely inaccessible due to the changing terrain, the distances that hindered logistical support, natural features such as fast-flowing rivers in the rainy season and the width of the Cunene River with a limited crossing at Xangongo only and, most importantly, the threat of FAPLA forces.

The large operations map at our Tactical HQ at Ionde displayed these towns on its outermost edges, with enemy bases situated at such places only noted, but posing the biggest challenge for any future invasion. They were the ultimate prize. I didn't believe for a moment that we could stike over such distances, but SADF commanders had other ideas. The silence would soon be broken.

North of the 150-kilometre line (from the cut-line) was considered a no-go area for 32 Battalion; this was the SAAF's domain and, with their ongoing airstrikes against anything military, we could not risk becoming a SAAF target. However, farther north, the Recces gathered intelligence, observing airfields and enemy movements as far north as Menogue, Cahama, Cassinga and Lubango, and also attacking enemy installations and infrastructure such as bridges and railway lines in a series of hit-and-run strikes.

However, a meaningful strike against FAPLA/SWAPO was only possible with a large all-arms combination and a huge logistics tail. Operation Askari was an opportunity to break the impasse and show the enemy that the SADF could strike wherever they chose.

Askari was primarily aimed at destroying targets at Cahama, Mulondo and Cuvelai. Later, Caiundo was also earmarked for attack, as was Techamutete which was captured quite unexpectedly by 32 Battalion. Askari was to become the watershed in the war.

D-Day for Operation Askari was initially planned for 9 November 1983, but was postponed to 9 December due to South African Foreign Affairs Minister, Pik Botha, embarking on a series of talks with African and other political leaders during this period. The element of surprise, always important in an operation, was thus forfeited in the process.[2]

Operation Askari consisted of the following phases:[3]

Phase 1: Deep penetration by Special Forces, followed by a SAAF attack on the Typhoon-Volcano SWAPO base at Lubango, between 1 November and 30 December.

Phase 2: The offensive reconnaissance and isolation of Cahama, Mulondo and Cuvelai, planned from 16 November to the mid January 1984. By attacking these targets, enemy communication and logistic lines were to be cut deep within enemy territory, to demoralize SWAPO and force them to withdraw northward.

Phase 3: To establish and dominate the area from west of the Cunene River, through Quiteve, Mupa, Vinticete and Ionde, by February 1984.

Phase 4: To halt SWAPO incursions once and for all, with these general guidelines applying:[4]
a.   The enemy must be stopped externally
b.   Deep reconnaissance coupled to offensive actions must be commenced at an early stage
c.   Maximum use of mobile elements for follow-ups must be made
d.   Security forces must operate proactively, not reactively
e.   Security forces must maintain the initiative
f.   A SWAPO infiltration during 1984 must simply not take place. Not even ten terrorists will be permitted to successfully infiltrate

The SAAF aims for Askari were as follows:[5]
a.   To gain and maintain a favorable air situation over Cahama–Mulondo–Cuvelai
b.   To prevent the expansion of enemy air-defence capabilities in the Mulondo–Quiteve–Cuvelai areas
c.   To expand the SAAF interdiction programme:
     i.   up to Chibemba
     ii.   north of Mulondo
     iii. up to Cassinga
d.   Extend *Maanskyn* (Impala night operations) north of the 150km line

The aim was also described as the continuance of normal operations to cause the maximum losses to SWAPO 'detachments', before their yearly attempt to infiltrate South West Africa.

The general guidelines were to stop SWAPO infiltration from reaching the border, to perform deep reconnaissance and offensive actions during the early stages, and to make use of maximum mobility during follow-up actions.

The SADF strike force consisted of a 5,399 troops, commanded by Brigadier Joubert, and was made up of of four major combat groups: Task Force Echo Victor (Colonel Eddie Viljoen), Task Force Fox (Commandant Tobie van Schalkwyk), Task Force Victor (Commandant Faan Greyling, the Citizen Force elements) and Task Force X-Ray (Commandant Ep van Lill, on 12 January replaced by Commandant Welgemoed). There was a fifth force, Combat Group Delta Foxtrot, also referred to in its initial stages as a joint Sector 20 force (Colonel Deon

Ferreira), consisting of a company-based combat group from Sector 20, Echo Company of 1 Parachute Battalion and one company from 32 Battalion.[6]

The other commanders in Task Force X-Ray were:

- Combat Group 1: Capt J. Buisson
- Combat Group 2: Maj C.P. du Toit (Maj Dries van Jaarsveld)
- Combat Group 3: Maj I. Johnson
- Combat Group 4: Capt Grundlingh
- 1/4 Recce: Maj D. Steyn
- 54 Recce: Capt Jacobs
- 53 Recce: Maj C. Meerholz

Task Force X-Ray, with its operational HQ situated at Xangongo, was made up of 61 Mechanized Battalion, plus attached units consisting of three motorized infantry companies, an armoured car squadron, two troops of mobile rocket launchers, one artillery battery, two anti-aircraft batteries, a reconnaissance element and a troop of engineers (with elements from 102 Battalion also giving support).

The two mechanized combat groups of Task Force X-Ray consisted of two mechanized companies of 20mm Ratels, one motorized company with Buffalo vehicles, an armoured car squadron consisting of five troops of 90mm Ratels (not to be confused with the Eland 90 armoured cars), 20mm Anti-Aircraft Troop, 3 Reconnaissance Commando, Engineers Troop, medics, four 81mm mortar groups with eight weapons in total and four sections of storm troops mounted on Buffalo vehicles, all spread over four combat groups. Ten composite artillery regiments were also included, as follows:

- Papa Battery: 8 x 155mm G4 guns, manned by the so-called 'old guard' from 61 Mechanized Battalion.
- 142 Battery from 14 Field Regiment: 155mm G4 guns (with a maximum range of 24 kilometres). This was last time the G4s were used.
- Quebec Battery: 8 x 140mm G2 guns from 7 Medium Regiment, and with Combat Group Delta and 82 Mechanized Brigade, in support of Task Force Victor.
- Romeo Battery: 7 x 127mm MRLs, 143 Battery troop of 4 SA Infantry Battalion, divided into one troop in support of Task Force Victor and a Foxtrot troop in support of Task Force X-Ray.
- Sierra Battery: 8 x 140mm G2 guns, the so-called 'new guard' from 61 Mechanized Battalion, and 14 Field Regiment in support of Task Force X-Ray.
- 4 x 120mm M5 mortars in support of Task Force Delta Foxtrot.
- Cymbeline radar set on a Samil 50.[7]

Interestingly, these SADF guns overshadowed FAPLA's artillery, including its standard gun, the D-30 (122mm howitzer) with a range of 15.5km, the BM21 mounted on a URAL 375 truck with a range of 21km, the 130mm gun with a range of 27km, the D-74 122mm gun with a range of 22km, the 76mm gun with a range of 13km, the 120mm mortar with a range of 5.7km, and the 82mm mortar with a range of 3.5km. During Cuito Cuanavale, the range of FAPLA's M-46 (27.5km) was again outclassed by the G5's and G6's range of 39–47km, the longest accurate range in the world at that time.

Due to the poor mobility of the G4 guns, they were primarily used in areas where they had access to roads. Therefore they could not be deployed during the Cuvelai stage of the operation.

A 4th battery from 7 Medium Regiment was used in support of Combat Group Delta. I include information regarding the SADF Artillery's involvement during operations, as is provided by Clive Wilsworth in his book: *First In, Last Out* (pp 220–240).

Task Force Victor consisted of a core force, Combat Group Delta, from 82 Mechanized Brigade with its operational HQ at Ongiva.

Task Force Delta Foxtrot had its operational HQ at Rundu in Sector 20.

Combat Group Tango was also a small force that consisted of Recce teams and armoured cars, which operated near the targets at Mulondo and Cuvelai. Several secondary operations were conducted within Operation Askari, one being Operation Shark, consisting of Recce teams in the Mulondo and Quiteve areas. Another was Operation Blesbok consisting of a Recce team, a company at the HAA which operated at platoon or section strength, and also a mortar group, operating in the Chibemba, Cahama and Cuvelai areas. Operation Javelin consisted of elements from 1 Parachute Battalion, 101 Battalion and 8 South African Infantry Battalion at Xangongo. Operation Fox was formed in an attempt to capture the advanced FAPLA SA-8 ground-to-air systems during the last stages of the offensive at Cahama.

Task Force Echo Victor of 32 Battalion consisted of A, C, D and E companies and an 81mm mortar group, with their total strength at 617 troops.

The South African Air Force conducted several missions during the operation: ten Impala jets attacked Cuvelai, with four direct hits; four Canberra aircraft accurately bombarded Cuvelai; eight Impala jets attacked Caiundo; two Impalas destroyed anti-aircraft gun positions at Caiundo; two Impalas performed reconnaissance missions on the road north of Caiundo; and four Canberras bombed Caiundo. The SAAF supplied six Alouette gunship helicopters and two Puma helicopters in support of Task Force X-Ray.

The Signal Corps had two fully equipped Ratels, with HF/VHF radio facilities and direction-tracking equipment to locate EF HQs.

Several appeals were made to consider only SWAPO bases as targets, however, it was inevitable that in attacking SWAPO, their FAPLA hosts would also fall foul of the SADF. SWAPO's major positions were ten kilometres northwest of Dongo and west of Lubango, eight kilometres northeast of the airfield and 25 kilometres northeast of the town centre, housing two brigades, respectively—and were all well plotted by the SADF. They were behind the Cahama/Mulondo/Cassinga frontier and reachable by clandestine Recce deployment and aerial attack by the SAAF. These areas hosted 700 SWAPOs each; the Western SWAPO group would also be moving to Dongo before commencing with their infiltration.

As at 30 November 1983, SWAPO's strength was 79 artillery reconnaissance cadres, 81 B10 troops, 140 82mm mortarmen, 94 RPG operators and 600 SWAPO Special Unit infantry, 320 of whom completed their training in December 1983, to be deployed with the Shield Battalion in the Cassinga area. Twenty-two SAM-7 operators were sent to the THTC on 28 November to practise with MiG aircraft.

Based at Camene was the 10th SWAPO 'Salute' Battalion, and 40 kilometres east of Lubango SWAPO's Alpha 'Shield' Battalion. Based at Cahama was the SWAPO Western Areas HQ (WAHQ). At SWAPO's Ongulumbashe bases were their Front HQ, Leningrad base, Logistics base, Marxist Youth Centre and the Greenwell Matombo Training Centre.

Further intelligence was gathered on 15 December that also pointed to SWAPO's Eastern Areas HQ (EAHQ) bases situated in three positions, three and a half kilometres north of Cuvelai. On 16 December it was reported that four kilometres west of Caiundo,

FAPLA bunkers had been identified. As at 22 December FAPLA bases were identified four kilometres northeast, five kilometres north, three kilometres northwest, four kilometres north-northeast, five kilometres north-northeast, six kilometres north-northeast and seven kilometres north-northeast of Cuvelai.

SWAPO was also organized into a number of complexes: Complex 1, the HQ 53 Brigade plus one platoon of Cuban advisers, 120mm mortars, two BTR 152s and two BRDM-2s, manned by a 100-strong force; Complex 2 consisted of one battalion from 53 Brigade; Complex 3 consisted of 400 troops, armed with four 120mm mortars, six 82mm mortars, three BTR 152s, two BRDM-2s, one MTU and several 14.5 /12.7mm anti-aircraft guns. At Menongue were stationed a number of helicopters, four MiG-21s, four MIG-17s and four Pilatus PC-7 reconnaissance aircraft

SWAPO's Special Units operational commander was Michael Ashipala aka 'Danger', with Kapoko the second-in-command. Dino Hamaambo was the overall commander of SWAPO's armed forces.

At Matala were based the 6th FAPLA Brigade with 1,200 men and a Cuban regiment with 1,500 men. Their armoury consisted of SA-3 and SAM-9 missiles, 39 x T-54 tanks, MiG aircraft and M1-8 helicopters and radar. At Dongo was a 150-strong Cuban tank company. Jamba hosted a Cuban regiment of 1,500 men and the SWAPO logistic base.

Based at Techamutete was a company of 11th FAPLA Brigade, four 23mm AAA. SWAPO's 8th Battalion was based 30 kilometres east of Techamutete, as was SWAPO's Bravo Battalion consisting of 250 men.

Cuvelai hosted three battalions of the 11th FAPLA Brigade, one battalion ODP (local militia), 14 x T-34 tanks (later discovered to be T-54s), 4 x PT76 amphibious tanks and a number of BRDMs. Also included were 57mm AAA weapons, BM21 multiple rocket launchers, 122mm and 76mm artillery, 82mm and 120mm mortars and possibly SA-8 and SAM-9 missiles.

Other FAPLA brigades included the 53rd Brigade at Caiundo, the 3rd Brigade at Cahama, the 19th Brigade at Mulondo and the 3rd Brigade at Chiane.

FAPLA's 53 Brigade was based at Caiundo, consisting of the Brigade HQ and three battalions, including an ODP battalion. Thirty Cubans and 80 Russians were located a Caiundo, along with 120mm mortar groups, six 82mm mortar groups, 14.5mm anti-aircraft guns and SA-7 missile teams, and 60mm mortars. Between 5,000 and 6,000 civilians lived in the Caiundo area.

The initial stages of Operation Askari consisted of the usual planning of the operation, ongoing intelligence gathering and the consolidation of the various units and their deployment. Two Pumas departed from Xangongo on 3 November to deploy Recce teams (three Reconnaissance commandos were involved) at a position 35 kilometres west of Chibemba. This was the largest Recce involvement in the war. Consisting of five teams, they were then deployed west of Cahama, east of Cahama and in the vicinities of Mulondo and Cuvelai, to provide tactical intelligence from which the operational planning was done.

To summarize, two commandos were on the road northwest of Cahama to serve as cut-off groups, with a Recce group on the road between Quiteve and Mulondo to isolate Quiteve, supported by Task Force X-Ray.

On 7 December reports were received from the 32 Battalion Recce Wing that SWAPO had already withdrawn from the target area during March 1983, and that the Cubans had withdrawn in November 1983.

During the period 10–20 December, ten SAAF Mirage F1AZ fighter jets were on immediate standby for deployment, also lodging air attacks against enemy 57mm and 23mm anti-aircraft positions. Recce teams were positioned west and north of Mulondo to serve as cut-off teams for any EF movement in their direction. More airstrikes by Impalas were made to stop further EF vehicle movement.

Task Force Tango commenced an artillery bombardment on EF targets at Mulondo. This was met with return fire.

On 27 December the SAAF almost lost an Impala after the aircraft, piloted by Captain J. van der Berg, was hit in the tail section by a SAM-9 ground-to-air missile. Fortunately, the damaged aircraft landed safely at Ongiva airport.

QUITEVE

On 28 December 1983, a force of 230 FAPLA troops was confirmed in the area just south of Quiteve.

Combat Group 1 of Task Force X-Ray now consisted of two mechanized platoons and two Ratel 90 armoured car troops, an engineers section and Sierra Battery with its 140mm guns. Combat Group 2 consisted of three mechanized infantry platoons, three armoured car troops, an anti-aircraft troop, an engineers section and an MRL troop, Foxtrot Troop.

The term used was 'fighting element' and not 'platoons', as four cars had infantry platoons and four cars from the armoured car troop were integrated to form a small fighting team. Combat Group 1 could form two fighting elements and Combat Group 2 three.

Task Force X-Ray sent an element (Combat Groups 1 and 2) west of the Cunene River to capture Quiteve and fix the enemy at Cahama. Therefore, after achieving these objectives, the western flank of Task Force X-Ray was protected from attack by FAPLA and SWAPO reinforcements. Thereafter, Task Force X-Ray linked up with Combat Group Delta to attack Cuvelai. Combat Group 3 of Task Force X-Ray was deployed at Katagwera.

The area between Quiteve and Vinticete was completely deserted; it was discovered that the villages in the area had been torched.

On 11 December Task Force X-Ray, under the auspices of Operation Shark, arrived in the vicinity of Quiteve and attracted EF mortar positions. Two Impala jet aircraft spotted two T-54 tanks and EF infantry approaching the OF on foot, who disengaged from their pursuit, left the main road and sought cover in the dense bush. A SAAF Mirage fired at the target and hit a T-54 tank.

The SADF used the Landnav system for the first time in combat. It was a first-generation global positioning system that could position one within a 300-metre-accuracy range.

The EF southeast of Quiteve consisted of two infantry platoons. A stronger EF was present north of Mulondo.

Combat Group 2 would attack Quiteve from the north, while Combat Group 1 would remain with the echelon; both combat groups formed a TB ten kilometres from Quiteve.

A Reaction Force (RF) from Task Force X-Ray made contact with EF on 15 December, 21 kilometres east-southeast of Anhanca, and another RF had a contact ten kilometres west of

Mupa, killing one enemy soldier An SADF Buffalo detonated a landmine eleven kilometres east of Anhanca, injuring three soldiers.

142 Battery headed to Cuvelia, while an attack commenced on Quiteve.

S Battery directed reactionary bombardment at Quiteve, with R Battery positioned at locations northeast of Quiteve to cut off SWAPO members escaping.[8] SWAPO moved into a wooded area and opened up with their MRLs but without effect.

Quiteve was taken by 61 Mechanized Battalion on their way to Cahama on 16 December with almost no resistance. It was preceded by an artillery and MRL bombardment on the target, and to the south to ward off any possible EF threats from that direction. The real breakthrough came when 61 Mechanized Battalion advanced on 16 December. This was met by round-the-clock FAPLA bombardments. Quiteve was placed under UNITA control and OF withdrew from the area

On 22 December, 16 kilometres northwest of Quiteve, a Recce team from 53 Reconnaissance killed four EF members during a contact.

On 28 December a force of 230 men from UNITA was deployed south of Quiteve, with 650 more troops to follow. UNITA also had 400 men 62 kilometres east-southeast of Techamutete on the Equendiva–Evale road. On 2 January 1984, Combat Group Tango withdrew from Quiteve when the operation closed.

CAHAMA

To give a brief summary of the operation, Task Force X-Ray was operating in the western operational area in the Cahama, Quiteve and Mulondo zones. Their prime task was to undertake 'choking' actions directed at the EF; because of this Quiteve was captured on 16 December.

EF with two T-54 tanks and infantry approached the OF from Mulondo. Mirage and Impala fighter jets launched several attacks on the EF position but the camouflage used by the EF was very effective and none of the targets was hit.

The next day, SADF MRLs were used against targets south of Mulondo, where Cuban and Russian advisers were present. EF messages were intercepted reporting, "The situation is very bad due to artillery fire."

A combat group from Sector 70 with the 144mm guns took control of the area from 15 December, releasing Task Force X-Ray, which moved 25 kilometres southeast to regroup for the attack on Cahama. The combat group received a new commanding officer, a strange decision in the heat of combat. The next night, a new formation set up a TB, causing much confusion that lasted for six hours before a further attempt was then made to get things right.

The EF had a recce element known as Gato; consisting of five operators, they were very effective. In one case, a radio message was intercepted giving exact accounts of OF strengths.

On 15 December OF reconnoitred the Chicusse area, 14 kilometres from Cahama. When the OF combat element moved behind the high ground 800 metres from Chicusse, they attracted heavy EF artillery fire. The OF took up their positions and, at 1200, commenced

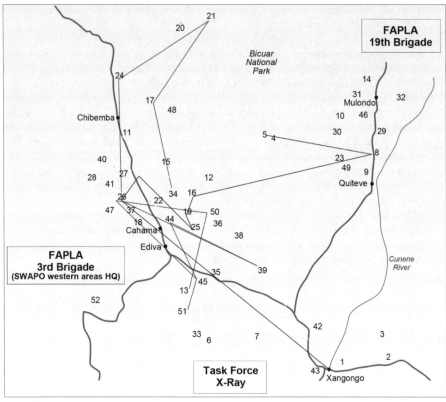

Map of Cahama showing SADF (Task Force X-Ray) movements and positions.

Legend

1. TASK Force X-ray 06/12/1983 (day 1)
2. Task Force Victor: Combat Group 2 06/12/1983 (day 1)
3. Task Force Victor: Combat Group 2 06/12/1983 (day 1)
4. Combat Group 1 12/12/1983 (day 5)
5. Combat Group 2 12/12/1983 (day 5)
6. Recce Team 13/12/1983 (day 5)
7. Recce Team 13/12/1983 (day 5)
8. Combat Groups 1 and 2 13/12/1983 (day 5)
9. Task Force X-ray 14/12/1983 (day 6)
10. Recce Team 14/12/1983 (day 6)
11. Recce Team 14/12/1983 (day 6)
12. Combat Groups 1, 2 and 3 16/12/1983 (day 8)
13. Task Force X-ray 16/12/1983 (day 8)
14. Combat Group Tango 17/12/1983 (day 9)
15. Combat Group 2 17/12/1983 (day 9)
16. Combat Group 1 18/12/1983 (day 10)
17. Combat Group 3 17/12/1983 (day 9)
18. Task Force X-ray 18/12/1983 (day 10)
19. Combat Group 1 18/12/1983 (day 10)
20. Combat Group 3 18/12/1983 (day 10)
21. Combat Group 3 19/12/1983 (day 11)
22. Combat Group 1 19/12/1983 (day 11)
23. Recce 19/12/1983 (day 11)
24. Combat Group 3 19/12/1983 (day 11)
25. Combat Group 1 19/12/1983 (day 11)
26. Combat Group 1 20/12/1983 (day 12)
27. Combat Group 2 20/12/1983 (day 12)
28. Combat Group 3 20/12/1983 (day 12)
29. Recce 20/12/1983 (day 12)
30. Recce 20/12/1983 (day 12)
31. Combat Group Tango 20/12/1983 (day 12)
32. Task Force Victor + MVL 6-12/12/1983 (days 1–6)
33. Combat Group 3 20/12/1983 (day 12)
34. Task Force X-ray 21/12/1983 (day 13)
35. Task Force X-ray 21/12/1983 (day 13)
36. Task Force X-ray 22/12/1983 (day 14)
37. Combat Group 1 22/12/1983 (day 14)
38. Combat Group 2 22/12/1983 (day 14)
39. Combat Group 3 22/12/1983 (day 14)

artillery fire simultaneously with 30 rounds per piece. However, a single shell from a 76mm EF gun landed in the middle of the OF position, but with minimal casualties. The OF immediately increased the depth of their trenches from three feet to five feet. They then began a hasty withdrawal, but the gun tractors got stuck in the trenches. After they had successfully managed to extricate themselves and redeploy, they held a prayer meeting to give thanks. But they had to reposition themselves twice, as the 76mm guns kept harassing them. On 20 December the MRLs fired a ripple at the 76mm positions; enemy fire was instantly silenced.

Cahama was now being threatened from the northwest by EF trying to occupy the higher ground to the west. After the deployment of Combat Group 3, the G4 guns commenced firing at targets at Cahama and Ediva, the positions of the 130mm enemy guns.

The first contact was made with EF on 16 December, 17 kilometres southeast of Cahama, killing two EF and wounding one.

On 18 December OF were shelled by EF mortars, but OF replied with their 140mm guns. Anti-aircraft gun positions were destroyed with the help of the SAAF. On 18 December Task Force X-Ray commenced artillery fire at targets in Cahama with 140mm guns. Elements of the force moved north of Cahama, after handing control of Quiteve over to the UNITA forces in the area. On 20 December OF received EF artillery fire from Cahama. Five or six T-55 tanks with dismounted infantry were visible two and a half kilometres ahead. The T-55 tanks with their 2.7km range compared to the 1.2km range of the Ratels, posed a real threat. G4 artillery began firing on the T-55s, with one round scoring a direct hit. For a while, smoke boiled from the tank, but it simply pulled away and drove off. The T-55s were pinned down by effective artillery fire which also caused great losses to the enemy infantry. Meanwhile, the OF commander's vehicle was suffering mechanical problems, but, even as he was being towed away, the commander continued issuing orders although he was now already behind a hill. During the action, an order had been given over the VHF radio network for the OF artillery to withdraw. The commander in the stricken vehicle only had HF communication and did not realize this. Everybody had left the scene, save the commander and his small force, with T-55s heading towards his position. The T-55s posed a serious threat to the G4 guns. However, one T-55 was destroyed and the OF made good their withdrawal.

One combat group remained north of Cahama to seek and destroy SWAPO bases southeast of Chibemba. In the meantime, an echelon was taking effective BM21 fire from south of Chibemba. The firing fell 15–20 metres from the Ratels, but their armour was sufficient to protect the troops.

A G4 battery joined the Task Force to relocate in an easterly direction; however, they experienced great difficulty in moving the guns as they had just fired 30 rounds each within one and a half hours (the MRLs fired three ripples) and were well and truly embedded after their bombardment. It took 42 minutes to get them mobile again.

61 Mechanized Battalion moved on to the 20th northern line to a position north of Cahama.

FAPLA's 11th Brigade was at Cahama. Despite numerous air strikes against Cahama, it was never the SADF's intention to capture Cahama prior to this operation. The plan was to fix the enemy at Cahama to prevent him sending reinforcements to their forces on the eastern front. However, the decision was taken, mainly due to the presence of enemy SA-8 missile systems, to either isolate Cahama completely or, preferably, take it. 61 Mechanized Battalion and attached artillery were given the task of performing the assault.

Recce teams continued operating on the road north of Cahama, between Cahama and Chibemba to cut off enemy logistic lines. The SAAF continued with air strikes against Cahama, trying to force FAPLA to withdraw.

61 Mechanized Battalion was positioned between Cahama and Chibemba and manoeuvred in such a manner to avoid being flanked by the enemy.

S and Q batteries conducted harassing fire during the night and were met with FAPLA return fire which was ineffective.[9]

On 20 December a combat group proceeded to Chibemba; SWAPO was aware that Chibemba was a primary target, with Lubango, their operational HQ, next in line. The EF reaction was to dispatch a column of T-55 tanks and armoured personnel carriers. A number of Ratel armoured vehicles were hit by tank fire, causing several OF casualties.

Several SADF soldiers were killed in action and two wounded. Official records indicate that six members of 61 Mechanized Battalion were killed: Rifleman G.C. Schonborn (on 21 December), Rifleman S. Pretorius (on 27 December), Rifleman N.W. Niemand (on 28 December) and Riflemen M.C. Smit, G.P. Pretorius and D.J. Schronen (on 31 December). A soldier from 5 Maintenance Unit driving a resupply vehicle from Ondangwa fell asleep next to his truck and was driven over and killed by a Ratel in the dark.

On 20 December FAPLA suffered severe casualties from retaliatory SAAF air strikes. Two Mirages bombed roads used by EF, two Impala aircraft served as air protection for the Puma helicopters and OF commenced its artillery barrage on Cahama. The EF responded with a T-54 attack on OF, but one tank was taken out by OF defensive action. More BM21 EF firing was directed at OF ten kilometres northwest of Cahama. Recce teams served as cut-off groups on the road between Cahama and Chibemba, south of Chivemba. Eight EF members were killed and three EF members were wounded.

On 21 December, six kilometres east-southeast of Chibemba, three EF vehicles drove into an OF ambush, consisting of a Ratel 90mm and 40 Recces. Three EF vehicles, a Jeep in front, a truck with 20 FAPLA and Cuban soldiers 100 metres behind the Jeep and another truck 100 metres farther back, were engaged. The Ratel fired at the Jeep but missed. It then fired at the following truck and scored a direct hit. The EF fled into the dense bush and fierce fighting broke out. During the action, two EF vehicles were destroyed, four Cuban soldiers and one FAPLA soldier were killed and one Cuban soldier was captured. Two EF members were also wounded.

Also on 21 December OF took up artillery positions to form a trap for the EF artillery. 142 and Q batteries occupied positions to the east of Cahama, while the attack was launched from the north.[10] The OF were using advanced electronic equipment, including the *Cook-klos*, also referred to as the Invals Mk I, a sound-measuring system developed by the CSIR in Pretoria, and still in its prototype stage. They had three observation positions 1,500 metres to each side. OF then commenced firing at 20:00 with G4 and 144mm guns ('five-fives') at enemy targets in Cahama. Enemy artillery immediately responded with return fire, forcing the OF to seek cover in their trenches. A target was identified at Mile 1020; the EF 122s were fiercely engaged and effectively destroyed. Enemy BM21s were also firing at the OF but could not be silenced.

On 23 December OF artillery opened fire from their location 19 kilometres east of Cahama, while two Recce teams and a company of 102 Battalion served as cut-off groups, 35 kilometres northeast of Chama. Another Recce team began harassing firing at Ediva. Elements of 102 Battalion were situated 40 kilometres west-southwest of Cahama.

The SAAF attacked Cahama during the night of 24/25 December, at 241600B December 1983, with a full-scale airstrike conducted by three Canberras and eight Impalas. Cahama was bombed every night thereafter to break EF morale, with attacks taking place at irregular and infrequent intervals. The EF continued to aggressively return fire, but the SADF soldiers became so used to this and did not bother taking cover unless the rounds landed in among their positions. FAPLA was now facing a severe shortage of ammunition and was forced to fire only three guns with minimal fire at specific targets only.

On 24 December the combat group command Ratel detonated a triple landmine 29 kilometres south-southeast of Chibemba, injuring its occupants. A SWAPO base was identified west of Cahama, consisting of 200 SWAPO members. Realizing that they had been spotted, they quickly abandoned their position and fled to Cahama to seek refuge.

While the attack on Cahama was under way, an OF MRL commenced firing on a target west of Mulondo. 142 Battery was still at Cahama firing at selected targets, before being redeployed northeast of Cahama to the mechanized combat group situated between it and Cahama. S Battery was north of Cahama, a combat group to the west, with 61 Mechanized Tactical HQ positioned on the tar road that skirted Cahama.

One important purpose of the attack was to capture the SA-8 missile batteries located southeast of Cahama. These missile systems were a much-sought-after prize, having never been captured by any Western force. A sub-operation within Askari was Operation Fox, which called for a coordinated air and ground bombardment in such a pattern that the SA-8 batteries would be forced to change their position and move south. The SAAF continued with several air strikes against Cahama on 25 December. It was expected that the SAM-8s would be moved to prevent them from being captured.

At H-Hour on 24 December one combat group wheeled left and three kilometres south. FAPLA T-54 tanks were reported to be on the move in the area. S Battery commenced firing but an order came through to break contact.[11] The two combat groups withdrew in great haste, as FAPLA BM21s opened up on them. However, Impala strike aircraft arrived on the scene and the problem was quickly resolved.

Cahama was then attacked again, this time from the southeast, to capture the SA-8s. Heavy FAPLA artillery fire was encountered with 142 Battery delivering an intense counter-bombardment.[12]

On 25 December 61 Mechanized Battalion had a contact and killed one FAPLA soldier, 31 kilometres south-southeast of Chibemba. A Ratel detonated a landmine 29 kilometres north-northwest of Cahama and was totally destroyed. Conducting harassing fire, Task Force Victor shelled Cahama; a number of their shells were painted with goodwill Christmas messages. Task Force Tango performed ambushes on the Mulondo–Quiteve road.

Task Force X-Ray, with one combat group from 61 Mechanized Battalion, contacted a six-man FAPLA reconnaissance team, killing one FAPLA member.

On 27 December the Chief of the SADF laid down new priorities for the operation at Cahama:

1.   Operation Fox shall proceed to capture an SA-8 system/s at Cahama
2.   It is no longer a priority to capture and occupy Cahama

3.   The expected infiltration by seven SWAPO companies [into SWA] should be avoided at all cost

4.   The main target of the operation is Cuvalai which must be captured.

61 Mechanized Battalion was on the outskirts of Cahama, but was reassigned to support other forces at Cuvelai now facing the threat of being cut off by FAPLA's 11th Brigade.

Due to the relatively high toll—according to SADF standards, a few casualties were regarded as 'high'—the combat group then withdrew from Cahama to Xangongo to reorganize and regroup with only 142 Battery remaining at Cahama. It was also reported that a 700-strong FAPLA force was heading towards the SADF force at Cuvelai, and so reinforcements from Task Force X-Ray had to be reassigned to this location. After Task Force X-Ray had laid 30 landmines near Mulondo on 27 December, it withdrew part of its force. They then began building a bridge at Humbe to cross the Cuculuvar River.

On 27 December, while disembarking a Ratel, a hand grenade attached to a soldier's belt exploded when the safety pin snagged on the door. He was killed instantly and three soldiers inside the vehicle were wounded. Under extremely hostile conditions, a Puma, flying very low, managed to evacuate the wounded.

On 28 December a Ratel received a direct hit from artillery fire while moving to the higher ground west of the road, 13 kilometres east-southeast of Cahama. The shell struck the Ratel on the right side above its hatches, opening up a one-metre gap in its 12mm solid steel armour. One OF member was killed and three wounded, one being left totally blind.

The withdrawal of the main force was officially ordered from Cahama on 30 December. Combat Group 3 now consisted of 563 soldiers with 72 vehicles.

On 31 December a 122mm missile exploded 30 metres from a Samil 100 truck, ten kilometres east-southeast of Cahama, setting the vehicle on fire. The entire combat group broke contact with Cahama and withdrew to Xangongo, crossing the Cunene River after successful completion of the mission. 142 Battery remained behind at Xangongo. 82nd Brigade HQ then arrived at Xangongo to to occupy the area.

Combat Group Delta (Task Force Victor), accompanied by Q Battery, then moved towards Cuvelai.[13] 61 Mechanized Battalion crossed the Cunene River over a temporary bridge and arrived in the vicinity of Cuvelai during the evening of New Year's Day in record time (16 hours). 61 Mechanized Battalion and S Battery joined up with Combat Group Delta after only a ten-hour rest, before joining the battle at Cuvelai almost immediately.

By the end of December, all action against Cahama had ceased in order to now concentrate on the attack against Cuvelai, where more SA-8 missile systems were reported to be deployed, 22 kilometres west and 23 kilometres west-southwest of Cuvelai, as well as at Chiange and Televemba.

Operation Fox

On 30 December Operation Fox was opened with the following components:

Combat Group 1
3 x mechanized platoons
3 x armoured car troops
1 x 81mm mortar group
1 x G2 artillery battery

Combat Group 2
2 x mechanized platoons
2 x armoured car troops
1 x 81mm mortar group.
Engineers

Combat Group 3
1 x mechanized platoon
1 x armoured car troop
20 x 20mm anti-aircraft troop
1 x G4 artillery battery

Reserve Force
2 x motorized platoons
1 x Recce team

Operation Fox consisted of the following phases:

Phase1: Building of a bridge across the Cunene River, at a crossing ten kilometres northwest of Xangongo.

Phase 2: Combat Group deployed at a location 14 kilometres east-southeast of Cahama, providing fire support for the Tactical HQ and Combat Group 1; the Reserve Force to deploy at 33 kilometres south-southeast of Cahama.

Phase 3: Capturing of a complete SA-8 missile system.

Phase 4: Withdrawal of force to Xangongo

The remotely piloted vehicle (RPV), codenamed the 'Gharra', had earlier been deployed at Xangongo, primarily to locate the Soviet SA-8 missile systems present in the area.[14] But, only much later during the war, on 5 October 1987, was a complete SA-8 missile system captured during Operation Modular. Commandant Johan Lehmann was awarded the Honoris Crux for his bravery in this operation. However, during Askari the SADF did manage to lure SA-9 missile systems from the enemy.[15]

On 23 December, two kilometres west of Cahama, an SA-8 ground-to-air missile was

Remotely piloted vehicle, the 'Gharra'.

fired at a Gharra, damaging its cockpit with shrapnel. The RPV managed to land safely back at Xangongo.

On 25 December Recce teams reconnoitred Ediva in search of SA-8 launching sites. South of Humbe, engineers erected a bridge to allow Combat Group 1 to cross a fast-flowing river before the attack on Ediva could commence from the northwest. Unbeknown to the combat group, the crossing point was a pre-set EF mortar target and they were subjected to an intense bombardment. It was therefore decided to attack Ediva from the southwest; this also attracted EF mortar fire.

At 311600B December, five or six T-55 tanks supported by infantry attacked the combat group. Two of the tanks were immediately hit by OF fire. In a fierce engagement three OF soldiers and great number of EF infantry were killed. The SADF dead and wounded were evacuated by Puma helicopters which had entered the 30km no-fly zone at great risk to perform the casevacs.

An OF gun truck was hit 50 kilometres from Cahama on the tar road.

Twelve T-54 tanks and 50 EF vehicles carrying a great number of troops were deployed south to avoid being cut off by the OF combat group.

An EF 81mm mortar bomb detonated when it hit the branch of a tree above a Buffalo vehicle, killing three soldiers and injuring four more: a fluke shot as, a few centimetres either side of the branch, the bomb would have exploded on impact with the ground and have done no damage to the vehicle's impressive side armour.

Combat Group 1 evacuated the area and regrouped at Xangongo for its next mission at Cuvelai. While Combat Group 1 had been engaged at Ediva, Combat groups 2 and 3 opened fire on targets at two river crossings. The Gharra later reported that one target had been destroyed. However, a 76mm round exploded 600 metres behind the combat groups' position. A second shell then hit a gun truck from which ammunition was being unloaded; it blew up immediately, causing huge flames and smoke to fill the air, further indicating their position to the enemy artillery spotters. The troops were ordered to recover the ammunition vehicle at all costs. It took a train consisting of a recovery vehicle and five Ratels to drag it to an accessible position and a further three hours to cover 20 kilometres towing the vehicle to the safety of the nearest tar road.

CAIUNDO

Sector 20 elements were deployed in the east to divert attention from the main force in the central and western areas. On 14 December three OF members were killed. The OF was reinforced with more personnel from 32 Battalion, with more attacks planned to commence from 25 December.

One battalion and one brigade of FAPLA's 53rd Brigade were located on the Caiundo–Ionde road. A political commissar and schoolteachers were reported to have been present in Caiundo town. The EF consisted of three battalions, supported by 122mm single-shot missiles, B10-anti-tank guns, together with anti-aircraft guns.

The enemy's operational preparedness was reported to be low at Caiundo. Reports were also received that an extended trench system ran through the town. Only on 8 January 1984 were the exact locations of FAPLA targets confirmed at locations five kilometres north of Caiundo, with 122mm anti-aircraft guns at three and five kilometres north and north-northwest of Caiundo respectively.

By 19 December the SADF force for the operation against Caiundo was positioned 45

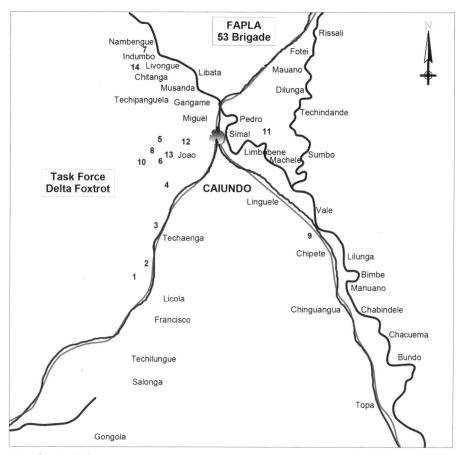

Map of Caiundo showing SADF (Sector 20 Task Force DF) movements and positions.

Legend

Operation Askari: 6/12/1983 – 13/01/1984
Sector 20 / Task Force Delta Foxtrot (Colonel Deon Ferreira)

1. Sector 20 Rifle Infantry Platoon 16/12/1983 (day 9)
2. Sector 20 Armoured Car Troop 16/12/1983 (day 9)
3. Sector 20 Rifle Infantry Platoon 16/12/1983 (day 9)
4. Sector 20 Rifle Infantry Platoon 16/12/1983 (day 9)
5. Sector 20 Rifle Infantry Platoon 16/12/1983 (day 9)
6. Sector 20 Rifle Infantry Platoon 16/12/1983 (day 9)
7. 3 SADF soldiers killed 18/12/1983 (day 11)
8. Sector 20 Task Force 30/12/1983 (day 22)
9. Sector 20 Task Force 31/12/1983 (day 23)
10. Task Force DF: Combat Group 1 01/01/1984 (day 24)
11. Task Force DF: Combat Group 2 05/01/1984 (day 28)
12. Task Force DF: Combat Group 1 05/01/1984 (day 24)
13. Task Force DF: Combat Group 2 09/01/1984 (day 28)
14. Task Force DF: Combat Group 1 09/01/1982 (day 28)

kilometres south of Caiundo, consisting of four infantry platoons (one company) from 202 Battalion, two platoons from 7 South African Infantry Battalion, one armoured car troop, one 81mm mortar group, engineers from 24 Field Squadron, echelon elements and possibly two 20mm troops and four SA-7 teams. This force was later strengthened by a company from 1 Parachute Battalion, a company from 32 Battalion; the 7 SAI strength was increased to company strength, with another armoured car troop and Bravo Troop 141 Battery with 120 mm mortars added to the complement. The force was referred to as Task Force Delta Foxtrot, named after its commander, Colonel Deon Ferreira, the Sector 20 commander and a former 32 Battalion commander.

The operation was planned over five phases:

Phase 1: Mobilization of OF elements at Mashapi training base, including preparation for the operation and further training.

Phase 2: Overt movement of Combat Group from Mashapi to Kahenge, to display a show of strength.

Phase 3: The OF to advance along the western bank of the Cubango River towards Caiundo, covering a minimum of 50km per day.

Phase 4: Offensive to be conducted south, west and north of Caiundo.

Phase 5: Withdrawal.

The 359-strong SADF force, mounted on 35 Buffalo mine-protected vehicles and consisting of elements from Sector 20, would serve as a diversionary force to draw EF attention away from the Cuvelai area. There were concerns over the MiGs situated at Menogue.

On 16 December four EF underground bunkers were located four kilometres west of Caiundo.

On 18 December an OF infantry platoon and two SA-7 teams on three Buffalo vehicles, unexpectedly drove into a battalion-strength (500 men) FAPLA force deployed on foot. The SADF troops fled, leaving two of the vehicles behind at the scene. One driver managed to manoeuvre his Buffalo out of the contact area but was soon ambushed and the vehicle hit. He debussed and escaped on foot. Three OF members were killed during the contact, including Lieutenant L. Claasen and Sergeant Oosthuizen; three Buffalo vehicles were lost, one being the first SADF vehicle ever to captured by FAPLA. Predictably, the vehicle was displayed to the media for propaganda purposes. The following day the bodies were recovered in a follow-up operation, with close air support provided by SAAF Mirages and Impalas. Rifleman Kandjendje (83891937) of 202 Battalion was thought to have been captured and taken to Bimbe as a prisoner. He was later found in a healthy state at Menongue by UNITA soldiers.

On 30 December, the OF combat group opened the bombardment of Caiundo and moved from six to ten kilometres west of Caiundo.

The next day, with the SADF artillery barrage continuing to soften up the town, the combat group took up assault positions 12 kilometres southeast of Caiundo, where a HAA was established. FAPLA troops began fleeing in large numbers. An SADF armoured car detonated a landmine. OF troops north of the town bumped into two FAPLA soldiers and killed one.

OF positions at Caiundo were compromised when their presence was discovered by a FAPLA recce team, FAPLA dispatched a company to attack an SADF platoon, which was forced to withdraw.[16]

On 3 January 1984, Task Force DF destroyed 20 EF vehicles, including two BTRMs. Twenty FAPLA troops and one Cuban soldier were killed ten kilometres north of Caiundo. Seven OF members were wounded when their Buffalo vehicle detonated a landmine on a tar road.

On 6 January three Canberra bombers and eight Mirage fighter jets struck at enemy targets in Caiundo. This was followed by more airstrikes: three Canberras bombed targets four kilometres from Caiundo on the Menongue road, and six Mirages destroyed fuel depots in the town. Three FAPLA troops were captured on this day.

On 7 January an air strike against an enemy base was reported to have beeen only 50% effective. Twenty SAAF aircraft made two air strikes against the FAPLA Brigade HQ. Two direct hits were made, including one on the brigade commander's bunker. The brigade commander suffered severe smoke inhalation and was reported to have been severely traumatized.[17] Further FAPLA targets were identified five kilometres north of the town. 122mm rocket launcher sites and AAA positions were spotted three and five kilometres north and north-northwest of Caiundo respectively.

On this day, the task force assault group consisted of elements from 32 Battalion, 1 Parachute Battalion, 7 South African Infantry Battalion, two Engineers sections, one 120mm mortar troop, one 81mm mortar platoon, one armoured car troop and two SA-7 teams.

Due to the low cloud cover in the area, no fire support was available for Combat Group 2 operating east of the river. The plan of attack was amended for Combat Group 1 to capture the western part of the EF target on the high ground west of the river. Artillery and mortar fire would be directed at enemy AA and mortar positions. The EF Brigade HQ and Battalion HQs were positioned east of the river. Electronic warfare assets were required to determine the EF response to these attacks before further SADF strategy was determined. Two Puma helicopters and four gunship helicopters were now present at the HAA. Combat Group 2 was deployed by Puma helicopters in 26 flights. SADF mortars eliminated the B10s near the airfield. By last light, a third of the enemy targets had been captured but the OF had to withdraw due to bad light.

An enemy AA installation and an armoured vehicle were destroyed. Four FAPLA troops were killed and two wounded in a contact. Enemy vehicles began withdrawing to Bambi, accompanied by a flood of FAPLA troops anxious to vacate the stricken town.

A Samil 100 logistics vehicle detonated a landmine seven kilometres west-southwest of Caiundo.

It was finally resolved to discontinue the attack on Caiundo and, on Monday 9 January 1984, Task Force Delta Foxtrot was ordered to withdraw.

The next target was Techamutete, situated north of Cuvelai and south of Cassinga. The attack was to be spearheaded by 32 Battalion.

TECHAMUTETE

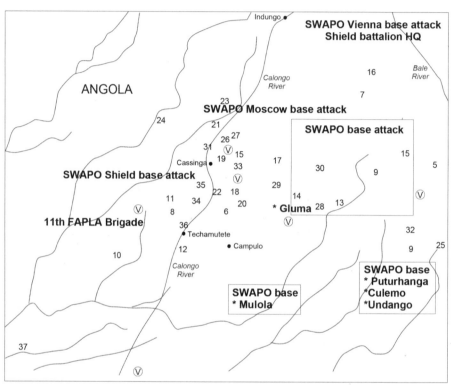

Map of Techamutete showing SADF (32 Battalion/Task Force EV) movements and positions.

Legend

1. 32 Battalion Tactical HQ at Ionde 06/12 (day 1) (not on map)
2. 32 Battalion 07/12 (day 2) West of Nauxindo (not on map)
3. 23 Battalion Recce 07/12 (day 2 North east of Ionde (not on map)
4. 23 Battalion Recce 08/12 (day 3) North east of Ionde (not on map)
5. 23 Battalion A 11/12 (day 6)
6. 23 Battalion E 11/12 (day 6)
– 23 Battalion D 11/12 (day 6)
7. 23 Battalion Mortar section 12/12 (day 7) East of Delta (not on map)
8. 32 Battalion Mini HAA 17/12 (day 12)
9. 32 Battalion Recce X3 teams 17/12 (day 12)

10. 23 Battalion A 18/12 (day 13)
11. 23 Battalion D 18/12 (day 13)
12. 32 Mini HAA 18/12 (day 13)
13. 23 Battalion D 19/12 (day 14) (Attack)
14. 23 Battalion E 19/12 (day 14)
15. 23 Battalion A, D 20/12 (day 15)
16. 23 Battalion E, C 20/12 (day15) (Attack)
17. 23 Battalion D 22/12 (day17)
18. 23 Battalion C 23/12 (day 18)
19. 23 Battalion A 22/12 (day 17)
20. 23 Battalion D, E 23/12 (day 18)
21. 23 Battalion Recce 25/12 (day 20)
22. 23 Battalion A,E 23/12 (day 18) (Attack)
23. 23 Battalion D,C 23/12 (day 18)
24. Puma down 27/12 (day 22)
25. 23 Battalion C 22/12 (day 17)
26. 23 Battalion C 26/12 (day 21) (Attack)

27. 23 Battalion A 26/12 (day 21)	33. 23 Battalion A 31/12 (day 26)
28. 23 Battalion D 26/12 (day 21)	34. 23 Battalion E 31/12 (day 26)
29. 23 Battalion E 26/12 (day 21)	35. 23 Battalion A 31/12 (day 26) (Bridge)
30. 23 Battalion D, C 29/12 (day 24)	36. 23 Battalion HAA 02/01/1984 (day 28)
31. 23 Battalion Recce 28/12 (day 23)	(Techamutete)
32. 23 Battalion D 31/12 (day 26)	V = Task Force Victor

32 Battalion's 596-strong force was dispatched to probe enemy defences and engage the SWAPO headquarters and logistic base five kilometres northeast of Cuvelai. Several SWAPO bases were expected in the Techamutete area. On 28 December 1983 the exact location of FAPLA forces, consisting of 400 troops, was confirmed east-southeast of Techumatete. More FAPLA troops were confirmed eight kilometres north of Cassinga on 31 December. 32 Battalion took Techamutete town on 2 January 1984. 32 Battalion, also serving as stopper groups, captured a large number of FAPLA troops who had fled north from Cuvelai during the OF attack.

32 Battalion consisted of:
- 35 x officers (including 9 x PF)
- 50 x non-commissioned officers
- 81 x SP (black) non-commissioned officers (including 31 PF)
- 55 x troops
- 366 x SP troops
- 5 x UNITA guides

On 5 December 1983, logistic supplies were delivered to 32 Battalion Tactical HQ at Ionde in preparation for Operation Askari, consisting of:[18]

- Diesel: 9,000l
- Avtur: 42,000l, 13,000l tanker and 19 x 210l drums (helicopter fuel)
- Avtur: 90,000l and 60 x 210l drums
- Petrol: 4 x 210l drums
- Avgas: 3 x 210l drums (aviation fuel for piston-propelled aircraft)
- Diesel for convoy: 47,000l and 10 x 210l drums
- 3,300 x ration packs at Ionde and 14,600 on the convoy

32 Battalion first established an HAA near the Bambi River, exactly east of Techamutete. On 7 December three EF members were killed and one OF member was wounded during a ground-air attack on enemy positions.

On 9 December two UNITA soldiers and 15 locals were captured by SWAPO east of the Vingombe River. A 'Black Widow' landmine was detonated on the same day. One UNITA soldier captured earlier escaped. Two SWAPO bases were spotted at the junction of the Chiocha and Bale rivers. Discussions with UNITA began regarding their role in the forthcoming operation.

As mentioned. the final passing-out function for a group of national servicemen who had completed their military service with 32 Battalion was held on 10 December at Rundu HQ, including the author. The remaining leadership team of 32 Battalion involved in Operation Askari consisted mainly of volunteers and CF servicemen.

On 10 and 11 December, five locals were interrogated after it was discovered that they were in possession of FAPLA and SWAPO brochures. On 14 December an enemy soldier was captured. On 16 December two OF Recce groups crossed the river at the junction of the Bale and Cubango rivers, but lost their equipment in the strong current. Heavy rainfall was experienced. Peter Williams's small 32 Battalion Recce team was pinned down by enemy fire; however, a platoon of 32 Battalion quickly came to their rescue and fended off the attack.

SWAPO camps were regarded to be situated in the Mulola area, 20 kilometres southeast of Techamutete, Chinanba in the Winelands area, the Soviet Point east of Techamutete, at Gluma, Puturhanga, Culemo and in the Undango area near the Bale River. SWAPO's Eastern Area HQ was situated here, as well as transition camps from where infiltrations into South West Africa were launched. SWAPO's HQ was at Lumbambula, much farther north of the railway line. This was not within reach of 32 Battalion. No orders were received to advance this far; in any event, SAAF aircraft would not be available to support any such attack, so it was never on the cards.

Broadly, 32 Battalion was conducting search and destroy missions in the Techamutete area north of Cuvelai. Disappointingly, little sign of SWAPO was found during Operation Askari. Later, General Eddie Viljoen, 'Big Daddy', said that Operation Askari had very little to do with eliminating SWAPO but was directed more at FAPLA targets. FAPLA's war in Angola was against UNITA. Since 1978, the SADF had become more and more distracted, focusing on FAPLA which, in turn, allowed SWAPO more freedom of movement. Had the SADF persisted with its pre-1978 policy of striking only against SWAPO, that organization might well have been eliminated entirely. Viljoen went on to state that the SADF persisted in their efforts against FAPLA during Operation Askari, as FAPLA forces at Cahama, Cuvelai and Caiundo were easily recognizable targets.[19]

On 17 December a SWAPO base was attacked with 81mm mortar fire. On 17/18 December, eight members of 32 Battalion Recce Wing (c/s 81) were attacked. One EF member was killed and the attack was foiled.

On 18/19 December Task Force Echo Victor's C and E companies of 32 Battalion were ordered to attack a suspected 30-strong enemy base known as the Vienna Base, which included SWAPO's Shield Battalion HQ. Four Puma helicopters were made available for the attack. Five SWAPO troops were killed and one captured without OF loss. On 19 December three EF members were killed 31 kilometres east-southeast of Cassinga.

On 20 December a cache was located at the SWAPO Berlin base; its contents were destroyed. Nine SWAPO members had been in the base with another 21 patrolling close by. However, all fled in a northwesterly direction.

On 21 December, at 06:40, the SADF made contact with enemy troops and killed four. Two companies of 32 Battalion were airlifted by Puma helicopter to a location east of Cassinga.

At 18:30 on 22 December, eight kilometres east-northeast of Cassinga, 32 Battalion made contact with a ten-15-strong EF group; however, five 32 Battalion soldiers were wounded in the engagement. Another contact took place 13 kilometres southeast of Cassinga with a ten-strong EF group; one 32 Battalion member was wounded. Eight kilometres east of Cassinga, 32 Battalion killed three EF members and 46 kilometres east of Cassinga, 30 EF members were engaged, with three enemy killed.

The next day, 32 Battalion killed one EF member and captured another, two kilometres east of Cassinga. General Geldenhuys and his party of senior officers were now present at the 32 Battalion HAA and mini-HAA, positioned at RV 660280XP and 330330XP respectively.[20] Geldenhuys was accompanied by General Meiring, Brigadier Packering, Colonel Dick Lord, Commandant Lombard, Brigadier Joubert, Chaplain Jordaan and the RSM of the Army,

Sergeant-Major Holiday. The HAA was primarily for 32 Battalion's use, however, the Alouette gunships now relocated to Ongiva each day before sunset. On one occasion, the HAA came under FAPLA artillery fire but, due to the HAA's location behind high ground, it was ineffective. Gunship pilots rushed to their helicopters and scrambled to flee in great haste, causing some amusement for Big Daddy's group.[21]

A request was made for the deployment of 32 Battalion's C and E companies by Puma helicopter to be utilized as cut-off groups north of Cuvelai, and to support UNITA in laying night ambushes. Reconnaissance missions were also underatken on an enemy base.

Pamphlets were distributed to local civilians, alerting them of the imminent SADF strike against Cuvelai, at the same time serving as a diversion while 32 Battalion hit SWAPO targets elsewhere. The SADF generally communicated with the local population in this manner prior to launching a major strike.

On 24 December enemy communications were intercepted by an EW team, reporting that SAAF helicopters had been spotted at Chalas and Mbale. Two EF members were captured on this day. Twelve kilometres north-northeast of Techamutete, 32 Battalion killed one EF soldier in a contact. It was suspected that a group of more than 200 SWAPO troops were operating in this area.

On 25 December, at targets three kilometres south of Cassinga, 32 Battalion attacked SWAPO's Moscow Battalion in their base, killing five and capturing one. Two 32 Battalion soldiers were wounded. SWAPO's 8th Battalion base was located ten kilometres south of Cassinga. Two other bases, 17 kilometres south and 22 kilometres southeast of Cassinga, were already deserted. At 06:00 32 Battalion made contact with three to five EF and discovered a cache of ammunition and equipment. At 07:50, a 32 Battalion recce team and one company had a contact with 20 EF, killing six and capturing one, while three SADF soldiers were killed.

The next day, 32 Battalion attacked a SWAPO base situated eight kilometres north of Cassinga. Alouette gunships had spotted the base and opened firing immediately, killing four EF members and wounding one. This was the Red Square Battalion base, SWAPO's Central HQ and the Moscow Battalion's logistics base. Seven companies of SWAPO Special Units were reported to be operating near Indungu.

On 27/28 December, a Recce team and two platoons from 32 Battalion's D Company conducted a recovery operation of the helicopter, Puma 155, that had crash-landed earlier, 12 kilometres northwest of Cassinga. Puma 155, with its eleven passengers, had been piloted by Captain Manie Gildenhuys and co-pilot Captain Terry Chaplain. Major Arthur Walker was the pilot of a second accompanying Puma. Puma 155 was uplifting a stick of 32 Battalion at a location 20 kilometres southeast of Techamutete when its engine failed while getting airborne. It crashed into the bush and the soldiers evacuated the aircraft in great haste. Seven 32 Battalion members were slightly wounded as the aircraft ignited and burned out. Only after the aircraft had been uplifted, was a body of a 32 Battalion soldier discovered trapped under the wreckage. Eddie Viljoen had had to make an urgent plan to remove the wreckage, but it was still too hot to handle. Waiting for the metal to cool down, the crash site attracted a great deal of interest from the enemy. Eventually, on 29 December, the wreckage was loaded onto several Samil 100 trucks and removed. As a result of the incident, an attack at Indungo was cancelled. (Manie Gildenhuys told an amusing story related to this incident. For a while after the crash he wore a 'Do not step' sticker on his forehead. This is the sign that appears on the mudguards of Puma's wheels to warn soldiers not to step on them. During the evacuation of the aircraft, the deplaning soldiers had all stepped on Manie's head.[22])

FAPLA had completely destroyed a bridge, which had to be rebuilt on 31 December. In turn, 32 Battalion destroyed a bridge four kilometres south of Cassinga.

On 28 December, OF members erected a bridge over the Cuvelai River using logs cut from nearby trees. Viljoen embarked on a series of new deployments for 32 Battalion. E Company was instructed to search for SWAPO's special forces, A and D companies were to perform patrols in the area and D Company and the Recce team were to ambush roads; C Company, with one 81mm mortar group, was to serve as protection for the HAA, which had by now amalgamated the nearby mini-HAA. A UNITA force of 104 troops was deployed northwest of the HAA, with further UNITA soldiers patrolling north of the Bale River.

Viljoen had received specific instructions to avoid the FAPLA brigade-strength force at Techamutete. However, on 31 December, in light rain, 32 Battalion saw EF movement in front of them, just below some high ground. A few shots were fired but without any significant EF response. Then suddenly, scores of FAPLA were seen scrambling in all directions in an effort to escape. Vehicles were abandoned and even the crews of the T-54 tanks opened their hatches and fled in the general direction of Cassinga, totally abandoning their equipment.

On 2 January 1984 32 Battalion engaged a group of 12 FAPLA on patrol a kilometre northwest of Techamutete. The enemy abandoned their gear, with 32 Battalion capturing four 23mm anti-aircraft guns and six vehicles. These 23mm guns were then put into effective use on the nearby road. On the same day, 32 Battalion destroyed a bridge eight kilometres southwest of Cassinga.

32 Battalion was accompanied by 127mm MRLs and a platoon of Ratels from 61 Mechanized Battalion. 32 Battalion was now also armed with 23mm guns. The firepower of these weapons was to cause great distress to FAPLA, with the din of continuous firing on the T-54 tanks instilling panic among the crews. FAPLA, unaware that 32 Battalion was in the area, was to take heavy fire on their flanks and, lacking any decisive leadership, this sowed further panic.

32 Battalion's spoils of the battle were a number of GAZ trucks, GP Russian vehicles and six T-54 tanks; quite an achievement considering that 32 Battalion was not equipped with any anti-tank capability.

32 Battalion destroyed three more bridges at two kilometres north-northwest, one kilometre west and six kilometres north of Techumutete; another bridge was also destroyed eight kilometres southwest of Cassinga.

Viljoen assessed the situation and realized that he had unexpectedly stumbled upon the now deserted FAPLA base just south of Techamutete. This was the alleged brigade-strength base "to be avoided at all costs", but it had housed only a small force.

32 Battalion then advanced on the town of Techamutete, capturing it on 3 January 1984. Advancing through the western side of this mining town, they headed towards the main mineshaft to the south. Viljoen signalled Brigadier Joubert at the Tactical HQ that he was now in control of the town. Joubert received the message with almost total disbelief, ordering Viljoen to occupy the town and remain there.

The ease with which 32 Battalion took its target was in contrast to the difficulties that faced the Task Force at Cuvelai to the south of Techamutete. Here a battle of attrition was under way, with Ratels engaging T-54 tanks and 23mm anti-aircraft fire raking the ground troops.[23]

Viljoen then moved his Tactical HQ to Techamutete. A shed was being used to hold several FAPLA captives; one such prisoner told Viljoen that he was a FAPLA engineer. He escorted Viljoen to a bunker and showed him all the drawings and plans of the minefields situated at Cuvelai. He was immediately airlifted and the information proved invaluable to SADF sappers as these minefields could now be traced and further damage to vehicles and personnel avoided.

Viljoen then ordered the release of the FAPLA prisoners, but they refused to leave, stating that they would be shot by their officers for deserting their posts.[24]

One night the crews of three Ratels accompanying 32 Battalion were preparing to sleep on the one side of a Ratel when they were ordered to move to the other side. A well-directed 127mm MRL rocket landed right in their earlier spot, leaving scratches on the side of the Ratel. All would have perished had they not moved to the other side.

One Sergeant-Major Thomas was instructed to recover the six captured T-54 tanks, as 32 Battalion did not have the capacity to utilize such weaponry. Thomas suddenly fell very ill and was casevaced to Ondangwa hospital where he died of malaria. Sergeant-Major Koos Krokodil then took over the tank recovery. Parking the T-54s on some high ground, he loosed off a few shots in the EF's direction just for the fun.[25]

32 Battalion was aided by four Task Force artillery guns, which were then deployed defensively and offensively on the high ground around Techamutete, and from where they could open fire in Cassinga's direction. The Colomba, Bale, Danga and Quele rivers were the major features in the area, with the high ground southeast of Techamutete occupied by 32 Battalion. From this position 32 Battalion commanded a wide view of the area, and from here the artillery found many targets, including approaching BTRs and B21s vehicles. Two EF vehicles were destroyed and five FAPLA members were wounded in one such action.

The HAA was transferred to Techamutete, at YN 550503, on 6 January,[26] where it remained until 20 January.

Three FAPLA soldiers suddenly appeared in Techamutete, asking to speak to the officer in charge. They were introduced to Colonel Viljoen. The three FAPLA soldiers, one of them a lieutenant, put down their rifles and made themselves at home, being supplied coffee and food While eating, Viljoen asked, "Who do you wish to speak to?"

"The Cubans," replied the FAPLA officer.

"Who do you think we are?" asked Viljoen.

"Cubans?"

"Wrong. Guess again," said the South African.

"East German?"

"Wrong. Guess again."

"Russians then?" asked the FAPLA officer apprehensively.

"No, guess again"

"We don't know. Who are you?" asked the now thoroughly alarmed Angolan.

"We are the South Africans," was Viljoen's reply.

Upon hearing this, one of the FAPLA soldiers was so startled that he dropped his plate of food, the three of them momentarily paralyzed. They looked around and started shouting at one and other, trying to blame each another for falling into the hands of the South Africans,[27] who waited until their outbursts subsided and made them prisoners of war.

FAPLA opened artillery fire from Cassinga, dispatching the Bida Brigade to attack 32 Battalion. On 5 January several FAPLA vehicles and T-54 tanks were seen approaching OF positions, four kilometres to the northwest. Six Milan anti-tank-missile Ratels, deployed with 32 Battalion, were instructed to prevent the enemy breaking through the OF defensive lines. One tank that attempted to break through got stuck in the mud and was abandoned by its crew. Six FAPLA members were killed and another five captured in this engagement.

The FAPLA Bida Brigade, under the command of Colonel Chiloya, was now threatening to cut off 32 Battalion from the main SADF force. The SAAF were requested to put in an airstrike on three T-54 tanks, ten kilometres north-northwest of Techamutete, but the strike was aborted due to low cloud cover.

On 9 January 32 Battalion had a contact with 15 enemy troops northeast of Techamutete. One enemy soldier was killed, along with two members of 32 Battalion: 81553596S Rifleman J. Dala and 80830409SP Rifleman I. Milongo, both of E13. OF platoon guards had spotted the approaching enemy and withdrew to their positions in the company to form up for battle. However a ten-strong enemy detachment flanked the OF, killing the two soldiers.

By this time, 32 Battalion's support units were withdrawing to Ionde, and the HAA was relocated to Cuvelai, while the four 32 Battalion companies remained at Techumatete. On 12 January, one platoon and one troop of Ratels arrived 30 kilometres north of Cuvelai to recover the captured T-54 tanks.

Colonel Viljoen filed a report describing 32 Battalion's involvement in Operation Askari. 32 Battalion had accounted for 48 SWAPO killed and five captured and 14 FAPLA captured and unknown number killed. 32 Battalion losses were four dead and 23 wounded. The battalion captured one SWAPO Land Cruiser, one Jeep, two URAL and four GAZ trucks and six T-54/55 tanks.

CUVELAI

The attack against FAPLA targets at Cuvelai in the Central Area, by Task Force Victor, was performed using 'choking' actions. Combat Group Delta (from Task Force Victor) was deployed at Cuvelai, approaching from the south and the west. Four companies from 32 Battalion were deployed north of Cuvelai in the area of Techamutete to cut off retreating enemy. On 20 December 32 Battalion attacked a SWAPO base that has very recently been evacuated. The attack at Cuvelai was successfully concluded by these task forces and, as mentioned in the previous section, 32 Battalion captured Techamutete with little effort.

FAPLA's 11th Brigade, with an estimated 6,000 troops, a number of Soviet advisers and an unknown number of SWAPO troops, was positioned at Cuvelai. The force comprised four battalions, a company of T-55 tanks (previously not expected to be present), a platoon of PT76 amphibian tanks, a battery of 122mm guns, a battery of 76mm guns, single-shot 122mm missile launchers, 82mm mortars, two anti-aircraft batteries, 57mm anti-aircraft guns, two SA-9 missile systems, SAM-7s and a machine-gun platoon armed with the new 30mm grenade launchers.

On 22 December the locations of the EF targets were confirmed in the following areas around Cuvelai: four kilometres northeast, five kilometres north, three kilometres northwest, four kilometres north-northeast, five kilometres north-northeast, six kilometres north-northeast and seven kilometres north-northeast. Farther north, a threat was posed by more FAPLA forces, with their bases confirmed to be situated at ten kilometres west, 17 kilometres south, 22 kilometres southeast, ten kilometres south (8th Battalion) and 17 kilometres south of Cassinga.

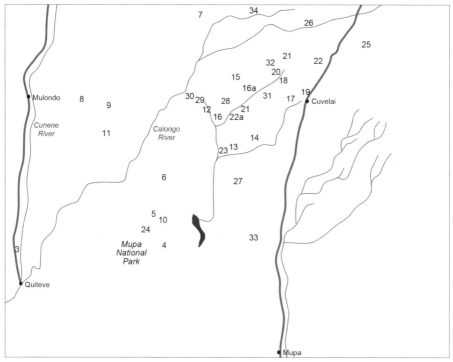

Map of Cuvelai showing SADF (Combat Group Delta/Task Force Victor) movements and positions.

1. Task Force Victor: Combat Group 2 07/12–12/12 Mongua road (not on map)
2. Task Force Victor: Combat Group 3 07/12–12/12 North of Mongua (not on map)
3. Task Force X-ray
4. Task Force Victor: Combat Group 3 15+16/12
5. Task Force Victor: Combat Group 1 15+16/12
6. Task Force Victor: Combat Group 1 13/12 (day 6)
7. Task Force Victor: Combat Group 2 17/12 (day 10)
8. Task Force Victor: Combat Group 1 7-13/12
9. Task Force Victor: MVL 16-19/12
10. Task Force Victor: Combat Group 3 19/12 (day 12)
11. Task Force Victor: HQ 20/12 (day 13)
12. Task Force Victor: HQ 22/12 (day 13)
13. Task Force Victor: Combat Group 1 22/12 (day 15)
14. Task Force Victor: Combat Group 1 22/12 (day 15)
15. Combat Group Tango 22/12 (day 15)
16. Task Force Victor: Artillery 22/12 (day 15)
16a. Task Force Victor: Combat Group 2 22/12 (day 15)
17. Recce 22/12 (day 15)
18. Task Force Victor: Artillery 22/12 (day 15)
19. Recce 22/12 (day 15)
20. Task Force Victor: Combat Group 1 23/12 (day 16)
21. Task Force Victor: Combat Group 2 23/12 (day 16)
22. Task Force Victor: Combat Group 3 23/12 (day 16)
22a. Task Force Victor: Combat Group 3 25/12 (day 18)
23. Combat Group 2 25/12 (day 18)
24. Combat Group Tango 26/12 (day 19)
25. Task Force Victor Ambush 26/12 (day 19)
26. Task Force Victor: Combat Group 1, 2, 3 28/12 (day 21)
27. Task Force Victor: Echalon 28/12 (day 21)
28. Task Force Victor: MVL 29/12 (day 22)
29. Task Force Victor: Combat Group 1, 2, 3 30/12 (day 23)
30. Task Force Victor: Tactical HQ 31/12 (day 23)
31. Combat Group Tango 31/12 (day 23)
32. Task Force Victor: MVL 31/12 (day 23)
33. Task Force Victor 01/01/1984 (day 24)
34. Task Force EV: 32 Battalion Mini HAA

D-Day for the attack on these FAPLA targets at Cuvelai was initially planned for a day between 17 and 21 December 1983.[28]

Task Force Victor was divided into three combat groups, consisting of three heavy infantry combat groups and one lighter infantry combat group positioned to the south.

On 17 December OF at positions 65 kilometres west of Cuvelai opened fire at EF targets in Cuvelai for 30 minutes after receiving EF artillery fire from the 11th FAPLA Battalion. The OF positions for the 140mm guns were at RV 3408, the 127mm MRLs ('Valkiris') at RV 3608 and the 155mm guns at RV 4492. Combat Group Delta and Task Force Victor crossed a river with the 127mm MRLs. The OF artillery consisted of two batteries of five-fives, Sierra and Quebec batteries from 82 Mechanized Brigade, and the MRL troop with two launchers. Gunships were used as spotters in this densely vegetated area. Up against the SADF artillery were aan EF battery of 57mm guns, a number of 23mm guns and two batteries of 122mm guns. Air support was urgently requested by the SADF forces.

On 18 December Recce teams made contact with EF 20 kilometres southeast of Cassinga. To escape the enemy pursuit OF helicopters were called in to airlift the troops.

On 20 December Task Force Victor made contact at 48 kilometres east of Cassinga, killing three SWAPO members and capturing one.

On 22 December the SADF directed increased firepower on the various EF targets. The next day, EF artillery opened fire on Combat Group Delta at their position seven kilometres southwest of Cuvelai. On 24 December an OF diesel tanker was destroyed when it detonated a landmine ten kilometres north of Cuvelai. Task Force Victor moved its Tactical HQ. North of Cuvelai, two companies, a mortar platoon and Combat Group 3 (an armoured car troop and one platoon) commenced harassing fire on Cuvelai.

On 26 December Task Force Victor directed 127mm MRL fire at Cuvelai, while its main echelon was situated 40 kilometres southeast of Mulondo. The SAAF conducted airstrikes to illuminate anti-aircraft installations three kilometres north of Cuvelai. A Buffalo vehicle detonated a landmine ten kilometres north-northeast of Namacunde.

On 28 December four Canberras attacked Cuvelai, delivering their bombs at 0920B. On 29 December four Buccaneers attacked the Tobias Hanyeko Training Centre (THTC), just outside Lubango. This SWAPO training centre had over the years been responsible for training thousands of SWAPO recruits. An airstrike was put in on EF targets to prevent the enemy from launching SA-8 missiles at the SAAF aircraft, OF members also laid 30 landmines on EF routes.[29]

At 1735B on 29 December, OF at Chama da Sacagsube opened fire on EF targets.[30] A signal was relayed to Brigadier Joubert and Colonel Lord to alter the original plan of Operation Askari, as low cloud cover made observation and air support for Task Force Victor impossible. There was also no support from artillery east of the river, which made for a dangerous situation. The plan was amended by one company from the Task Force occupying the high ground (rising to a mere 50 feet, the trees were also very high, making any observation from this area impossible) situated to the west of the river. Gunships were to be made available at the HAA.[31] Artillery west of river was to deliver restricted fire on EF AAA positions, mortar installations, as well as on the enemy Brigade HQ, positioned east of the river. Two Puma helicopters and two Alouette gunships were placed on standby at the HAA, with a further two Pumas on standby to perform casevacs. A Bosbok fixed-wing aircraft was on standby to become airborne after the weather had cleared.

As the weather cleared, the SADF commanders re-evaluated the operation. It now appeared unlikely that the planned assualt would take place on time. It was decided that should the attack be called off, OF troops were to withdraw south across the *shonas* before dark. It was decided that once reports were received from intercepted enemy communication by the EW team, the EF response would be evaluated and a plan of action implemented accordingly.

By 29 December, a large area near the target at Cuvelai was now occupied by OF.

Three OF members of Combat Group Delta were wounded at a location 20 kilometres west of Cuvelai by an accidental, spontaneous ignition of a 127mm MRL rocket. Other reports stated that a rocket was launched by accident through its crew compartment. The 127mm MRL system had recently being modified and was being used in combat while still in its testing stage.[32]

OF artillery fire on 30 December proved inaccurate, eliciting no enemy response. Three vehicles from 61 Mechanized Battalion were destroyed by EF fire, a Ratel got stuck in a minefield, which the enemy then blew up with explosives.

On the same day, 30 December, instructions were issued to capture three SA-8 missiles, along with enemy radio equipment, expected to be in the area. Thereafter, this equipment was to be transferred directly to the Sector 10 HQ. The radio settings were to remain undisturbed for close inspection.

One Recce team and D Company of 32 Battalion laid ambushes on the road to Indungo, ten kilometres north of Cassinga. The next day they sabotaged the railway line to Techamutete. Task Force Victor was positioned with its combat groups 1, 2 and 3 and the Tactical HQ 25 kilometres west of Cuvelai, awaiting logistical resupply and much needed fuel supplies. By now, elements of 61 Mechanized Battalion from Task Force X-Ray, with one mechanized company, an armoured car squadron and a medium battery had joined Task Force Victor. The approach route was from the east of Cuvelai, with the 127mm MRL positioned 15 kilometres west-northwest, the artillery ten kilometres west-northwest and the echelon 25 kilometres west of Cuvelai. A stationary force was deployed south of the target, while two combat groups were to penetrate the target and clear the area; a third armoured car group was ready to combat any tank threat. On D-Day, 31 December, at H-Hour, 12:00, members of Combat Group Delta were positioned on the left flank, with the Calongo River to their right.[33]

The initial planning at 310000B December 1983, for D-Day of the attack, was as follows:

Phase 1: OF river crossing on 2 January, at a location 24km south-southeast of Cuvelai.

Phase 2: Movement to jump-off positions.

Phase 3: One combat group to approach EF from the tactical terrain south of the EF positions south of the river.

Phase 4: Three combat groups to break through EF lines, and enter EF positions from a southeasterly direction.

Phase 5: Capture of the target.

Phase 6: Withdrawal.

Enemy targets at Cuvelai were:
* Target 1   just north of Cuvelai
* Target 2   just northwest of Cuvelai

- Target 3   3km northeast of Cuvelai
- Target 4   4km northeast of Cuvelai
- Target 5   5–6km northeast of Cuvelai

Two OF companies were positioned north of Techamutete and south of Cassinga and one company was positioned on the road north to prevent EF movement north towards Cassinga. One OF company was to prevent EF occupying positions at Techamutete, and to prevent an EF counter-offensive from Jamba and Camene.

At 13:00 on New Year's Eve one EF member was killed. Two OF members from Combat Group Delta were killed when an RPG-7 rocket hit the turret of their Ratel six kilometres northeast of Cuvelai, and four OF members were wounded by enemy small-arms fire while debussing from their vehicle. A combined FAPLA-Cuban force, with Soviet advisers, ambushed a unit of Combat Group Delta near the town of Cuvelai. The OF had reported that an area had been discovered where the vegetation had been cut knee-high, clearly for enemy fields of fire. When the enemy spotted the approaching Ratels, they immediately opened fire with their 23mm and 14.5 mm anti-aircraft guns. While the Ratels were withdrawing, Rifleman Callie Fourie, a Citizen Force soldier, was fatally wounded.[34]

On the same day, just outside Cuvelai, call sign 19 Juliet, a light infantry rifle company mounted in Ratels, with an Eland 90 armoured car escort, approached a FAPLA target. Unexpectedly, they encountered a large FAPLA force with T-34 and T-54 tanks. In such dense, tall bush, the outdated Elands were simply no match for the tanks. The Ratels came to an abrupt halt as a furious firefight erupted. A round from a 23mm AA cannon pierced the armour of one Ratel right below the turret, killing Lieutenant Piet Liebenberg instantly.

JANUARY 1984

Task Force Victor (Combat Group Delta) consisted mainly of Citizen Force members called up for duty from their civilian lives. This was the first time that a complete Citizen Force Combat Group had been formed to attack enemy bases.[35]

It was decided to reassign 61 Mechanized Battalion, under command of Commandant van Lill, who were on the outskirts of Cahama, to assist the embattled Combat Group Delta. Task Force X-Ray, with S Battery and 61 Mechanized Battalion, then hooked up with Task Force Victor to attack Cuvelai.

The advancing SADF forces drew accurate mortar fire from the EF, but smashed into FAPLA's 11th Brigade; the battle raged for three days. The FAPLA brigade was backed by a company of Soviet-supplied T-54 tanks, which launched an attack on Combat Group Delta. During previous operations, FAPLA had used T-34 tanks in stationary hull-down positions, meaning that the crews dug trenches and almost buried the tanks in such a way that only their turrets were visible above ground level. Now it was different, with FAPLA using their T-54 tanks in an offensive manner, charging and firing at the oncoming SADF. The operation had turned into a full-scale conventional battle. Assessing the situation later, General Meiring said, "The security forces did not have heavy calibre arms with them and had to fight against much more powerful firepower."

A bombardment commenced against EF targets, with 52 tonnes of artillery ordnance directed at Cuvelai, but the enemy simply moved to other pre-arranged positions.

Heavy enemy fire was experienced, which was considered a fire plan to scare off OF. By now, enemy morale was reported to be very low. Five FAPLA members deserted, with EF members reported to have expressed concerns over the safety of the Cuban solders in the area.

On 1 January 1984 reports were received that the extensive enemy radar system had detected SAAF aircraft movement, providing the enemy with sufficient early warning to seek cover in their underground bunkers; however, five FAPLA troops were wounded and one killed in a subsequent air attack. Two EF vehicles were destroyed. Cuban advisers were reportedly hiding in bunkers at the enemy HQ.

After three days of continuous battle, FAPLA's 11th Brigade withdrew, forfeiting their T-54 tank company in the process to the inferior firepower of the Ratel 90mm armoured troop carriers. Twelve T-54 Soviet tanks were knocked out by the Ratels. The Ratel crews were better trained and more disciplined than their counterparts and, in spite of its inferior firepower, the Ratel was better able to find its target in thick bush, due to its higher silhouette and superior manoeuvrability.[36]

On 3 January the attack on the wider area of Cuvelai commenced when the Task Force invaded a third of the target area. Enemy AAA opened up on the advanving SADF forces at H-Hour, 04800B January 1984, OF artillery and airstrikes pounded enemy installations with bombs exploding everywhere. However, the Task Force was experiencing navigational problems due to the dense vegetation and had to withdraw from the target area due to bad light. Nevertheless, a section of the EF brigade HQ position had by now been taken. Dozens of enemy troops were found dead in the bunkers, having been unable to escape.

A 32 Battalion soldier, Rifleman T. Manganhes, had been killed and one member of 7 SA Infantry Battalion wounded. OF members destroyed 60 enemy vehicles in a vehicle park, with a further 15 destroyed at other locations.

The OF delivered harassing fire, *kwelvuur*, from west of the river, with a 120mm mortar attack against FAPLA's 11th Brigade HQ. The bulk of the Task Force was now situated east of the river. The enemy was reported to be in a state of total chaos, with a severe paucity of any leadership element.[37]

Following the airstrikes against Cuvelai over 27/28 December, with the SADF task forces

approaching the town, a further aerial assault against Cuvelai took place over 3 and 4 January, conducted by ten Impalas and four Canberras. Together with the air strike at Cangamba of August 1983, this airstrike was regarded to have been one of the most successful airstrikes of the war.

A typical HAA inside Angola.

The OF had to deal with the defensive minefields encircling the town after a number of Ratels had detonated landmines. On 3 January, 25 kilometres north of Mupa, 53 Battalion made contact and killed two enemy troops and wounded one. A Ratel detonated a landmine, and the next day three more Ratels suffered the same fate in the minefields three kilometres south of Cuvelai. An OF ambulance also detonated a landmine. As previously mentioned, this situation was soon resolved when 32 Battalion captured extensive sketches showing the location of the enemy minefields.

On 4 January a 61 Mechanized Battalion Ratel from Delta Company 4 SA Infantry Battalion was destroyed by a T-54 tank, five kilometres northeast of Cuvelai. The Ratel had got bogged down in a minefield after detonating a landmine and sat there as a static target for an advancing tank. The Ratel was bombarded with shell after shell and stood no chance. Some SADF members were incinerated where they sat while others left desperate claw marks on the closed metal hatches in a desperate attempt to escape. The corpse of the Ratel driver had apparently shrunk to half its body size due to the heat of the explosion. Five of the bodies had to be identified through dental records and surviving 'dog tags'.[39] Rifleman J.L. Pretorius was actually the final serviceman to be included on the list of those who had perished, but his remains had not been identified due to the intesity of the incineration. Only on 2 February 1984 was he first reported missing when his personal mail was discovered unopened. It was ruled out during an inquiry that his remains could still be in Angola as he had no doubt died in the stricken Ratel, which was eventually recovered to South West Africa. Those who died were Lance-Corporal W.T. Steenkamp and Riflemen P.D. Pretorius, L.E. Pearson, G.A. Lennox, B. Geen, D.A. Louw, H.A. Heyns and J.L. Pretorius. This was the battle's worst single incident for the SADF and a dark day for Combat Group Delta and 4 SA Infantry Battalion.[40] During the subsequent pursuit, eleven T-54 tanks were knocked out, including four destroyed.

The enemy death toll rose rapidly with 50 bodies found at one target alone. More were to be counted over the following days; a total of 324 enemy bodies were discovered at Cuvelai. The southern part of Cuvelai was by now totally void of the enemy and, by 5 January, Combat Group Delta was in full control of the entire Cuvelai area the first time in the history of the bush war.

On 3 January Rifleman A. Aurelio of 32 Battalion detonated an anti-personnel landmine and was killed. An OF member was wounded when an ambulance arrived on the scene and detonated a landmine. On 6 January Combat Group Delta performed a final sweep of the target area, clearing all enemy positions. On 7 January a Ratel detonated a landmine; during its recovery another landmine was detonated. Three EF members were wounded at an observation post when SAAF launched a bombardment on EF installations.

On 8 January SADF troops captured two SA-9 ground-to-air missile systems from the EF base, although it was expected that the lesser known and more sophisticated SA-8 missile systems were present in the area too. The unknown AGS -17, the first of its kind to be examined by western forces, was also captured at Cuvelai. The capture of these state-of-the-art weapons was indeed a very significant discovery. The complete Soviet mobile SA-9 (NATO codename 'Gaskin')

The Ratel that was hit by a T-54 tank, killing its occcupants.

ground-to-air missile defence system was a critical component on the comprehensive anti-aircraft defence network in Angola, which far exceeded that country's defensive requirements. The SA-9 is bigger, faster and far more manoeuvrable than the SAM-7, designed to explode near a target and doesn't need to make contact with an aircraft to bring it down. The missile-launching tubes of the captured SA-9 were mounted on an adapted Soviet BRM2 amphibious armoured vehicle. The system is easily deployable and only takes 90 seconds to load the missile tubes. The AGS-17 is a 30mm air-cooled automatic grenade launcher, described by General Meiring as, "one of the most sophisticated weapons of its kind in the world". A circular drum magazine holding 29 rounds is simply inserted into position and, machine-gun-like, the grenades are hurled for distances of up to 1,730 metres.

Also on 8 January, five more T-54 tanks were destroyed and three FAPLA troops were captured. An OF Samil 20 transport vehicle detonated a landmine and a gun tractor was put out of action by FAPLA 120mm fire. The SAAF launched an airstrike at further enemy installations, destroying a fuel depot. A number of church services were held at the HAA on this day. Also on this day, requests were made for four gunship helicopters to provide air support. A specific request was made for Captain Anderson to pilot one, due to his experience. Four Bosbok fixed-wing aircraft were present overhead, providing communication. The Task Force was deployed west of the river but, attracting very accurate enemy fire, had to be

Far left: Commandant Faan Greyling with Brigadier Joep Joubert (back).

Left: An SA-9 missile system captured during Operation Askari.

redeployed. A Kwêvoël transport vehicle detonated a landmine.

On 10 January, 15 enemy troops were killed and two wounded. A 201 Battalion Buffalo vehicle detonated a landmine, killing Riflemen I. Malonga and J. Dala of 32 Battalion and wounding four.

On 11 January two TM-57 landmines were discovered on the road, one on top of the other. OF members continued to perform river protection and the clearing the EF area.

The Task Force, including 61 Mechanized Battalion, then withdrew from the area as the operation came to a close.

The AGS-17 is a 30mm air-cooled automatic grenade launcher.

MULONDO

After Cuvelai had been taken, the SADF effort was directed against Mulondo, where FAPLA's 19th Brigade was stationed. The same ground forces that had taken Cuvelai were used to attack Mulondo. Here FAPLA used their D-30 guns to good advantage, as their range was three to four kilometres longer than the SADF artillery. 7 Medium Regiment attached to Combat Group Delta proceeded to Mulondo, where a fierce artillery engagement took place. The SADF artillery then quickly withdrew. Once Mulondo was captured, UNITA forces were to occupy and dominate the area.

On 22 December, at a location 25 kilometres south-southwest of Mulondo, four EF members were killed when their vehicle detonated a landmine. Also on the same day, the former Sector 10 Reserve, now known as Combat Group Tango (as of 16 December) opened with accurate mortar fire on enemy targets from ten kilometres southwest to five kilometres east-northeast of Mulondo.

On 23 December Mulondo was attacked by Impalas. One Impala was hit in its tail section by a shoulder-launched SAM missile. The pilot was forced to do an emergency landing but safely landed the damaged aircraft at Ongiva.

On 29 December Combat Group Tango delivered further harassing artillery fire against Mulondo. The combination and the SAAF airstrikes and the artillery barrages was to force the 19th Brigade out of Mulondo, with 107 of its troops killed and several T-54 tanks destroyed.

At the end of January 1984, 32 Battalion commenced with Operation Opsaal. Colonel Viljoen was ordered to withdraw from Techamutete to Cuvelai. He made the mistake of destroying a bridge during the withdrawal, only to receive orders soon afterwards to return to Techamutete; the bridge had to be rebuilt by driving captured GAZ trucks into the river and using makeshift logs.

On their return leg, Impala aircraft provided air cover for 32 Battalion. One pilot was asked to monitor any vehicle movement behind the convoy. The pilot responded with: "Which vehicles ... which road actually?" Viljoen's riposte over the radio was to the effect that he now understood why Impala pilots wore masks over their mouths: they needed a good supply of oxygen for their brains.[41]

After the SADF had withdrawn from Askari operations, 32 Battalion remained in the area

for phase 3, the wrapping-up of the operation. Three companies of 32 Battalion were based at the Tactical HQ northeast of Techamutete, two companies 27 kilometres southeast of Cassinga, with one company, one platoon and an element of the Recce group deployed around Techamutete.

At the end of January, 32 Battalion was ordered to withdraw from the Cuvelai and Cassinga areas. The battalion was then ordered to erect tents and facilities for the JMMK, the Joint Military Monitoring Commission which

Impala tail section showing damage caused by an SA-9 missile.

was to implement the ceasefire, at Cuvelai. Dignitaries from FAPLA and SADF arrived in grand style in their helicopters. Among the SADF were Generals Geldenhuys and Meiring, members of the Department of Foreign Affairs and sundry hangers-on whom Viljoen referred to as 'Rubber Necks', who were, in fact, high-ranking SADF officers wearing brand-new nutria-brown uniforms and displaying virginal holsters carrying virginal 9mm pistols.[42]

As of September 1984, 32 Battalion, still under the command of Viljoen, embarked on Operation Forte, this time in a totally new role. While the SADF had officially withdrawn from Angolan territory, 32 Battalion stayed behind. Wearing issued civilian clothes, the troops changed their diet to that of UNITA and were thus able to move freely around the Techamutete area posing as UNITA soldiers. The difference now was that they could no longer rely on air support from the SAAF. However, they had regular contacts with SWAPO, often relying on information passed secretly from sympathetic officers at the JMMK. Once information was received that an ememy convoy was underway, its position was signalled to Viljoen's forces via the secret new DET signals equipment. The target was then taken out with relative ease as SWAPO was glibly unaware that dirty tricks were at play. Naturally, UNITA was blamed for such violations.[43]

On 11 February 1985 Captain Frank Kranenburg's Charlie Company of 32 Battalion walked into a SWAPO base in search of desperately needed water. Seven of the company were killed in the ensuing firefight and several wounded. The secret DET signals equipment was lost and could not be retrieved as SWAPO had crossed an imaginary north-south line imposed by the JMMK that forbade UNITA from traversing. During the evacuation, undertaken by a platoon of Bravo Company in Mercedes-Benz trucks, several of the wounded died. A funeral was arranged at Buffalo, the largest in the unit's history. Colonel Viljoen protected Kranenburg when ordered by General Geldenhuys to have him court martialled, stating that if there was any blame to be apportioned, as the commanding officer, it was his and his alone.[44]

ASSESSMENT OF OPERATION ASKARI

On 6 February 1984 a conference was held at the South African Army College to reflect on Operation Askari. Various lessons were learned from the experience gained during the operation.[45] Some of the points that came out of the conference are listed below, in no particular order:

- The SADF pursued SWAPO to Cuvelai, where FAPLA intervened and attacked the SADF.
- The SADF decided not to take Caiundo as SWAPO had by that time already evacuated the town.
- The SWAPO bases, Volcano and Dongo, were not destroyed during the operation.
- The SWAPO DHQ was thoroughly destroyed.
- SAAF airstrikes against Cuvelai were effective, but similar airstrikes at Mulondo and

Caiundo were questionable.

- 61 Mechanized Battalion and 32 Battalion received high praise for achieving their goals during Operation Askari.
- The Eland 90 armoured car used in support of the Ratels was found to be unfit for modern service and, with its poor mobility, was decommissioned as a combat vehicle.
- It was shown that SADF equipment had stood up well to the extremely wet conditions, but had put undue pressure on commanders during the preparatory stages of the various operations. It was recommended that more cognizance be taken in future of the weather conditions, and that a degree of flexibility be allowed when planning deadlines such as D-Days and H-Hours.
- The result of the airstrikes at Cahama were not known; the attack on Ediva was not successful due to T-54/55 tank activity in the area.
- The attack on Cuvelai was hampered by poor weather. By the time Cuvelai was eventually attacked, 32 Battalion had already taken Techamutete.
- The presence of enemy T-54/55 tanks and their utilization in an offensive role were not expected by the SADF. Neither aerial nor ground reconnaissance had confirmed the tank presence.
- As a result of Operation Askari, SWAPO was no longer able to use the central and eastern areas of southern Angola; it was expected that SWAPO would use the western region through to infiltrate South West Africa, where the terrain was more suitable for the SADF.
- From their bases inside Angola, SWAPO guerrillas now had to carry all their weapons and equipment a further 100 kilometres, increasing their trek to the border to 300 kilometres.
- The SADF signals links during operation Askari were of a very good quality.

In a letter to the UN Secretary-General, dated 6 January 1984, Angolan President Eduardo dos Santos confirmed that the SADF bombardment of Cuvelai killed 78 FAPLA troops, 64 were wounded and 36 were missing in action.

Total enemy losses during Operation Askari were: FAPLA: 426 killed and 3 captured; SWAPO: 45 killed and 11 captured; Cubans: 5 killed and 1 captured.

Total SADF casualties (killed in action, died on active service and wounded) during the period of Operation Askari, including normal operations inside South West Africa unrelated to Askari, amounted to a total of 294, of which 206 were suffered on Angolan soil, with the balance occurring in South West Africa.[46] As below, SADF casualties in Angola are outlined in more detail:

- 13 Dec: artillery wounded 2
- 14 Dec: POM-Z AP mines wounded 3
- 19 Dec: POM-Z AP mines wounded 3
- 22 Dec: contact, 4 wounded
- 24 Dec: landmine wounded 1 and killed 9
- 25 Dec: contact, 2 wounded
- 28 Dec: contact, 3 wounded
- 29 Dec: POM-Z AP mines wounded 2
- 29 Dec: contact, 1 wounded
- 31 Dec: contact, 9 wounded and 5 killed

- 1 Jan: contact, 1 wounded
- 2 Jan: POM-Z AP mines wounded 6
- 3 Jan: contact, 4 wounded
- 4 Jan: 81mm mortar wounded 4
- 4 Jan: contact, 5 wounded
- 4 Jan: contact: Ratel destroyed by RPG-7 or T-55 shell, 10 wounded and 5 killed
- 5 Jan: contact, 1 wounded
- 7 Jan: contact, 1 wounded
- 8 Jan: contact, 1 wounded
- 10 Jan   contact, 2 wounded and 2 killed

OF casualties due to own conduct inside Angola:

- 11 Dec: claymore mine killed 1 and wounded 3
- 27 Dec: hand grenade killed 1 and wounded 6
- 10 Dec :   1 shot and killed
- 24 Dec: Puma helicopter crash killed 1 and wounded 9

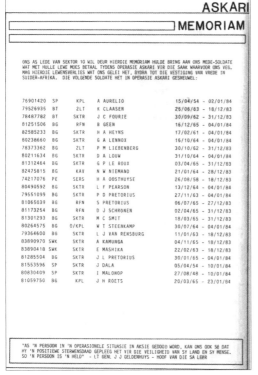

Roll of honour of SADF members killed during Operation Askari[48]

SADF vehicle accidents injured 11 soldiers during this period. Military personnel casevaced inside Angola:

- 62 from contacts
- 47 from landmine explosions
- 40 from accidents
- 5 for general reasons
- 6 for psychological reasons
- 36 for medical illnesses

In terms of matériel, SADF losses were: 3 x Ratel 90 APCs, 1 x Ratel 20 APC, 1 x Samil gun-towing truck, 1 x Samil fuel tanker, 2 x Samil 100 trucks, 1 x Samil 20 truck, 4 x Buffalo APCs (including 1 captured by FAPLA), 1 x Puma helicopter and 7 x Impalas damaged by missiles, AAA and small-arms fire.

Some of the more significant enemy armaments captured by the SADF at Cuvelai consisted of: 11 x T-54 tanks, 5 x 122mm D-30 cannons, 11 x 23mm anti-aircraft guns, 73 x SA-7 missile launchers, 13 x BRD 82mm cannons, 2 x 57mm radar-controlled AA cannons, 7 x 75mm tank cannons and 5 x 122mm rocket launchers.

T54-tank captured by the SADF at Cuvelai.

Private Petro Torrez, the Cuban soldier captured near Cahama during Operation Askari (Photo South African Department of Defence Archival Services)

Notes

1 National Museum of Military History, Johannesburg, archives
2 South African Department of Defence Documentation Centre, original sources
3 *ibid*
4 *ibid*
5 *ibid*
6 *ibid*
7 Wilsworth, Clive, *First In, Last Out: The South African Artillery in Action, 1975–1988*, (Johannesburg: 30° South, 2006) pp. 220-240
8 *ibid*
9 *ibid*
10 *ibid*
11 *ibid*
12 *ibid*
13 *ibid*
14 Lord, Dick, *op.cit.*, p. 399
15 Bridgland, Fred, *op. cit.*, p. 151
16 South African Department of Defence Documentation Centre, original sources
17 *ibid*
18 South African Department of Defence Documentation Centre, original sources
19 Interview with Brigadier-General Eddie Viljoen
20 South African Department of Defence Documentation Centre, original sources
21 Interview with Brigadier-General Eddie Viljoen
22 *ibid*
23 *ibid*
24 *ibid*
25 *ibid*
26 South African Department of Defence Documentation Centre, original sources
27 Interview with Brigadier-General Eddie Viljoen
28 South African Department of Defence Documentation Centre, original sources
29 Lord, Dick, *op.cit.*, p. 308
30 South African Department of Defence Documentation Centre, original sources
31 *ibid*
32 *ibid*
33 *ibid*
34 Kruger, Anthony Korporaal, *My Herinneringe van Hierdie Operasie*, http://www.61mech. org.za/pages/demo-story2?height=400&width=400http://www.justdone.co.za/roh/main. php?page=View_Person&PersonNumber=1169 (Accessed February 2012)
35 National Museum of Military History, Johannesburg, archives
36 South African Department of Defence Documentation Centre, original sources
37 *ibid*
38 Dick Lord, p. 307
39 Wall, Dudley Colonel, *Operation Askari 1983–1984 Southern Angola*, http://www.warinangola. com/Portals/31/Op%20Askari%20SWA.pdf (Accessed February 2012)
40 South African Department of Defence Documentation Centre, original sources
41 Interview with Brigadier-General Eddie Viljoen
42 *ibid*
43 *ibid*
44 Bothma, Louis Johnnes, *op.cit.*, pp. 306-309
45 South African Department of Defence Documentation Centre, original sources
46 *ibid*

PART 6:

WARFARE IN AFRICA

THE SIGNIFICANCE OF THE BATTLE OF CUITO CUANAVALE

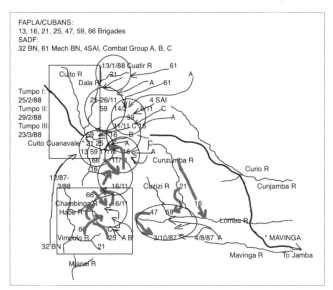

Map of the Battle of Cuito Cuanavale.

By the end of Operation Askari in 1984, SWAPO's forces were on the brink of collapse. The ceasefire that followed, however, allowed SWAPO to regroup in Angola. On 15 April 1985 Operation Dikmelk commenced and the SADF withdrew from southern Angola after the failure of the JMMK. A military parade was staged north of the border at Santa Clara; FAPLA representatives were expected to attend. However, FAPLA's offensive against UNITA increased to the extent that the SADF found itself drawn further into the conflict between FAPLA and UNITA. Their war was one that did not directly concern the SADF apart from protecting the northern border of South West Africa from SWAPO invasion. It was clear that a UNITA collapse would favour SWAPO's cause; this was something to be avoided at all costs. This story came to an end not in 1984 but only in 1988. Therefore, we need to gain a proper understanding of the significance of the Battle of Cuito Cuanavale, which was the final chapter in the Angolan bush war.

Cuban President Fidel Castro was desperately in need of an opportunity to display

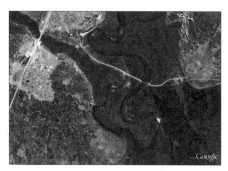

Aerial photograph of the bridge at Cuito Cuanavale.

Cuban military prowess to be able to pull out of Angola with a modicum of honour. The military objective of FAPLA, backed by Cuban forces based in Cuito Cuanavale, was to capture Mavinga, and thereafter Jamba, both controlled by UNITA, in southeastern Angola. The objective of UNITA, backed by the SADF was to defend Mavinga and prevent it from falling into FAPLA/Cuban hands. Mavinga is approximately 120 kilometres southeast of Cuito Cuanavale and Jamba farther southeast. It is more correct to refer to the operation as the 'Battle for Mavinga' and not Cuito Cuanavale. Cuito Cuanavale was a ghost town, 400 kilometres from the Namibian border. The MPLA government made several attempts to implement its rule across Angola, including UNITA-controlled areas in the southeast. The SADF, on the other hand, wanted to make sure that southeastern Angola did not fall to FAPLA in case of a UNITA defeat. FAPLA control of Cuando-Cubango would have meant that SWAPO's PLAN and even the ANC's MK guerrillas would easily cross into Namibia and Botswana via Kavango and Caprivi and thereafter into South Africa itself.

SWAPO needed these areas to be able to infiltrate Namibia via Kavango and Caprivi. UNITA forces were determined to defend their strongholds against FAPLA and Cuban forces, while SADF wanted to prevent SWAPO guerrilla incursions into Namibia through Kavango and Caprivi. Hence, the prospect of FAPLA controlling Cuando-Cubango, attracted SADF interest in helping UNITA militarily to frustrate FAPLA efforts. UNITA's presence opposite Kavango and Caprivi served as a buffer zone, so much so that the SADF could deploy its troops elsewhere.

In 1985, and again in 1986, the Angolan armed forces attempted to occupy Mavinga, a town halfway to UNITA's main base at Jamba, 200 kilometres to its south. Both offensives were mercilessly beaten off by UNITA, backed by the SADF. Eighteen FAPLA brigades were assembled and ready to be thrown into the assault.

Intelligence estimated that the MPLA's warplane strength was 30 advanced MiG-23 fighters, eight Sukhoi-22 fighter-bombers, 50 MiG-21 fighters, 16 older MiG-17 fighters, 33 Mi-24 'Hind' helicopter gunships, 27 Alouette assault helicopters and 69 Mi-8 and Mi-17 transport helicopters. I have included in the appendices the specifications of the MiG-21 and the MiG-23 aircraft.[1] The FAPLA tank force consisted of 350 T-55s, 150 T-34s (also described in the appendices) and 50 amphibious PT-76s.[2]

From 1974 to 1984, the MPLA had received US$4 billions' worth in military aid from Moscow.[3] By 1985, the MPLA had received a further US$1 billion's worth of the latest Soviet weaponry.

In August 1987 the FAPLA/Cuban forces deployed the following forces in their 1987/88 suicidal offensive: Brigades 8, 13, 16, 21, 25, 47, 59 and 66, plus the 50th Cuban Brigade, artillery and MiG jets, as well as Hind Mi-24 helicopters piloted by Cuban and Soviet 'advisers'. They had close to 20, 000 heavily armed troops in total. The Cuban field commander was General Leopold Cintra Frias and the FAPLA regional commander was General Mateus Angelo, aka 'Vietnam', assisted by operational FAPLA commander Lieutenant-Colonel Ngueto.[4]

As a reaction to FAPLA and Cuban deployment, UNITA deployed seven conventional battalions and commandos. They were also heavily armed with artillery and anti-aircraft weapons, including US-made Stinger missiles. They had a total of 5,000 armed men. UNITA's operational command was led by Generals Renato Campos Mateus, Joao Batista Tchindandi aka 'Black Power' and Altino Sapalalo aka 'Bock'. The overall UNITA military commanders for this operation were Generals Demosthenes Amos Chilingutila, and Arlindo 'Ben-Ben' Pena[5]

The stated FAPLA and Cuban objectives for the Mavinga/Jamba campaign were as follows:[6]

- to occupy the UNITA-held town of Mavinga and then proceed to Jamba
- to weaken UNITA by destroying its main base at Jamba
- to open up the Namibia/Angola border in the northeast for SWAPO guerrillas to infiltrate into the Kavango and the Caprivi

They failed in all three objectives. The stated SADF and UNITA objectives were:

- to halt and reverse the FAPLA/Cuban advance on Mavinga/Jamba
- to inflict maximum casualties on the retreating FAPLA and Cuban forces
- to force the FAPLA/Cuban troops to retreat to the west of the Cuito River

This was exactly what had happened.

The SADF force consisted of 61 Mechanized Battalion, 32 Battalion, two APC-mounted companies from the Ondangwa-based 101 Battalion, Special Forces (Recces), long-range artillery, including G5 guns (later G6 mobile guns were briefly deployed), as well as SAAF jet aircraft and helicopters. The SADF had 3,000 heavily armed men in total. The overall SADF commander of the 20th South African Brigade was Colonel Deon Ferreira, assisted by Colonel Jack Harris and Commandants Robbie Hartslief, Kobus Smit, Mike Muller and others. The bloody encounter that was to follow, is described by Fidel Castro as one of those "absurd offensives towards Jamba in remote southeastern Angola ... with disastrous consequences as always".[7]

Operation Modular and the Lomba River

Based at Cuito Cuanavale, the FAPLA and Cuban 47th, 59th and 21st Brigades started their advance towards Mavinga on 17 August 1987 and by 30 August were just north of the Lomba River, within 25 kilometres of Mavinga.[8]

32 Battalion, under Commandant Jan Hougaard, was operating in the area with UNITA. A battery of G5 guns was deployed to give support to 32 Battalion;[9] they were capable of delivering a variety of 43.5-kilogram shells up to 42 kilometres or as close as three kilometres. The computer-controlled G5s delivered fragmentation shells, detonating 20 metres above the target and blasting down 5,000 steel shards and slivers which killed or maimed anyone in their path and penetrated soft-skinned vehicles. Mirage F1AZs and Canberra bombers pounded the enemy daily. Mirage IIIs, escorted by Mirage F1CZs, collected intelligence by taking aerial photos of the battle zone.

On 2 September Lieutenant Glynn, and Commandant Johan du Randt were directing the first G5s shots of the war from a Bosbok spotter aircraft. The plane became the first casualty of the battle when it was shot down by a powerful long-range ground-to-air missile.[10]

47th and 21st Brigades were formidable opponents, accompanied as they were by a tactical armoured group with tanks; the 21st also carried chemical weapons in its armoury.

4th SA Infantry Battalion was organized into two artillery-supported combat groups: Combat Group Bravo, consisting of 32 Battalion, 101 Battalion from Ovamboland, supported by UNITA's semi-regular 3rd Battalion, was tasked with preventing FAPLA from crossing the river; Combat Group Alpha, consisting of 61 Mechanized Battalion, supported by 32 Battalion and UNITA's semi-regular 5th Battalion, was tasked with halting FAPLA's movement east along the river.

FAPLA's D-30 artillery and BM-21 'Stalin Organs' commenced firing gas shells to drift over the South Africans with severe consequences. Fortunately for the South Africans, the wind direction changed, with the gas drifting back in the enemy's direction.[11]

On 10 September four Ratel 90 anti-tank armoured cars and companies of 101 Battalion in 30 Casspir infantry combat vehicles, with 32 Battalion's Major Nortman's four Ratels in reserve, approached the enemy. Nortman received instructions from Colonel Ferreira to neutralize a BRDM armoured scout car and a GAZ truck which were then hit by ZT3 anti-tank missiles, the first time these weapons had been deployed in action. The missile's 3.5km range was the longest achieved by any anti-tank weapon at that time.[12] Thereafter, three T-54 tanks were knocked out. In the follow-up, 21st Brigade was virtually destroyed. Twelve days later the Combat Group Alpha was recalled due to more reports of gas. After they returned to the battlefield with Combat Group Bravo, the enemy retreated rapidly, mowed down by 7.62mm machine-gun and 20mm high-explosive cannon fire. More than 300 FAPLA soldiers from the 21st were killed, but this figure could have been as high as 600. On 13 September 200 more FAPLA were killed by Hartslief's Ratel 90s using their AP shells. This coincided with the 200-round ammunition belts from the 7.62 mm machine guns being fired in less than a minute, mortar fire and 7.62mm R4 assault rifles firing through the slits of the Casspirs. (The R4 was developed from the Israeli Galil assault rifle.)[13]

32 Battalion's Captain Mac Macallum's Ratel was destroyed by fire from a T-54 tank, killing him.[14] The T-54 was capable of shooting more accurately and faster than the Ratel 90; it carried a much larger 100mm gun, had thicker armoured protection and a stabilizing system that allowed it to shoot on the move.[15] However, the dense bush allowed close combat within 15 to 25 metres' range and so the Ratel, with a smaller turning circle than the T-54's, could get behind them and shoot them out. The Ratel 90's range was 1200 metres compared to the T-55's 2,000–2,500 metres,[16] and coupled with the tank's superior armour, the Ratel sometimes had to fire up to five shots before the soft spot of the T-55 was hit.[17]

On 27 September 21st Brigade was ordered to pull back, now at a third of its strength. It was now Combat Group Bravo against the 59th and 21st and Combat Group Alpha against the 47th Brigade. Also on 27 September, Captain Arthur Piercy's F1CZ Mirage was hit by enemy fire and, on landing at Rundu, his aircraft overran the runway, with the pilot paralyzed as a result of the crash.[18]

Colonel Ferreira was now focusing on distracting the 47th Brigade.

The RPV, the Gharra, used during Askari for the first time, also played a major role in the battle, [19] attracting dozens of SA-8 missiles, which simply gave away the positions of the enemy missile emplacements. They gathered vital information of enemy movements and strengths, giving the SADF essentially what was live coverage.

On 3 October Combat Group Alpha with 61 Mechanized and 32 battalions were unleashed on the 47th. Fifty Ratels advanced in three lines; the enemy moved into an open area where they were caught and 600 FAPLA soldiers were killed. The MiGs, with potential air superiority throughout the battle, flew at too high an altitude and could not identify their targets. Their primary role became to destroy their own abandoned vehicles and equipment before they fell into the hands of the SADF. Among such abandoned equipment was a complete SA-8 missile system, much-anticipated by the SADF who became the first anti-communist force to capture such a prize.[20]

Colonel Ferreira became the first South African commander with an opportunity to destroy an entire brigade, which successfully did that day.[21] FAPLA pushed 22 tanks into the battle while the SADF had none. Only one Ratel was destroyed and one SADF soldier was killed while 600 FAPLA troops were killed.[22]

On 5 October, the 59th, 21st and 16th Brigades and the remains of 47th Brigade began their withdrawal; however, the SADF could not give chase due to fatigue and their extended lines. An additional force of 4th SA Infantry Battalion, a squadron of 13 Olifant tanks, an additional battery of eight G5-guns and a troop of three G6 guns (for their first deployment) were on their way. The Olifant tank had a Centurion chassis as its base, but had been totally remodelled by Armscor with extra electronics added.

Combat Group Alpha and Charlie, backed by Combat Group Bravo, followed suit on 8 October. Captain Chris van Zyl formed Task Force Delta before Combat Group Charlie was dissolved. Alpha (350 infantrymen from 61 Mechanized battalion in Ratels) now fell under Bok Smith, and Bravo (32 Battalion and 101 Battalion troops with UNITA) came under Hartslief. Task Force Delta was incorporated into Bravo.[23] Five UNITA units joined up with the 3rd UNITA Battalion.

The next assault took place on 17 October. The 59th Brigade became isolated and was now being softened up with artillery.[24]

A MiG-21 was hit by a Stinger missile and the two Cuban pilots were taken prisoner on 24 October. The G5s, now firing within range of Cuito Cuanavale, destroyed two Hind helicopter gunships. The bridge at Chambinga was also destroyed by G5 gunfire.

On 9 November the assault on 16th Brigade commenced. A T-55 was taken out by an Olifant tank,[25] as dozens of Ratel 90s, Ratel 20s and Olifants advanced with infantrymen deployed 600 metres ahead. A Ratel also took out a T-54 but two Ratels were then hit, killing their occupants. Five T-55s were destroyed and one captured. By that night the SADF had advanced through the 16th's positions. Charlie destroyed ten T-55s and captured three.[26] Three of the destroyed tanks were credited to G5 hits. FAPLA suffered 75 dead while the SADF lost only seven men; this was clearly a great victory for the SADF. However, the 16th managed to escape and Charlie's advance was halted, one of the main mistakes of the war.

The attack resumed on 11 November. But due to threatening MiG attacks, the SADF force was ordered to withdraw, much to to their dismay. By that time, more than 300 FAPLA troops had been killed and 14 enemy tanks had been destroyed.[27] SADF suffered five killed and 19 wounded.[28] The routed FAPLA and Cuban troops were in the process of staging a disorganized retreat of 120 kilometres to their point of departure: Cuito Cuanavale. According to FAPLA's own record of events, they were "obliged" to pass from offensive tactics to a defensive strategy "to avoid the worst".

On 31 October another raid took place on Cuvelai by the SADF in the west, hitting a SWAPO base, with 150 SWAPO and 12 SADF soldiers killed.[29]

On 10 November, FAPLA's 59th began heading towards the Tumpo Triangle, close to Cuito Cuanavale.[30] On 16 November the 16th, 21st and 25th escaped from Combat Group Charlie's clutches and the chance to destroy the fleeing brigades was lost. By mid November, all the FAPLA brigades were back where they had started in July.

During the fighting on 16 November, 130 FAPLA troops were killed and seven tanks were destroyed. The G5s destroyed 300 vehicles at the bridge over the Chambinga River on 17

November.[31] The MPLA admitted that it had suffered major losses: 4,000 soldiers killed or wounded, and 90 tanks, eleven SA-8 and SA-13 missile systems, 20 BM21s and more than 300 other vehicles were admitted to have been destroyed. In the first half of November, the SADF suffered 17 killed and 41 wounded.

The three G6s were withdrawn at the end of November. On 25 November FAPLA forces consisted of 5,000 men east of the Cuito River;[32] the SADF had a force of 3,000 men on the ground. An attack commenced on this day against the 25th Brigade as Operation Modular came to an end. Operation Hooper was opened on 13 December.

Operation Hooper: western offensive
32 Battalion, under Colonel Jan Hougaard, began an assault on FAPLA's supply lines between Menongue and Cuito Cuanavale during December, causing huge losses to vehicles, equipment and supplies.[33]

On 13 January the 21st Brigade came under fire from the 4th SA Infantry Battalion (Commandant Jan Malan), 61 Mechanized Battalion (Commandant Koos Liebenberg) and UNITA. 61 Mechanized Battalion was issued a further eleven Olifant tanks; 4 SAI was at the time regarded as the most formidable South African combat group since World War Two, consisting of 1,000 men mounted on Ratels and service vehicles, with eleven Olifant tanks.[34]

The Olifants systematically took out the bunkers but the Ratel, with its thinner armour, took a hammering from the enemy 23mm guns. Two Ratels were put out of action. Two T-55s were destroyed by the Olifants. UNITA, with a captured ZU-23, shot down a MiG-21. By 14 January, seven enemy tanks had been destroyed and five captured and three SA-8s (not complete) were also captured. FAPLA lost 15 dead and wounded and one SADF soldier was wounded. UNITA lost four dead and 18 wounded. 32 Battalion on the Menongue route did not take part in this operation, but the enemy was severely demoralized and low on personnel due to 32 Battalion action.[35]

The 21st reoccupied the positions they had lost on 13 January, now with 50 T-54/55 tanks. Castro set up an operations room in Havana from where he could direct operations.[36]

The SADF now had 59th in their sight.

On 3 January the bridge at Cuito Cuanavale was hit by a secret H-2 'intelligent' laser-guided missile, taking out 20 metres of the bridge.[37]

On 14 February, the 54th was attacked. 4 SAI (Commandant Schoeman) destroyed four T-54s and then found the 54th HQ already abandoned. 61 Mechanized Battalion was led by Commandant Muller at this time.[38]

A close fight with T-54s then ensued, with Cubans now serving at the forefront for the first time.[39] Seven T-54s were destroyed. For the first time since October 1987 the SADF achieved a clear victory over FAPLA: the 59th was destroyed and the 21st and 25th were pouring into the Tumpo Triangle, with 400 FAPLA troops killed and 14 T-54/55s destroyed, while 61 Mechanized Battalion suffered four killed and three wounded when a MiG dropped a bomb right on a group of 4 SAI.

On 6 February 32 Battalion attacked Menongue, killing seven Cubans and 37 Angolan Air Force personnel; one MIG-21 was put out of action.[40]

On 19 February Major Ed Every's Mirage F1AZ was hit and he was killed. One hundred and forty-three Cuban and FAPLA troops inspecting the Mirage wreckage were killed when 32 Battalion fired a ripple of 96 rockets at the crash site.[41]

In total, one Mirage, one Bosbok and three RPVs were shot down during the battle.

On 19 March another Mirage crashed in northern South West Africa and Major van

Coppehagen was killed. FAPLA's air strikes, with up to 60 sorties a day, were largely ineffective. Only four SADF and two UNITA members lost their lives as a result of these.

Tumpo I, II and III and Operation Packer

Tumpo I commenced on 25 February with mainly 61 Mechanized Battalion accompanied by 20 Olifant tanks. Three tanks lost their tracks in a minefield. FAPLA's artillery knocked out seven vehicles that day. Tumpo I failed due to no night follow-up assault being ordered when FAPLA was on the run.[42]

Tumpo II opened on 29 February, with only 16 of the 22 Olifant tanks operational at that stage. It failed because the SADF over-estimated FAPLA's tank strength. Only two, and not ten T-54/55s were in the area as was reported.[43] FAPLA's 25th lost 15 men, but the brigade was not destroyed as it received more tanks, with elements of the 66th Brigade and the 16th Brigade and the Cuban-mounted 3rd Tank Battalion joining the fray.

Operation Packer opened between 4 and 8 March, consisting of 82 SA Brigade (trained by Colonel Paul Fouché), Ratel Regiment Mooi River and G5 guns from Potchefstroom University Artillery Regiment, made up of mostly CF troops.

Tumpo III opened on 23 March in what was basically an artillery action.[44] Eleven Olifant tanks were deployed. UNITA's strength was only 200 fighters and not the 700 that formed a battalion.[45] A and a B Olifant squadrons of Regiment President Steyn, plus Regiment Mooi River Ratel squadron and two mechanized infantry battalions of Regiment De la Rey and Regiment Groot Karoo participated in the attack. They were supported by a G5 battery, and ancient G2s, with a range of only 16 kilometres. The 44th Parachute Brigade provided 120mm mortar support and the 19th Rocket Regiment a troop of four MRLs. Major van Staden commanded three 32 Battalion companies

Tumpo III was directed at 25th FAPLA Brigade. Two Olifant tanks were crippled and permission was asked to destroy them. Another was abandoned and two more were captured, a propaganda boon for SWAPO. Tumpo III was the only defeat that the SADF ever suffered during the war.[46]

It was clear that FAPLA could only be destroyed from the east by a massive armament build-up and a large loss of life.

The SADF laid vast numbers of landmines. By the end of Operation Packer on 30 April 1988, only 1,000 CF members remained serving with 82nd SA Brigade.[47]

The 'Battle of Cuito Cuanavale' was over, with dire results, particularly on the FAPLA and Cuban side, the scoreboard reading as follows:

1 x FAPLA brigade (i.e. 47th Brigade) was effectively annihilated
4,768 x FAPLA soldiers were killed
94 x FAPLA tanks were destroyed or captured (and handed over to UNITA)
8 x MiG-23 and 4 x MiG-21 jets were shot down

On the SADF/UNITA side:

> 1,000 UNITA soldiers were killed
31 x SADF soldiers were killed
3 x Olipfant tanks were destroyed
11 x armoured cars and APCs were lost (including four Ratels)
1 x Mirage was shot down

Recent photo of the bridge at Cuito Cuanavale.

Looking at the figures it is overwhelmingly clear that the SADF/UNITA forces had the best of the battle. The FAPLA/Cuban forces did not capture a single SADF soldier during the entire campaign. The FAPLA/Cuban force did not capture Mavinga or destroy UNITA's Jamba HQ. The FAPLA/Cuban advance to Mavinga was stopped at the Lomba River and the FAPLA troops were "obliged" to retreat 120 kilometres back to the western side of the Cuito River, after which the SADF destroyed the bridge, to ensure FAPLA/Cuban forces would not be able to cross to the eastern side any time soon after the SADF had departed.

Moreover, the actual FAPLA/Cuban defeat was a nightmare for Arnaldo Tomas Ochoa Sanchez ('El Moro'), commander of the Cuban forces in Angola since November 1987.[48] He complained that he was dispatched to "a lost war" so that he would be blamed for "the defeat". General Ochoa did in fact become the scapegoat and was executed on 12 July 1989 following accusations against him by President Fidel Castro of "serious acts of corruption, dishonest use of economic resources, and drug trafficking". He took the fall for the shameful Cuban defeat in Angola that is now sugar-coated and presented to a gullible international public as the "victory of Cuito Cuanavale".[49]

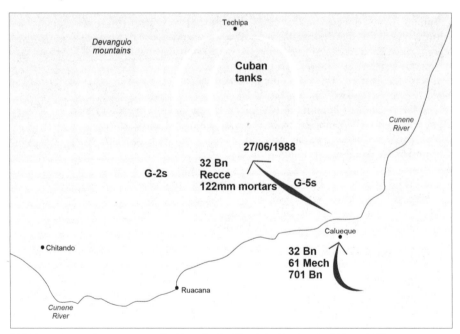

SADF positions and movements at Techipa, the final battle inside Angola, 27 June 1988.

THE FINAL CUBAN OFFENSIVE FROM TECHIPA

By January 1988, 3,500 Cuban soldiers were deployed in southwestern Angola, posing a threat to the SADF on a totally new front in the west.[50] The terrain was much different from the area in the southeast of Angola as it is a mountainous desert area, with limited protection to be sought in trees and undergrowth.

During June 1988, 32 Battalion Recce Wing reported that a Cuban force was being assembled at Techipa, a town west of the Cunene River and 50 kilometres north of the border with South West Africa.

Things in the west changed drastically with the Cubans erecting of a bridge over the Cunene River at Xangongo and the upgrading of airfields at Xangongo and Cahama. MiG-23s had now been stationed much closer to the border, at Cahama and no longer only at Lubango. These MiGs now frequently entered South West African airspace, and came as close as 20 kilometres to the Sector 10 HQ at Oshakati.

Commandant Jan Hougaard was brought in and he set up a Tactical HQ at Ruacana on 9 May.

32 Battalions Recce teams reported that the Cuban force was advancing on the Techipa road to within 25 kilometres of the strategic Calueque dam. The Ruacana power scheme to its south was their main target.

On 27 April the Cuban Major-General Francisco Crus Borsao made an attempt to fly to South West Africa to defect to the United States with 26 people on board an Antonov-24 transport plane, including a number of military officers.[51] When the aircraft's pilot ignored orders to land the aircraft, it was shot down by MiGs and all on board were killed.

The Cubans had 11,000 infantry soldiers from Castro's elite 50th Division positioned in the west. With them were 100 T-55s and also the more advanced T-65 Soviet tanks. Three integrated SWAPO-Cuban battalions were divided between Techipa, Xangongo and Mupa.[52]

As the enemy HQ was at Techipa, Commandant Hougaard was ordered to attack this location with three companies of 32 Battalion, consisting of 300 soldiers, while a larger conventional force was being formed, which would consist of 14,000 Citizen Force members, to prepare for attack from the South West African side of the border. 32 Battalion's Colonel Michau Delport would command the initial Task Force.

Hougaard had two companies deployed south of Techipa, with the third company 20 kilomtres south of Xangongo. During their first encounter with BRDMs a Cuban was killed by rifle fire. However, more Cuban tanks were coming at them. 32 Battalion retreated quickly, and loaded all their kit onto two Unimog vehicles. Both vehicles were destroyed, containing the precious B22H radios with their hopping-encoding capability. A group of 32 Battalion soldiers escaped to the north, and ran 100 kilometres in two days to avoid the Cubans. Every soldier was ultimately accounted for.

Commandant Jan Hougaard was nearly shot down on board a Bosbok by an SA-6 missile (effective at distances of 60 kilometres). It had been decided to destroy seven Cuban missile systems and while the ground was being prepared by the Recce teams, an attack by the SAAF was ordered and then cancelled and then ordered again. Hougaard desperately needed to contact his Recce teams and boarded the Bosbok to make contact with them on their ground-to-air radio network. The missile came within a whisker of downing the plane.

To defend the Calueque dam at all costs, a force from 61 Mechanized Battalion was mobilized, consisting of one squadron of eleven Olifant tanks, two infantry companies in Ratel 20s, a platoon of eight anti-tank Ratel 90s, 12 81mm mortar-mounted Ratels and a troop of four 120mm mortars. 32 Battalion was in support with four anti-tank ZT3 guided missiles mounted on Ratels, an additional Ratel 90, a troop of four MRLs, two Recce teams, four infantry companies and a light artillery support company, plus G5s and G2s.[53]

The G5s crossed the bridge at Calueque on 16 June 1988. On 22 June Combat Team Charlie, under Mike Muller, crossed the dam after a bridge was strengthened in haste by the 25th Field Engineers. Task Force Charlie was then divided into three combat groups.

On 26 June the advance commenced with 32 Battalion infantry spread out over a front of 12 kilometres, followed by eight Ratel 90s and four Ratel-TZ3s, followed by Olifant tanks with two infantry companies on their flanks.[54] Hougaard was on a hill in the distance to coordinate the attack. The Cuban SAM-6 positions were identified by luring them into firing at two tempting Impala aircraft flying past and fake weather balloons. The positions were then blasted continuously for six hours, by G5s, G2s and 120mm mortars, causing ontold destruction.

During the advance, Muller came up against T-54 with his Ratels, and one Ratel was immobilized. In return, they shot out a T54-tank, two ZU-23 guns, several halftracks and killed 60 infantry soldiers. A Ratel 90 was then hit by a T-54, killing Lieutenant Meiring and wounding three soldiers. An Olifant tank hit a T-54 tank and the enemy soldiers riding on the tank were all killed. By now two Cuban tank companies of eleven tanks each were approaching Muller's force from two directions.[55] Eight MiG-23s from Lubango attacked the Calueque dam wall and the ramp erected to cross the Cunene River. Six bombs hit their targets. On the second approach, eleven SADF members were killed next to their Buffalo vehicle, while on a supply mission. A 20mm gun hit a MiG, which crashed on its return.[56]

The SAAF had been caught off-guard by the low-flying MiGs. The reason why they were not detected earlier was that the MiGs managed to maintain radio silence. A great toll was paid for engaging the Cubans without air superiority.

On 27 June the SADF withdrew over the Cunene River at a crossing not targeted by the Cuban MiGs. Three hundred FAPLA troops had been killed during the battle; the SADF had lost 12 men. If needed, the SADF would force a stand-off on the South West African border against any approaching Cuban invasion force, where the SADF could engage from their permanent bases and, importantly, with air superiority.

The Buffalo destroyed by a MiG-23 airstrike, which killed eleven SADF troops. (Photo *At Thy Call We Did Not Falter*, Clive Holt, 2004)

If Fidel Castro was losing militarily, he was winning economically. The bill for the South African government to run the war was now estimated at R2 million a day[57] Soon the cost—political, economic and technical—of maintaining its Angolan military adventure was to prove unsustainable for South Africa. Moscow was providing Cuba with US$10 million in aid a day. However, Soviet President Mikhail Gorbachev was pursuing his Perestroika and Glasnost policies of openness towards the west. He had already begun withdrawing his forces from Afghanistan as of 28 July 1986, after some heavy defeats. In February 1988 Gorbachev announced the full withdrawal of Soviet forces from Afghanistan.[58] he started cutting foreign aid to his Soviet allies and during May 1998, Cuba's fuel supply was down to just one week's reserve.

Brigadier-General Dick Lord sets the number of SWAPO insurgents to security force personnel at a ratio of 1:8. More significant was the fact that able-bodied South Africans were removed from participating in the economic workforce. He stated: "The war had become so predictable that it was difficult to foresee how this process of violence could be halted."

In September 1988, a mulit-party conference was held, attended by Neil van Heerden and General Jannie Geldenhuys on behalf of South Africa. The result, the Geneva Protocol, dictated that the withdrawal of all foreign forces from Angola would commence on 1 September. SWAPO was to remain north of the 16th degree of latitude.

On 13 December 1988, a further protocol was signed at Brazzaville. Among other issues, it was agreed that UN Resolution 435 should be implemented on 1 April 1989, and that the Cubans would finally depart from Angola 18 months from this date. A peace treaty was signed on 22 December 1988 on an island in New York harbour.[59] The last Cuban left Angola on 1 July 1991. During the Angolan bush war, a total of 400,000 Cuban troops had served in Angola.[60] Together with their family members, it is likely that the entire Cuban population of ten million people was indirectly involved.

But, on 1 April 1989, 1,600 SWAPO members, heavily armed, crossed the border into South West Africa. Perez de Cuellar and Martti Athisaari approved the release of SADF members from their bases in Oshivelo to assist the police in countering the SWAPO invasion, which was a clear breach of the peace treaty. Three hundred and five SWAPO members and 27 policemen were killed and the invasion was repulsed.

Eleven assembly points were established with all SWAPO members required to report to these areas by 11 April 1989.[61]

Finally, the war in South West Africa was over.

OTHER INCIDENTS OF TOTAL CARNAGE

The Angolan civil war and the South West African/Angolan bush war were conflicts where external forces, such as the SADF, curtailed the war to one area. Such conflicts generally escalate and result in many innocent civilians being drawn in and caught in the middle of the fighting. As they are forced to show their allegiance to one side, a recipe for carnage is created on a grand scale. The Angolan bush war was not the first case of civilians being implicated in this manner.

On 3 February 1960 the British Prime Minister Harold Macmillan made his 'Winds of Change' speech to the Parliament of South Africa, Cape Town. Macmillan said: "The wind of change is blowing through this continent. Whether we like it or not, this growth of national consciousness is a political fact." He was commenting on European nations who ruled over African colonies and how these colonies were now seeking independence from their European overlords.

Africa is the second largest continent in the world, houses the second largest population and has the most countries, each with a diversity of tribes and languages. Yet during the second part of the 20th century, many of these countries experienced the worst possible transition from colonialism to sovereignty. Before subjugation by its European colonialists the country was pristine, with large areas unspoiled by human habitation. Traditional inter-tribal strife aside, the diversity of the land and the friendly and nature-loving temperament of its people left them uninterested in modernization and industrialization. Furthermore, the indigenous people of Africa were largely disinterested in land ownership, preferring a communal joint ownership under a single tribal chief. As European colonialists moved into Africa in the 19th century this tranquil existence was upset, even more so as the rich resources of the continent, not least its gold and diamond reserves, were realized. The thrust of materialism upon the African people produced a less than civilized response, and so the violence in Africa was instigated. However, we must remember that tribalism, xenophobia and violence by the state, is not, and never has been, confined to Africa. Mankind has always committed itself to war as an outcome to solve its problems. It all began, as the Bible tells us, when Cain slaughtered his brother Abel.

The Anglo-Boer War of 1899–1902 marked the first use of the 'concentration camp' which was the typify conflict in the 20th century. As Lord Kitchener became commander-in-chief, the British adopted new tactics to defeat the Boer enemy. Their main policy became known as 'Scorched Earth', which involved the systematic destruction of crops, homesteads and farms, the slaughter of livestock and poisoning of wells. The British then forcibly moved women and children into the concentration camp system. Within these camps 28,000 Boer men were held as prisoners of war, 25,630 were sent overseas, with more than 26,000 women and children perishing in the camps. This was the first example of systematic targeting, causing whole regions to become depopulated.[62]

In 1904 and 1905, the German army, led by General Lotha von Trotha, attempted to exterminate the Herero and Nama peoples of South West Africa using similar tactics. The German army poisoned wells and starved the natives of the Namib desert. In total, some 65,000 Herero (80 per cent of the total Herero population),and 10,000 Nama (50 per cent of the total Nama population) were killed or perished.[63] This was to be the first of many incidents of carnage and killing in the 20th century.

Throughout the century great deeds of carnage were committed under various guises. During the Nazi genocide and Second World War (1933–1945), approximately 11 million people were exterminated, of which six million were Jews.

With Operation Barbarossa, the Nazi invasion of Russia in June 1941, approximately 21 million Soviets, among them seven million civilians, were killed in the onslaught. Civilians were rounded up and shot in Nazi-conquered cities and, since the Slavs were considered 'sub-human', this soon became ethnically targeted mass murder. Yet the Nazis also killed other groups, such as those suffering from birth defects, mental retardation or insanity; homosexuals, prostitutes and communists, as part of a wider policy of mass murder.[64]

Yet the Russian people were by no means adverse to mass killings themselves. Estimates on the number of deaths brought about by Stalin's rule are hotly debated. The published results vary depending on a number of factors: the time when the estimate was made, the criteria and methods used and sources available. Some historians attempt to make separate estimates for different periods of Soviet history, with casualties for the Stalinist period varying from eight million to a staggering 61 million. Several scholars, among them Stalin's biographer, Simon Sebag Montefiore, and former Politburo member Alexander Nikolayevich Yakovlev put the death toll of Stalin's terror at 20 million. [65]

The Russian civil war also saw terror unleashed on civilians. The Red Terror, led by the Bolshevik government, culminated in the execution of tens of thousands of those declared 'enemies of the people' by the Cheka, the secret police. These people were allegedly involved in counter-revolutionary provocation, and were put to death as a result of the Kronstadt and Tambov rebellions of 1921. The White Terror, controlled by anti-Communists, followed a similar vein. The White Army targeted communist sympathizers and Soviet revolutionaries, again causing tens of thousands to be murdered or sent to prison camps.

The Chinese Communist Party came to power in the wake of a long and bloody civil war. The policies and political purges of Mao Zedong, the party leader who seized power in 1949, had already directly and indirectly caused the deaths of tens of millions of people. Mao based his policies on the Russian experience and, as such, believed that violence was a necessary facet of society, especially one which was to have its foundations in Marxism. Mao's land reform policies envisaged one-tenth of the peasants would be destroyed to facilitate his agrarian reform programme. Those killed as a result are believed to be at least one million, although this is significantly lower than the 50 million deaths Mao envisaged. [66] Counter-revolutionaries were similarly a target for Mao as Kuomintang officials and intellectuals suspected on loyalties were also removed; 1.3 million were imprisoned in labour camps, 1.2 million were under subjected control and 712,000 were executed. [67]

The Communist government in North Vietnam launched a similar policy of land reform, a policy which, like so many others, aimed to remove class enemies. It is believed that in these campaigns against wealthy farmers and land owners as many as 900,000 may have perished. [68]

The Khmer Rouge regime controlled Cambodia in the wake of the Vietnam War (1975–79). It is noted that the regime murdered and buried around 200,000. Although, if we include those dying as a result of the regimes policies, which led to disease and starvation, the figure could be as high as 740,000, in a population of just seven million. [69]

On 15 March 1961, one of the factions inside Angola, the UPA movement (the *Uniao dos Povos de Angola* under Holden Roberto), entered the northern region of Angola from Zaire with the purpose of slaughtering whites, all *mestizos* (mixed race) and MPLA supporters. Reminiscent of the Congo when the Belgians left, 2,000 whites were massacred by the UPA. Body parts were hung on trees, women were raped and often crucified and men were roped to wooden planks and fed through sawmill machinery. Roberto had formed strong ties with President Mobuto of Zaire as he was married to his daughter. UPA became the FNLA. Later, in July 1964, the party's secretary-general, Jonas Savimbi, broke away from FNLA to form UNITA. [70] In July 1975, 180 trucks with UNITA followers negotiated a safe passage to leave Luanda to retire to its stronghold in central Angola. The MPLA laid an ambush and all but 12 people survived the massacre. On 21 August 1975, UNITA declared war against MPLA. [71] Furthermore, the MPLA (and the other 'liberation' movements) targeted the indigenous Bushmen in Angola and it is estimated that 25 per cent of the Bushman population was murdered[72].

The rule of Idi Amin Dada, the military leader and President of Uganda from 1971 to 1979, was characterized by political repression, persecution, corruption and nepotism. The death toll of his regime is estimated to be as high as half a million by international observers.

The Red Terror of 1977 and 1978 in the Democratic Republic of Ethiopia is said to have cost half a million lives. Victims were rounded up into churches which were then set alight and the systematic rape of women was undertaken by soldiers. President Mengistu Haile Mariam is even alleged to have killed political opponents with his bare hands.[73]

The Rwandan civil war fought between the Hutu regime and the Rwandan Patriotic Front (RPF) exacerbated ethnic tensions within the country. The consequent Rwandan genocide of 1994 was nothing short of mass murder, killing 800,000 from the small East African nation. Although some estimates as to the death toll of the 100-day spree differ, some quote the toll to have been between 500,000 to one million; in short, around 20 per cent of the country's population.[74]

The Second Congo War began in August 1998 in the Democratic Republic of the Congo (formerly Zaire) and officially ended in July 2003. It is the largest war in modern African history, directly involving eight African nations and 25 armed groups. By 2008, it was estimated that the conflict had cost 5.4 million lives, mostly from disease and starvation, making the Second Congo War the deadliest conflict worldwide since World War Two. This figure does not include the millions who were displaced or sought asylum in neighbouring countries.[75]

In one of the most remote places in Africa, Darfur, an insurgency began unnoticed under the shadow of the war in Iraq in 2003, killing 350,000 to 400,000 people in 29 months by means of violence, malnutrition and disease in the first genocidal rampage of the 21st century. The victims were the non-Arabic or African tribal groups of Darfur, primarily the Fur, the Massaleit and the Zaghawa, but also the Tunjur, the Birgid, the Dajo and others. These people have long been politically and economically marginalized, and in recent years the National Islamic Front regime, based in Sudan's capital of Khartoum, has refused to control increasingly violent Arab militia raids on African villages in Darfur. Competition between Arab and African tribal groups over the scarce primary resources of arable land and water has been exacerbated by advancing desertification throughout the Sahel region[76].

Evidently no single conflict in history has escaped some form of carnage. Tribalism and xenophobia thrive in Africa. The early colonizers of Africa experienced this from early times. Yet terror is not confined to Africa, even if this is where the origins of the concentration camp can be found.

GUERRILLA WARFARE

The situation in Angola during the late 1960s was perhaps no different to other conflicts on the African continent. The indigenous forces combined their efforts against the colonial authorities and thereafter they challenged each other for power.

Southern Africa was ripe for revolution. Numerous examples exist in conflict areas such as Zimbabwe, Angola and Mozambique, The People's Republic of the Congo and South West Africa/Namibia. In Rhodesia (now Zimbabwe) the revolutionary forces were the Zimbabwe African Peoples Union (ZAPU, with its ZIPRA, the Zimbabwe People's Revolutionary Army) and the Zimbabwe African National Union (ZANU, with its ZANLA, the Zimbabwe African National Liberation Army). ZAPU was aligned with the Soviet Union whose ideology was to mobilize the urban workers, whereas ZANU followed the Maoist doctrine from the People's Republic of China, directed at mobilizing the rural peasantry. It is also interesting to note that ZIPRA was in formal alliance with Umkhonto we Sizwe (MK), the ANC's military wing. MK was fighting the South African government at the time. This created the bizarre situation of South African Recces assisting ZIPRA against ZANLA and, indirectly, assisting its arch enemy, MK. Another bizarre alliance was briefly formed during the Angolan war when South African troops, most peculiarly, fought alongside SWAPO and UNITA against the FNLA.

In Mozambique, the latter RENAMO and earlier FRELIMO were the revolutionary forces who competed for absolute power, while the FNLA, UNITA and MPLA battled each other in Angola. When the Portuguese military staged a coup in Lisbon in April 1974 these countries became ripe for full-blown revolution. The Portuguese Armed Forces, *Movimento das Forças Armadas*, overthrew the government in protest at the ongoing colonial wars that seemed to have no end in sight, as well as in rebellion against new military laws that were to be enforced the next year. The left-wing revolutionary Portuguese government withdrew its overseas armies and agreed to a quick handover of power to the African nationalist guerrillas.

In the People's Republic of the Congo, the revolutionary forces consisted of the Congolese Labour Party (PCT) of the People's Republic of the Congo and the Pan-African Union for Social Democracy (UPADS, the *Union Panafricaine pour la Démocratie Sociale*).

These revolutionary wars extended over long periods and involved guerrilla warfare and ideologies that best suited the nationalists' cause, such as Maoism and Marxism. These 'freedom fighters', or terrorists, could not achieve their goals without the direct backing of the superpowers. They formed their revolutionary ideas having been trained and indoctrinated in the principles of war in the USSR, East Germany and China.

Various ideologies had great appeal to these revolutionary leaders. Mao's theories and political propaganda entails the "revolutionary struggle of the vast majority of people against the exploiting classes and their state structures". Mao termed it a "People's War". Different from Marxist ideology, it involved the peasantry, its military strategies utilizing guerrilla war tactics focused on the areas surrounding the cities, i.e. the countryside. Heavy emphasis was placed on political transformation of the lower classes of society, the masses. Mao's *Red Book* contains 427 quotations. It was widely published and provided the principles for revolution. Quotations from the book include:

- War is a continuation of politics, and there are at least two types: just (progressive) and unjust wars, which only serve bourgeois interests. While no one likes war, we must remain ready to wage just wars against imperialist agitations.
- It is the duty of the cadres and the Party to serve the people. Without the people's interests constantly at heart, their work is useless.
- The guerrillas must move among the peasants in the way fish moves through water, living off the land and learning from the people.[77]

The Cuban revolutionary leader, Che Guevara, was initially a disciple of the Marxist Soviet Union before, during and shortly after the Cuban Revolution. He later came out in support of Maoism and advocated and adopted the ideology throughout Latin America.

Whereas, in South Africa, Joe Slovo's Stalinists of the South African Communist Party (SACP) convinced the ANC to break away from the Chinese-Maoist influences to adopt the Marxist Soviet doctrine. The aim of Marxism, by nature, is to correct the inequality between the bourgeoisie, who are the wealthy minority, and the proletariat, who are the poorer majority. Soviet Marxism promotes, and believes in, the historical inevitability of a proletarian revolution, when the proletariat takes control of the government and then implements reforms to benefit their class. It confiscates private property which is taken under state control and run for the benefit of the people, rather than for private profit.

The freedom movements in southern Africa adopted guerrilla warfare as the method to combat government security forces. Guerrilla warfare is defined as in Wikipedia as: "A form of irregular warfare and refers to conflicts in which a small group of combatants including, but not limited to, armed civilians (or 'irregulars') use military tactics, such as ambushes, sabotage, raids, the element of surprise, and extraordinary mobility to harass a larger and less-mobile traditional army, or strike a vulnerable target, and withdraw almost immediately."

During the Angola bush war, the SADF's primary aim was to combat SWAPO's guerrilla insurgents inside South West Africa/Namibia. During the period prior to 1978, the SADF probably achieved it most notable successes when it adapted and refined it own modus operandi through trial and error. The SADF almost become a guerrilla force by adopting guerrilla tactics in the early stages of the war during Operation Savannah in 1975. Guerrilla warfare needs to be countered by insurgency tactics, i.e. counter-insurgency.

To form a clear understanding how to combat revolutionary warfare, a number of principles as outlined by Sir Robert Thompson (a counter-insurgency expert of the Malayan Emergency) should be analyzed. Here follow 12 principles that closely resemble the doctrine followed by the SADF during the bush war:

The people are the key base to be secured and defended rather than the territory
Support of the local population served as the key variable. In conventional warfare it is important to gain territory and inflict the highest possible casualties on the enemy, but not during counter-guerrilla warfare. While the guerrilla shall recruit members from the local population, purchase their provisions and seek shelter, the counter-insurgent force provides physical and economic security to the population. In South West Africa/Namibia, infrastructure such as power stations, electricity, roads, water supply and education were provided as part of government's service delivery to the local population, in an attempt to gain their support and trust.

Define a clear political counter-vision that can overshadow, match or neutralize the guerrillas'
The population is influenced through aggressive media campaigns which muster and integrate political, social, economical and propaganda, to overshadow that of the insurgents.

Practical action must be taken at lower levels to match comparative political vision
The population must believe they have a say in access to resources and the delivery of services.

Big-unit action is sometimes necessary
The SADF used military force with their task-force deployment of its mechanized divisions. The Ratel, with its 90mm gun, was specifically developed for such deployments. Cross-border sweeps and surprise assaults on guerrilla bases and logistic supply lines significantly broke large guerrilla concentrations into smaller groups and stretched their mobility and supply lines. The guerrillas were forced to work in very small units of between four and eight members, restricting them to sabotage, laying of landmines and focusing on soft targets.

They were not capable of taking offensive action against the larger, better-organized and better-trained SADF.

Aggressive mobility

During the Rhodesian conflict that took place during the 1960s and 1970s, the Rhodesian Light Infantry used a tactic referred to as 'Fireforce'.[78] In simple terms, it consisted of small sections of soldiers who were airlifted by mainly Alouette helicopters and dispatched to locations close to enemy targets and bases. This resulted in a sweep of the enemy target and during close combat the enemy was eliminated. With the element of surprise, these tactics were very successful. Troops were also airdropped in the close vicinity of targets, who then proceeded on foot to contact with the enemy. Chris Cocks in his book, *Fireforce,* describes these operations. Similar Fireforce tactics were also used by the SADF, but it had access to better military equipment, such as Puma helicopters, that could move more soldiers at a time to target. The SADF used the highly mobile Ratel, Buffalo and Casspir armoured vehicles. These vehicles were capable of covering vast distances over rough terrain in a short space of time. With Reaction Force (or Fireforce) teams, heavy formations were lightened to locate, pursue and destroy the enemy. With such SADF mobility, it was almost impossible for the enemy to predict when and where they would be hit next. The guerrilla was constantly on the run and harassed at every turn.

Ground-level embedding and integration

In South West Africa/Namibia the SADF formed a strong local militia. Many battalions were strengthened in this manner. CIA special units were involved in a number of guerrilla movements, providing advice, training and weapons. The US Stinger missile system was directly issued by the CIA to UNITA in Angola, forcing the Angolan Air Force to fly at such high attitudes, making accurate bombardment of ground targets ineffective. But the US never publically announced or demonstrated its commitment in deploying its own troops. During the Iraqi war in 2003, US special forces operated with Iraqi army units. These integrated forces were embedded in local areas to identify and empathize with the local population.

Cultural sensitivity

The local people's culture needs to be appreciated and understood. The local norms, language, customs and religions need to be respected and promoted. For example, Arabic-speaking interpreters and respecting the Koran in Iraq instilled trust in the local population.

Systematic intelligence effort

Every form of gathering intelligence should be utilized and integrated to form a proper picture and gain knowledge of guerrilla capabilities, movements and aims. Civilian suspects are exposed to casual questioning and structured interrogation. In South West Africa/Namibia the SADF captured hundreds of SWAPO guerrillas, re-orientated them to adjust their allegience, retrained them and then reintroduced them into the field to fight their erstwhile guerrilla masters. These double agents and bogus 'liberators' generally caused a great deal of suspicion and mistrust in SWAPO's ranks. It was so effective that SWAPO, through their 'cleansing efforts', probably killed more of their own than they did SADF soldiers.

Methodical clear and hold

The operational area in South West Africa/Namibia was divided into military sectors, providing an SADF presence over a wide area. Like an 'inkspot' it served to clear areas and retain its influence over such areas. When the 'inkspot' expanded, it systematically neutralized or eliminated guerrillas, forcing them off the grid. Each sector had its own priorities on how to clear and hold areas under its control.

Careful deployment of mass popular forces and special units
Short of adopting violent vigilante-style reprisal squads, the local popilation is given wider influence by forming self-defence groups, civilian militias organized for community defence and local security. Defectors could be incorporated into such groups, utilizing their training and influence over the community.

Foreign intervention to be limited
The foreign force should never be 'taking over' the local war. The SADF was actively involved in supplying, training and advising UNITA during the Angola bush war, but during the latter part of the bush war, the SADF was forced to do the fighting for UNITA at Cuito Cuanavale. They were drawn into a wider, foreign conflict. This changed the face of the conflict forever, placing the SADF in immediate contact with Cuban forces.

Time
During the Angolan bush war, no one would have predicted that the little police operation in 1966 at Ongulumbashe would result in large-scale conventional battles as seen at Cuito Cuanavale in 1988. Guerrillas prefer protracted conflict, wearing down the will of the counter-insurgent force. Enough time should be provided to get the job done. In Iraq and Vietnam the US government became more vulnerable as the war progressed, seemingly without end. Impatient demands for victory plays into the hands of guerrillas.

South African actions after 1986 against FAPLA were premature as the world order was already showing signs of dramatically changing with the total collapse of the Soviet Union later in 1989. How different could things have been if the bush war had lasted beyong this date. The Cubans would have being forced to withdraw, communist ideals would cease to exist and a more normalized environment would have been created within which opposing forces could engage in peaceful dialogue. But due to the South Africa's label as a racist apartheid regime, no foreign power could openly show its support for the SADF. The war only ever had one possible outcome: a grand withdrawal of opposing forces on both sides. Which is exactly that what happened in the end.

A NEW WORLD ORDER

South Africa engaged in a very expensive war in Angola. The logistical line between Pretoria and the border of Angola was extremely long, and troops had to be transported over vast distances to be deployed in the operational areas. The SADF was required to recruit a very large number of personnel to serve 'on the border'. The numbers varied, but no less than

15,000 South African troops served in South West Africa at a given time, supplemented by a large complement of the South West African Territory Force (SWATF). Here follows a record of the air movement of SADF troops between South Africa and South West Africa over an eight-month period in 1983:[79]

May 1983	Members entering SWA	1,446
	Members leaving SWA	1,308
Jun 1983	Members entering SWA	2,327
	Members leaving SWA	3,521
Jul 1983	Members entering SWA	5,084
	Members leaving SWA	2,885
Aug 1983	Members entering SWA	2,219
	Members leaving SWA	2,113
Sept 1983	Members entering SWA	2,665
	Members leaving SWA	3,422
Oct 1983	Members entering SWA	1,317
	Members leaving SWA	1,601
Nov 1983	Members entering SWA	3,250
	Members leaving SWA	1253
Dec 1983	Members entering SWA on 19 flights	1,488
	Members entering by vehicles	3240
	Members leaving SWA on 18 flights	1,059

The Angolan bush war finally ended in 1989. The war did not end with a victory for any one side, but all sides gained a great deal with its final conclusion. However, the large conventional battles of the war during Operations Modular, Hooper and Packer, showed the Cuban- and Russian-backed FAPLA forces that the SADF could not be defeated on the battlefield without paying a very high price. This realization, and global political factors, made the conclusion of a negotiated settlement unavoidable.

A new chapter would be written in the history of the southern African region. The result of the political negotiations was that SADF withdrew from South West Africa and Cuban forces withdrew from Angola. This brought an end to a war that had raged for over two decades. The new Namibia held democratic elections and gained independence.

It can be stated that none of the opposing sides achieved victory during the Angolan bush war. The SADF did not keep SWAPO out of Namibia as SWAPO was to raise its flag in Windhoek. SWAPO did not achieve power through the barrel of a gun. It came to power as a result of democratic elections after peace was restored.

The time was right to end the war at the end of the 1980s. The results would have been much different should SWAPO have gained power 20 years earlier. The SADF endured the conflict until the time was right to withdraw from the region.

Before the war came to an end, SWAPO strongholds from where insurgents were sent into South West Africa were located hundreds of kilometres from the border. SWAPO members had to carry heavy loads over long distances to reach South West Africa. This made them vulnerable to the SADF units who were able to stop their advances. Operation Askari was perhaps the most successful offensive by the SADF, as SWAPO bases were destroyed before they could be used as springboards from where they could enter South West Africa.

Internationally, the USSR and its close ally, Cuba, lost their grip on the world. The Cold

War ended on 9 November 1989, after the collapse of the Berlin Wall. On 22 December 1988 a trilateral agreement was signed by South Africa, Cuba and Angola, which officially ended South Africa's involvement in the war in Angola and the withdrawal of Cuban soldiers from Angola. The South African Minister of Foreign Affairs, Pik Botha, said four years later, that the negotiating concept that followed to achieve peace in South West Africa was the basis on which negotiations between South Africa and the ANC was conducted, which resulted in the first democratic elections in South Africa. Now, for the first time, freedom under a new South African constitution was possible. In South Africa, Nelson Mandela was released from prison and was elected president during the 1994 democratic elections.

On 22 February 2002 the Angolan war finally ended for the UNITA leader, Jonas Savimbi (67) when he was shot dead by FAPLA soldiers in the Moxico Province in Angola. He was loyal and fearless to the end, as his body was found lying in a shallow trench, where he'd fought and died alongside his troops.[80] The 27-year-long civil war in Angola was thus formally brought to an end. An estimated 500,000 people had been killed during this period. The Angolan civil war was one of the largest, longest and most prominent armed conflicts of the Cold War. Both the Soviet Union and the United States considered it critical to the global balance of power and to the outcome of the Cold War.

From a South African perspective the war in Angola achieved a great deal in establishing a new world order in southern Africa that was based on sound democratic principles and very much the result of the war. The aims had been to keep Soviet and Cuban forces away from South West Africa. For years, the SADF contained the enemy offensives, and were able to move almost unhindered within a vast area of Angola. As a result, SWAPO members were dealt with swiftly. The SADF always had the upper hand during all these operations into Angola, with 84% of all conflicts initiated by the SADF. General Meiring stated that SWAPO presence was traced within an average of six days after entering South West Africa, causing SWAPOs to flee and retreat back into Angola, proven by the large number of tracks that 32 Battalion reported moving from south to north. Large numbers of SWAPO members were captured and killed in the pursuits that followed.

The SADF was a winning force due to its proud history and reputation. Soldiers fighting in South West Africa and Angola were descendents of soldiers who had fought in both World Wars. Even earlier, the mighty British Empire was defeated during the first Anglo-Boer War, and many victories were claimed during the second Anglo-Boer War. Even earlier, Dingaan's Zulu kingdom was virtually destroyed at Blood River, when the first pioneers entered the interior of South Africa on horseback and in ox wagons.

But, South Africa has become a new nation with a new identity. Conflicts of this kind should no longer be necessary. For this we give praise and show our utmost respect to all those who suffered and died during the Angolan bush war.

EPILOGUE

The last day at Ionde. 2Lt Marius Scheepers and the Engineers officer 2Lt A.J. Theron. (Photo M Scheepers)

My stay in Angola was both a fruitful and wasteful personal experience. Although I dearly believe that the South African Defence Force achieved its goals during the Angolan bush war, I realize that I personally sacrificed a great deal while performing my service. I sacrificed a valuable two years of my young life serving this cause. I was totally isolated from normal civilian life. I was not able to do things or experience life like my friends were doing back in normal society. During this time, I always had a profound desire to rather be at home with my family and friends. Not a single day went by that I did not experience a longing for my family. It was due to many prayers and the support of my parents, family and friends, that made my task much more bearable.

I was fortunate to have had two surprise visits during this period from my father, Reverend D.J.J. Scheepers, a chaplain in the South African Air Force. I also found comfort and protection in my personal relationship with Jesus Christ. I believe God disapproves of all forms of violence and conflict.

Almost 30 years later, reflecting on all these major events, I made a startling discovery that many ex-SADF members were having difficulties in coming to grips with the war. Many had resumed their civilian lives while suffering from post-traumatic stress. This continues to this day, causing dysfunctional families, marriages and relationships at work, caused by the brutalities that were witnessed during this lengthy war. The SADF was not equipped to assist and did not fully appreciate that its soldiers needed counselling. The society which welcomed these returning soldiers was ignorant of the lasting effects that the war had on them. Senior officers were disfranchised from everything they stood for when this prolonged war came to a sudden end. They were no longer the powerful leaders and role models that everyone once admired. Their actions were soon forgotten. They did not receive the honours they deserved. During many conversations, I got distorted and bitter responses from such people. Many had resorted to hatred and accusing one another of "what if", or pointing fingers, blaming others. Those senior officers who continued their military careers with the new SANDF could not speak out and, under the guise of being professional soldiers, nullified their past.

This situation in South Africa is no different from other post-war situations. The same applied to the US after Vietnam, Russia after Afghanistan, the UK after the Falkland Islands and Iraq, and many more. Our experince was further exaggerated because returning SADF soldiers were not given proper recognition and were merely tossed back into society as if they had made no difference.

I managed to cope with all the guilt and strain that was caused by the war, when I made a decision to start over and join public life without expecting anything in return. I commenced with studies at University of the Free State and even joined a university hostel, Vishuis. Here

I was put through a dehumanizing and vigorous initiation process. I was actually forced to accept that I had returned to a society from which I could not expect any favours. I cherished my convictions and I joined a Christian fellowship at Moreletapark congregation, who consist of members serious about their relationship with the All Mighty God.

Years later, we revisited the former battlegrounds, to find the local population experiencing far more suffering due to the scars of the war, landmines and the loss of loved ones. We actively got involved with some of these communities and discovered that among these desperate conditions, were loving and caring people. We discovered remote rural areas where the war had left its scars. The Reverend Henk Olwage had joined the SADF, but after the war, he immediately realized the special needs of these communities. He continues to serve these people and provides them with comfort and the kind of hope that is only to be found in the Gospel. I was amazed to find among these people some individuals who were far more content with life than us who have more and who show a kind of pride that I was unaware existed. This outreach still continues. At Andara, a medical clinic was built near Buffalo base, where our outreach group also built a church. The community was taught about the passion of Christ and whole villages were converted. These people returned to the truth and cherish the values of the Bible. Post-war children who had completed their schooling are now fully integrated into society, successfully performing their roles as parents. This is truly a success story. It gives me much comfort to serve these people in such a humble way. But much needs to be done with other more remote communities in Angola. This is an expensive exercise and difficult to undertake. More ex- SADF members should get involved. By taking care of others' needs, absolute healing is achieved; the effects of the war may soon be alleviated, and one's sharing of the fruits of the Spirit, shall surely prevail.

"*Ons sal lewe, Ons sal sterwe, Ons vir jou Suid-Afrika.*"

A 32 Battalion Soldier

I was that which others did not want to be,
I went where others feared to go, and did what others failed to do.

I asked nothing from those who gave nothing
and reluctantly accepted the thought of eternal loneliness ... should I fail.

I have seen the face of terror; felt the stinging of cold fear;
and enjoyed the sweet taste of a moment's love.

I have suffered, pained and hoped ... but most of all,
I have lived times others would say were best forgotten.

At least now I am able to say that I am proud of what I was,
a 32 Battalion Soldier.

Author unknown

Notes

1 Bridgland, Fred, *op.cit.*, p. 15
2 *ibid*
3 *ibid*
4 South African Department of Defence Documentation Centre, original sources
5 *ibid*
6 *ibid*
7 *ibid*
8 Bridgland, Fred, *op.cit.*, p. 39
9 *ibid*, p. 48
10 *ibid*, p. 52
11 *ibid*, *p*. 62
12 *ibid*, *p*. 65
13 *ibid*
14 *ibid*, p. 81
15 *ibid*, p. 79
16 *ibid*, p. 75
17 *ibid*, p. 147
18 *ibid*, p. 105
19 *ibid*, p. 117
20 *ibid*, p. 136
21 *ibid*, p. 125
22 *ibid*, p. 162
23 *ibid*, p. 174
24 *ibid*, p. 176
25 *ibid*, p. 194
26 *ibid*, p. 198
27 *ibid*, p. 209
28 *ibid*, p. 200
29 *ibid*, p. 211
30 *ibid*, p. 214
31 *ibid*, p. 223
32 *ibid*, p. 230
33 *ibid*, p. 245
34 *ibid*, p. 256
35 *ibid*, p. 266
36 *ibid*, p. 267
37 *ibid*, p. 270
38 *ibid*, p. 272
39 *ibid*, p. 279
40 *ibid*, p. 288
41 *ibid*, p. 290
42 *ibid*, p. 297
43 *ibid*, p. 314
44 *ibid*, p. 323
45 *ibid*
46 *ibid*, p. 331
47 *ibid*, p. 333
48 *ibid*, p. 375
49 Wikipedia, *Arnaldo Ochoa*, http://en.wikipedia.org/wiki/Arnaldo_Ochoa, (Accessed February 2012)
50 *ibid*, p. 342
51 *ibid*, p. 345
52 *ibid*, p. 347
53 *ibid*, p. 356
54 *ibid*, p. 358
55 *ibid*, p. 361
56 *ibid*, p. 363
57 Steenkem, Wilem, *op.cit.*, p. 185
58 *ibid*, p. 228
59 *ibid*, 377
60 *ibid*, p. 374
61 *ibid*. p. 180
62 Wikipedia, *Herbert Kitchener*, http://en.wikipedia.org/wiki/Herbert_Kitchener,_1st_Earl_Kitchener, (Accessed: February 2012)
63 Wikipedia, *Lothar von Trotha*, http://en.wikipedia.org/wiki/Lothar_von_Trotha, (Accessed: February 2012)
64 Wikipedia, *Russian Civil War*, http://en.wikipedia.org/wiki/Russian_civil_war, (Accessed: February 2012)
65 Wikipedia, *Nikolayevich Yakovlev*, http://en.wikipedia.org/wiki/Alexander_Nikolaevich_Yakovlev, (Accessed: February 2012)
66 Wikipedia, *Mao Zedong*, http://en.wikipedia.org/wiki/Mao_Zedong, (Accessed: February 2012)
67 Wikipedia,, *Kuomintang*, http://en.wikipedia.org/wiki/Kuomintang, (Accessed: February 2012)
68 Wikipedia, *Steven Rosefielde*, http://en.wikipedia.org/wiki/Steven_Rosefielde, (Accessed: February 2012)
69 Wikipedia, *Khmer Rouge*, http://en.wikipedia.org/wiki/Khmer_Rouge, (Accessed: February 2012)
70 Stiff, Peter, *op.cit.*, p. 97
71 *ibid*, p. 103
72 *ibid*, p. 99
73 Wikipedia, *Mengistu Haile Mariam*, http://en.wikipedia.org/wiki/Mengistu, (Accessed: February 2012)
74 Wikipedia, *Juvénal Habyarimana*, http://en.wikipedia.org/wiki/Juv%C3%A9nal_Habyarimana, (Accessed: February 2012)
75 Wikipedia, *Second Congo War*, http://en.wikipedia.org/wiki/Second_Congo_War, (Accessed: February 2012)
76 Wikipedia, *Darfur*, http://en.wikipedia.org/wiki/Darfur, (Accessed: February 2012)
77 Stiff, Peter, *op.cit.*, p. 315
78 Cocks, Chris, *Fireforce: One Man's War in the Rhodesian Light Infantry*, (Johannesburg: 30° South, 2006)
79 South African Department of Defence Documentation Centre, original sources
80 Wikipedia, *Jonas Savimbi*, http://en.wikipedia.org/wiki/Jonas_Savimbi (Accessed February 2012)

APPENDIX I
32 BATTALION TACTICAL HQ SITREPS:
OPERATIONS DOLFYN AND ASKARI

The following serves as an exact record of the daily accounts of incidents and actions involving 32 Battalion, generally referred to as OF, and SWAPO, generally referred to as EF, as they were reported. Much of the contents of these sitreps have already been described, but they are provided here as a more complete list of all the events in chronological order.[1]

December 1982

2Lt M Scheepers, departed Rundu to Ondangwa on a Dakota; he was transported to the Tactical HQ, Ops Meebos.

4 Dec: Seven EF members attacked a Local Persons (Povo) settlement, where one Povo was accused of collaborating with OF. One Povo was killed and four wounded Povos fled south to Xangongo. Another Povo died at Ongiva.

6 Dec: A contact was made with two to four EF members in the Mupa area. The EF members moved north.

11 Dec: 32 Battalion, C/s 72, G Coy, 32 Battalion had a contact with EF members.

13 Dec : 2Lt M. Dames, the Signals Officer, was relieved by 2Lt M Scheepers at Tactical HQ, Ongiva, and trooped to Ondangwa airport.

16 Dec: One OF member of Platoon 2, C Coy, 101 Battalion was killed.

20 Dec: C/s 72 ambush EF members.

Scene from Ongiva airport. (SADF Archive)

January 1983

6 Jan: The new leadership team arrived at Ongiva for training.

10 Jan: A serious communication problem was experienced with all call signs. 200m south of Nehone, one Buffalo vehicle detonated a TMA3 landmine. The vehicle overturned and eight OF members were wounded. They were evacuated to Oshakati.

12 Jan: Pl 4, 1 Parabat Battalion detonated a TMA3 landmine with a Buffalo. The front wheel was damaged, and one OF member was wounded at 010510XM. He is the son of General Constand Viljoen, the Chief of the Defence Force.

13 Jan: Ongiva Tactical HQ consisted of:

- 1 x 3 SAI 81mm mortar group
- 1 x 32 Battalion 81mm mortar group
- 61 Mechanized Battalion armoured vehicles
- 1 x 103 Bty 10 LAA
- 1 x platoon, C Coy 1 Parabat Brigade
- 1 x platoon, C Coy, 32 Battalion
- Maintenance, Sappers, Signallers, LTW

The Xangongo base consisted of

- 1 x platoon, E Coy, 32 Battalion
- 1 x 3 SAI 81mm mortar group

Units present in Angola:

- 32 Battalion: A Coy, D Coy and E Coy
- 3 x platoons from 1 Para Battalion

Double TMA3 landmines were detonated without any damage to any vehicles. Pl 4, A Coy, 32 Battalion was deployed 15km east of Mupa. They had a contact with eight EF members. One FAPLA member was seriously wounded and transferred to Sector 10 HQ at Oshakati. The group of 20 EF members fled north, but it was impossible to pursue them due to bad weather.

14 Jan: Platoon 4, A Coy, 32 Battalion had a contact 15km north of Mupa with eight EF members. One FAPLA member was seriously wounded. Eight EF members' tracks were found moving north.

19 Jan: Operation Fakkel was completed. 32 Battalion Recce wing observed two EF MiG fighter aircraft at a height of 2000m.

20 Jan: The Administrator-General of the Transvaal Province, Mr Hough, Mrs Hough, Miss Hough, their farther, Mr Hough and General Lloyd stayed at Buffalo base.

21 Jan: 32 Battalion Recce wing reported loud

explosions 30km northeast of their position.

28 Jan: A member of 32 Battalion was reunited with his brother in Angola and both brothers returned to Buffalo.

29 Jan: 29 new recruits finished their training at Buffalo. A new SAWI shop opened for business at Buffalo. A foreign object, described as a high-altitude weather balloon was spotted floating in the area moving northwest.

31 Jan: 32 Battalion's strength consisted of 1,203 black soldiers, 680 women and 1,151 children.

February 1983

1 Feb: 32 Battalion A, D and E Coys deployed in Angola; the mortar group was present at Ongiva.

2 Feb: The Recce wing reported explosions 30km north of their position.

3 Feb: An EF cache was discovered, OF members laid an ambush for the EF.

4 Feb: Pl 3, A Coy, 32 Battalion had a contact with 40 EF members. Six EF members (other reports indicate 11) were killed, one EF member was captured and four OF members were wounded at NV 817477XM. Lance-Corporal Mario Oliviera was casevaced, with a wound involving a M60 rifle grenade embedded in his chest.

5 Feb: Two EF members' bodies were discovered, each carrying 6-10kg of explosives. 40 EF members' tracks were discovered moving southeast. Pl 2, A Coy, 32 Battalion was deployed north of Mupa to conduct ambushes. Landmines were discovered at Xangongo, camouflaged with fresh cow dung.

6 Feb: Three EF members' tracks were discovered at Mupa Mission. The EF members subsequently removed their boots and the tracks were lost. 20 EF members' tracks were found, carrying one EF member who was wounded. Tracks were moving north to Mupa.

7 Feb: Cmdt Viljoen and Capt Ratte arrived at Sector 10 HQ, Oshakati to hold discussions on Operation Fakkel.

8 Feb: A SWAPO member pointed out an EF ammunition cache. It was destroyed. Trooping of 32 Battalion companies took place. 32 Battalion B, C and F Coys were deployed in Angola as well as a mortar group.

10 Feb: Pl 3, A Coy, 32 Battalion had contact with 40 EF members. Six EF members were killed, four OF were wounded. One OF member stumbled with a MOI grenade launcher, one OF

was wounded in his leg. Trooping of 32 Battalion was taking place: 32 Battalion A Coy, D Coy, E Coy were relieved in Angola. An RPG-7 was detonated 40m from a Puma helicopter, after it was fired upon by EF members at RV 9008WN. A mini-HAA was established at RV 398960 XM. Gunships were present at mini-HAA.

11 Feb: 8 members of 32 Battalion Recce wing were trooped to Kaokoland for Operation Fakkel.

12 Feb: Pl 3, C Coy, 32 Battalion had contact at 18:30 at 520260XN with 20 EF members. One EF member was wounded. F Coy had contact with 60 EF members and discovered EF equipment. 40 EF members were moving in dense bush approximately 1km from the river. They follow the river for navigation.

14 Feb: 32 Battalion, C/s 71 has found 80 EF members' tracks.

15 Feb: Huge infiltration of EF members reported: 30 EF members' tracks were discovered east of Dova moving south, carrying a heavy load, probably ammunition. 40 EF members' tracks and 80 EF members' tracks from SWAPO specialized units were discovered moving south into Sector 20, SWA. They were carrying propaganda material.

16 Feb: 32 Battalion C/s 71 had contact with EF members at XN 482180. One EF was killed and 60 EF tracks were followed. 32 Battalion C/s 73 had contact with 14 EF members. The EF members joined the other group of 60 EF members. They moved in northern direction and then bomshelled. 32 Battalion C/s 61 had contact with 60 EF members.

17 Feb: 32 Battalion Recce wing heard six explosions within 20km from their location.

18 Feb: 100 SWAPO members walked into

32 Battalion soldiers. (Photo R. Griessel)

a UNITA base, 8km from Evale. One UNITA member was killed and 3 UNITA members were wounded.

19 Feb: 32 Battalion Recce wing heard 15 explosions within 20km of their location.19 EF members' tracks were found.

21 Feb: An EF cache was located consisting of ammunition.

22 Feb: 2Lt Notelovitz, Pl 24, F Coy, 32 Battalion reported contact with EF. One EF member was killed and one Povo woman was wounded. Lieutenant-Colonel D. Almog from the Israeli Defence Forces visited 32 Battalion HQ at Rundu. 32 Battalion companies were in search of 40 EF members in the general line between Nehone and Dova.

24 Feb: Resupply of 32 Battalion companies with 14 days rations was done.

25 Feb: It was reported that SWAPO have recently relocated a base from Calemo to Eu Putranyanga, just north of the northern boundary for the SADF operations.

26 Feb: Three EF members were fleeing, carrying one wounded EF member.

27 Feb: One 32 Battalion member was wounded in his leg.

28 Feb: Cpl W. J. Schoeman sustained a stomach wound.

March 1983

32 Battalion, C Coy, F Coy and B Coy were deployed in Angola.

3 Mar: A SWAPO sympathizer was captured at 32 Battalion's training base, Buffalo, who attempted to negatively influence 32 Battalion members. Contact was made with EF members. 3 EF members were wounded. EF members moved north ast.

6 Mar: 2Lt F.J. Louw reported that Pl 2, F Coy, 32 Battalion at Mupa, moved into their temporary base. They discovered EF members' tracks moving through an open area. They saw EF members in dense bush. One EF member was killed.

7 Mar: Contact was made with EF members. One EF member was killed and five to six EF members fled north. One Cuban uniform was discovered.

8 Mar: A Puma lifted a Recce group and passed in close proximity of a SWAPO base housing approximately 200 SWAPO members. The base was only two weeks old. All the SWAPO members fled, leaving behind equipment in the base in the

rush to escape. EF searched the SWAPO base for information. One EF member was killed.

10 Mar: Contact was made with EF members. Three EF members were killed and three EF members were wounded in the ambush. The EF initiated the attack. The EF members were pinned down for 15 minutes. 150 EF members then withdrew from the area in groups of 25 each. 10 EF members' tracks were moving south.

12 Mar: 2Lt J. Swart, Pl 6, B Coy, 32 Battalion reported contact at Mulola. C/s 60, 32 Battalion, was at the 30 degree line. They served to mislead EF that an attack was planned in their area as a decoy. Their area consisted of northern line: RV 782150WN, west of Cuvelai River, southern line: east of Vinticete, between Vinticete and Cuvelai. Contact was made with EF members after they entered an ambush. Four EF members were killed, and 10–20 EF members' tracks were moving northwest.

17 Mar: 32 Battalion, B and C Coys had a contact with 16 EF members, 15 EF members were killed and one EF member fled. He was later captured. Three EF members were captured and transported to Oshakati to be interrogated.

18 Mar: 2Lt B. van Dyk, Pl 8, B Coy, 32 Battalion reported a contact near Bambi. 32 Battalion B and C Coys had a contact with EF members. 15 EF members were killed and 16 EF members were wounded. The contact took place after an EF vehicle unloaded bags consisting of maize meal.

23 Mar: 600 UNITA members were transported with six Kwêvoël transport vehicles from Mongua to Anhanca.

25 Mar: 32 Battalion Recce wing and one 32 Battalion Coy were transported with six Ural vehicles (USSR made) which were supplied by UNITA, to a location, 8 hours' drive and then to travel by foot for four days to a destination at RV 4090 WM, the UNITA HQ at Sequendiva. A mini-HAA was established .The Evale airstrip was repaired and cleared of any possible landmines for possible use by a Dakota aircraft. C-160 planes dropped off fuel at the mini-HAA. Pamphlets were distributed in the area warning FAPLA not to engage the SADF while conducting operations in the area. Mirage and Impala fighter aircraft were placed on the alert to provide close air support. The deployment of 32 Battalion:

Call sign 51 at Ionde, southwest to Chitando

Call sign 52 between Chitando and Ionde
Call sign 53 between Evale and Acmela
Call sign 54 between Dova and Ionde
Call sign 55 at Xangongo
Call sign 56 also at Xangongo
Call sign 57 between Acmela and Nehone.Call sign V31 and V33 (1 Parabat Battalion) north of Anhanca..
Call sign V43 south of Anhanca
3 x 32 Battalion Coys generally operated in the area east of Mupa.

27 Mar: 32 Battalion's official anniversary was celebrated. 32 Battalion, C/s 72 had a contact with EF members. Six EF members were killed and 30-40 EF tracks were found moving west.

28 Mar: 60 EF members' tracks were found that were only 20 minutes old.

29 Mar: 30–40 EF members' tracks were found moving north. Contact was made with EF members by 32 Battalion C/s 73. 2 EF members fled east.

31 Mar: Two gunships were stationed at the HAA, and Impala fighter planes were put on standby. 20 EF members' tracks were found only 12 hours old. Contact was made by 32 Battalion, C/s 70. 2 FAPLA members were killed. 20 EF tracks were found moving east.

April 1983

Operations Dolfyn Tactical HQ, Ongiva consisted of the following units:

- 1 x troop 10 LLA (anti-aircraft guns)
- 1 x 81mm mortar platoon.
- Call signs 30 and 31 of 32 Battalion (2 platoons)
- At Xangongo was 1 x 81mm mortar platoon
- The HAA consisted of 1 x 81mm mortar platoon, and 32 Battalion call signs 51, 53 and 54 (3 platoons)
- A platoon of 1 Parabat Battalion was deployed at Ionde to serve as protection for the airfield

1 Apr: UNITA had contact with SWAPO.

3 Apr: Contact was made with EF members at Vinticete at RV 877479WN, by C/s 11 and C/s 14 while laying an ambush. Two OF members from 32 Battalion (Sgt A. Mande, and Rfn J.D. Kativa) were killed during the contact with EF members. 2LT G.W. Roos was wounded in his left arm, and sustained shrapnel wounds in his left leg. Five other OF members were also wounded. One EF member was killed and three EF members were wounded.

4 Apr: Contact was made with EF members, six EF members were killed and many more EF members were reported wounded. A 32 Battalion platoon had contact at the loading/landing zone while Puma helicopters were landing to perform a casevac of OF members. The EF members walked into the loading/landing zone area. A gunship reported that a road frequently used was spotted from the air at RV 840600SW. A 300-strong SWAPO base should be in the area.

7 Apr: A request was made for UNITA to supply guides to be sent to Ongiva.

8 Apr: Contact was made with EF members. 15 EF members' tracks were found.

9 Apr: 10 EF members' tracks were discovered, four hours old: One member of 5 SA Infantry Battalion was wounded in a mortar accident.

10 Apr: 50 EF members' tracks were discovered moving north.

11 Apr: 25 EF members' tracks were discovered moving southeast which were found to be only half an hour old.A report was received from Catholic nuns at Tchiulo that EF members from Lubango were in the area.

12 Apr: A large group of EF members were reported moving on Cuvelai road.

13 Apr: 3 UNITA members were killed in a contact with SWAPO.

14 Apr: 3 EF members' tracks were discovered.

19 Apr: (SWAPO founding day) and 25 April (SWAPO commemorating Cassinga Day) were celebrated by SWAPO. Increased enemy activity was expected in the area.

18 Apr: One Coy of UNITA (18 members) is moving to the Namaiaca/Naema area. UNITA members had contact with one SWAPO Coy. 13 UNITA members were wounded during the contact that lasted 15 minutes.

25 Apr: Initial planning for Operation Dolfyn, to commence on 1 May, was presented.

27 Apr: Two Pumas took medical staff and equipment to a landing zone (LZ) north of Ionde where 32 Battalion companies were deployed for Operation Dolfyn. Colonel Viljoen was present and was commanding the operation.

May 1983

Captain Willem Ratte wrote a report for the proposed deployment of a mobile task force at

Branch HQ Ionde.

1 May: Operation Dolfyn commenced. 32 Battalion was deployed north of Ionde.

5 May: Contact was made with five EF members. One EF member was killed. The Chief SADF visited Ongiva and Xangongo.

8 May: 90 EF members' tracks were found moving north.

11 May : An EF TMA2 landmine was discovered at Ionde airfield.

13 May: 32 Battalion deployed near Jaula, northeast of Techamutete during the initial stages of Operation Dolfyn. C/s V33 of 1 Parabat Battalion was ambushed. Six OF members were wounded. 20 EF members were moving south. One EF member was killed.

14 May: A Samil 100 fuel tanker and a Ratel 20 detonated landmines.

15 May: The noise of EF vehicles was heard and fresh tracks were found. An OF Ratel 20 from Task Force Bravo, detonated a landmine at RV 202134XM. Contact was made with five EF members. One EF member was killed.

16 May: 20 EF members' tracks were found. A Ratel 20 detonated a landmine.

17 May: Two EF members' tracks were found. Task Force Bravo had a contact with EF members at RV 0564XM. 2 EF members were wounded. Four EF groups fled into dense bush. The EF members were at the time bathing and fled naked.

18 May: 35 EF members were reported to be at Nete, 10km southwest of Xangongo. 3 PB women and five PB men were abducted by EF members. One PB was released.

19 May: Corporal C.W. Kindness was killed in a shooting accident. A report was issued by Captain H.J. Boshoff, to certify that the Ionde airstrip was cleared of any landmines. Later, several landmines were detonated at Ionde. UNITA were protecting the airfield at Ionde

20 May: An echelon of Task Force Bravo detonated a landmine in a Samil. Contact was made with EF members, 13 EF members fled southeast. Two EF members were killed and one EF member was wounded. News was received that a powerful car bomb had been detonated at the SAAF headquarters in Church Street in Pretoria. Operation Skerwe took place on 23 May, consisting of an SAAF attack at ANC targets in Maputo in Mozambique.

21 May: 12 EF members' tracks were found. Colonel Eddie Viljoen, and 20 members of 32

Battalion were flown from Omauni to Ongiva in a Dakota.

23 May: 32 Battalion Recce wing confirmed the position of SWAPO's Eastern Area HQ

24 May: Contact was made with 13 EF members. Three EF members were killed and two EF members were captured.

28 May: D-Day was planned for Operation Dolfyn. The attack actually started on 1 June.

29 May: A Ratel detonated a landmine.

32 Battalion soldiers. Photo R. Griessel

June 1983

32 Battalion mostly conducted patrols, manned observation posts and laid ambushes. Ionde was established on 16 June 1983 to serve as Tactical HQ. This was the centre where trooping' were coordinated and members swapped and replaced during operations, ensures the constant presence of 32 Battalion in Angola at all relevant times.

Operation Sevta: orders HQ Ongiva (Angola) for the period 3–27 September 1983

After their withdrawal from Ongiva, 32 Battalion tactical headquarters was relocated to Ionde. Colonel Serfontein was the new commander of Operation Dolfyn, also referred to as Operation Sevta, at Ongiva. Tactical Operations HQ at Ongiva was commonly referred to as HQ Ops Dolfyn and also known as HQ Ops Sevta. 32 Battalion operated in the Nehone, Dova and Mulola areas during this period, with the tactical HQ situated at Ionde. The operational area's parameters were as follows:

North: 8400 WN-1106 XN-6000XN
West: 8400WN–Road to Evale
South: Evale direct line to Nehone–050XM-
   6050XM
East: 6050XM-6000XN

No 32 Battalion platoons were allowed to enter north of the 30 northern measure (WN). Also, the Parabats were positioned at Xangongo to the west. The DISA (UNITA) force operated at Anhanca and Ionde to the east.

1 Jun: An attack was launched on a SWAPO base at RV 4679 XN, but it was already vacated prior to the attack. Unfortunately, tracks of a 32 Battalion platoon were discovered by SWAPO members earlier that alarmed the group of the SADF presence in the area. Earlier an HAA was established to be used during the attack at XN 360285. Brig Joep Joubert, Col. R.S. Lord, Brig van Niekerk and Brig Huyser were at the HAA.

The plan of the attack

Phase 1: Recce teams moved into position on 1 June to serve as stopper groups north of SWAPO base. Two Coys 32 Battalion, commanded by Commandant Eddie Viljoen attacked SWAPO from the south.

Phase 2: H-Hour was at 10:00 on 2 June. Impala fighter planes commenced with the attack, dropping napalm bombs east of the target. SWAPO members were expected to flee in a westerly direction.

At H-Hour + 3 minutes: A mortar group was flown in from the mini-HAA. 1 Parabat Battalion platoons were flown in as stopper groups.

At H-Hour + 5 minutes: gunships provided air support to the ground forces.

Phase 3: an attack commenced by two companies of 32 Battalion, and a mortar group, moving from south to north. Other forces that were on standby:

- 48 x paratroopers at the HAA
- 3 x Puma helicopters
- 4 x gunship helicopters
- 1 x Telstar spotter fixed-wing aircraft
- 1 x trooper fixed-wing aircraft
- 12 x Impala fighter aircraft
- Medical support at Ongiva

2 Jun: C/s 24 of 32 Battalion located a cache with ammunition.

3 Jun: The 32 Battalion commander withdrew from Tactical HQ at Ongiva.

4 Jun: The 32 Battalion companies withdrew from Tactical HQ at Ongiva.

5 Jun: Task Force Bravo had a contact with EF members. Two OF members were wounded, one EF member was killed and one EF member was captured. A 1 Parabat Battalion platoon and one mortar group served as protection at Ionde Airfield. A Samil 100 petrol tanker detonated a landmine.

6 Jun: Task Force Oskar had contact with EF members at Shatotwa. One EF member was killed and one EF member was wounded. A Ratel 20 detonated a landmine. The 5 Recce pathfinder group was dropped off by a Dakota.

7 Jun: 60 Recce Commando troops were deployed at an LZ near Mulemba for Operation Neptune. Supplies were provided at Ionde by aeroplane. A Samil 50 detonated a landmine.

10 Jun: Task Force Oscar had a contact with EF members at Vinticete. 20 EF members' tracks, moving northwest were found at 7747WN.

11 Jun: Task Force Bravo laid an ambush and had contact with five EF members. Two EF members were killed and one EF member was captured.

12 Jun: Contact was made with EF members. These EF members fled east.

13 Jun: The signals equipment at Tactical HQ Ongiva was relocated to Tactical HQ Ionde. 2Lt M. Scheepers is to install communication equipment at the tactical HQ at Ionde. An Eland 90 armoured vehicle detonated a landmine.

14 Jun: Two Puma and four gunships departed to the Vinticete area for operations. An EF base was discovered by 51 Recce group at GR 228575XM. The SWAPO commander of the base is reported to be Mondingi Mashado. Parabats and a task force commenced with an attack on a target that was reported by Blouwildebees troops. No SWAPO forces were engaged during the attack because the army blamed the air force for dropping off the stopper groups at the wrong LZ. A Ratel detonated a landmine.

17 Jun: A landmine was detonated at Ionde base. More landmines were later detonated on 29 July and 30 July 1983.

18 Jun: Trooping of solders was completed. 32 Battalion B and G Coys were at Mupa, and A Coy was at Ionde. 30 flights were conducted by Puma helicopters, flying 23.5 hours to replace 300 members of 32 Battalion. It was decided that the SAWI canteen vehicle could not travel to Ionde by road.

20 Jun: Contact was made with EF members, one OF member sustained a shoulder wound. EF members fled.

21 Jun: An enemy recce group of four members was observed, but no contact was made. C/s 72, 32 Battalion had contact with EF members when both groups walked into each other. One OF member was slightly wounded. Eight EF members were moving north.

22 Jun: Contact was made with EF members, who fled northeast.

23 Jun: Contact was made on the Mupa/Vintecete road, no one was killed. The opposing forces walked into each other.

24 Jun: Contact was made with two EF members who fled west. One EF member was wounded. 40 EF members' tracks were found.

25 Jun: All platoons were resupplied from the air by a Dakota.

29 Jun: Tracks were discovered of seven SWAPO members.

30 Jun: Five EF members' tracks were found moving south. Two PBs (local persons) were found returning from Cuvelai on the Mupa road. They indicated that 2 EF bases were in that area.

32 Battalion platoon. Photo R. Griessel

July 1983

The following new frequencies ('foxies') for radio communication during the winter months as from 1 July 1983 were assigned to Ionde Tactical HQ:

Between 8:00 and 9:00: 4702 MHz
Between 9:00 and 10:00: 5450 MHz
Between 10:00 and 17:00: 7679 MHz
Between 17:00 and 19:00: 5450 MHz
Between 19:00 and 20:00; 4702 MHz
Between 20:00 and 8:00: 3123 MHz
Spare: 8395 MHz

The frequency for ground-to-air comms was channel 9 (132,750 MHz) on A72 portable radios. During July 1983 32 Battalion's operations involved the Evale, Nehone, Anhanca and Cataue areas.

1 Jul: Contact was made with EF members at first light at Oshendje (XM 2560), southwest of Dova. Earlier, a stick of the platoon c/s 13 was left on patrol. The remaining stick remained in the temporary base (TB) when SWAPO members walked in a straight line into the OF group. The contact was reported at 210670XM. OF members were attacked by 30 EF members with 82mm mortars. OF members fled and lost some of their equipment. Two OF members were killed: Sgt G.H. du Randt (78226370PE) and Rfn E. Cassera (83708339SP) and four OF members were wounded: 2Lt Roos, Cpl P.G. Slabbert, Rfn P. Fygoctao and Rfn M. Moango. Three EF members were wounded, EF members fled east, then scattered. It was a surprise attack by EF members. B22 and A72 radios were captured by EF members. Reports were also received that an SA-7 ground-to-air missile was used during the contact. It was a victory for SWAPO, the only one of its kind during 1983. Blouwildebees Recce members were recovered by Pumas in the Oncocua area.

2 Jul: An attack was launched at an EF base (Operation Neptune). 32 Battalion members were operating in the Vintecete and Mupa areas. Four EF members' tracks were found. During the contact, one EF member was killed and one EF member wounded. One SA-7 missile was found. OF equipment and a radio were discovered. Five OF members who were wounded on 1 July were casevaced by vehicle. Two OF members who were reported missing after the contact on 1 July, were found at 610810.

3 Jul: During a contact, one EF member was killed, but 30 EF members fled north, west and south, then scattered. It was assumed to have been the same group that had contact with OF members on 1 July as various pieces of OF equipment waere found in the group.

4 Jul: At Ionde Tactical HQ, lights were reported north and northwest, 20–30km from the Tactical HQ. Impala aircraft were called to do an airstrike on the target. Shots were fired at the target and the lights went out. Later it was discovered that the source of the lights were most probably bushfires that were blazing in the area. Two EF members' tracks were found in the Mupa area. The Chief of the Army, General Geldenhuys visited Ongiva.

5 Jul: Two EF members' tracks were found which were two days old. Contact was made with one EF member.

6 Jul: 30 EF members' tracks were found but they were four days old.

9 Jul: Three groups of EF members' tracks were discovered, consisting of 20 members each at Nauxindo, Mupapa and Lupapa, moving south. Four EF members' tracks were discovered. Wounded OF members were casevaced by Puma. It was reported that SWAPO was receiving equipment and reinforcements from Cuvelai. It was expected that SWAPO will infiltrate through the Nehone, Mulola, Dova and Oshendje areas and lay ambushes against our own forces.

10 Jul: 20 EF members' tracks were found moving south that were two days old. EF detainees will show caches in area. A resupply was done at Dova.

11 Jul: 11–15 EF members' tracks were found moving north. 16 EF members' tracks were found carrying heavy supplies, probably to resupply the Ionde area.

12 Jul: 20 EF members' tracks were found moving in two groups.

14 Jul: 20–30 EF members' tracks were found.

15 Jul: 15 EF members' tracks were found. Ongutete area is reported to be the governing area for SWAPO members. OP orders were issued: under no condition were any OF members allowed to cross the 12 northern line, including the Mupa–Vintecete route as it was declared a 'hunting' area for only the air force. OF members who cross this line, may become targets.

16 Jul: Four EF members' tracks were found moving north. A Dakota landed at Ionde with supplies.

18 Jul: A contact was made with four EF members at 775082WN. One EF member was killed.

20 Jul: One EF member was captured and moved to Oshakati. 13 EF members' tracks were found. SWAPO members operating in the Nehone area have fled into the DISA (UNITA) forces' area to the east.

21 Jul: Contact was made with EF members at 610120WN. One EF member was killed and one EF member was wounded who died later. An OF member, Rfn A. Inossencio, was wounded. Four EF members moved south to north. Contact was made with two EF members. One EF member was wounded, but he later died. One EF member

was killed. 20–30 EF members' tracks were discovered moving north to south.

22 Jul: OF members investigated a feast which was taking place at a village, attended by 300 local people. 30 EF members were captured as it was discovered that their feet were soft due to wearing military boots.

23 Jul: 13 EF members' tracks were found moving north.

25 Jul: 30 to 40 EF members' tracks were moving into UNITA's area. Two groups of ten EF members' tracks were found moving into UNITA's area. Tracks were found of members of the local population at Ionde abducted by SWAPO.

25–29 Jul: Trooping took place between Ionde and Rundu.

29 Jul : A cache was found in a local village.

31 Jul: 32 Battalion was operating in the Mulola area. It was reported that two companies, of 8 Battalion EF members were in the area with Red Square Coy EF members to the south. 32 Battalion was deployed south of Dova, East of Dova and north of Nehone. Contact was made with EF members. EF members fled west. 50 EF members' tracks were discovered.

August 1983

2 Aug: Contact was made with EF members. One EF member was killed, and one EF member was wounded. An SA-7 missile was discovered

8 Aug: Reports were received that SWAPO is preparing to celebrate Namibia day on 26 August 1983. This will coincide with parades in Luanda, Cuanza and Lubango. They will target our own forces at the Air Force base Ondangwa. They are expected to lay ambushes at Ondangwa and Oshivello and to sabotage installations at Walvisbay, Tsumeb Mine and the Ruacana power line. "Wegstaan bestokings" (remote fire) of bases was expected. They were ordered to capture a SADF soldier. The response by OF was to conduct roadblocks and to sharpen the Border control. It emerged that SWAPO has withdrawn 700 members for action against OF and to utilize 200 members to attack Ondangwa on 22 August 1983. Five EF members' tracks were found moving north.

9 Aug: Three EF members' tracks were found moving south.

10 Aug: OF members fired shots at a single EF member, but he fled.

11 Aug: 15 to 18 EF members' tracks were found moving north.

12 Aug: 12 EF members' tracks and four EF members' tracks were found.

13 Aug: More than 200 Povos were in the immediate vicinity of Ionde base. Some required medical attention, food and water. Requests were made that provisions be supplied by Sector 10 HQ.

14 Aug: An OF member, Rfn Augusto, sustained wounds to his arm and chest from his own AK 47 rifle.

16 Aug: Three EF members' tracks were found as well as a Land Rover, which was left in the area six weeks ago at 730160WN. A recce was conducted on Vintecete.

18 Aug: It is reported that due to EF members' deployment of AAA installations in southern Angola, less air force support was provided in the area, and therefore limited air support was available for ground forces.

19 Aug: Four EF members were found in a kraal, one EF member was captured.

20 Aug: 20–30 EF members' tracks were found at Cafu moving from north to south. The captured EF members were transported by gunship. Four EF members were located in a kraal and one EF member was captured. An Impala flown by Colonel R.S. (Dick) Lord landed at Ongiva airfield.

22 Aug: Six EF members' tracks were discovered moving from south to north, only 12 hours old.

28 Aug: Lt A.D. MacCullam, sustained an eye injury, he is recovering at Ionde. Rfn J. Nambi was killed during a contact.

30 Aug: A trooping of OF members took place.

September 1983

1/2 Sep: 15 EF members' tracks were discovered at RV 450200XN moving from north to south, only one day old. Two platoons followed up on these tracks.

2 Sep: OF members trooping from Buffalo to Ionde arrived in Omauni. These troopings were done every six weeks to relieve and replace the three companies that operated in Angola at a time. As the 32 Battalion base was situated at Buffalo in eastern Kavango, they used the route Buffalo–Rundu–Omauni, where they crossed the border into Angola to Ionde. The convoy consisted of the following vehicles:

36 Buffalo vehicles to transport the members of the three companies

3 Buffalo vehicles to transport the mortar group

1 Buffalo vehicle to serve as a command vehicle.

2 Buffalo vehicles to be used as a tiffy vehicle by the mechanics

2 reserve Buffalo vehicles

3 Kwêvoël vehicles to carry members' equipment (one each per Coy)

2 Kwêvoël vehicles to carry ammunition

2 Kwêvoël vehicles to carry rations

3 Kwêvoël vehicles to carry general provisions

4 Kwêvoël vehicles to carry diesel

6 Kwêvoël vehicles to carry avtur aircraft fuel

2 Kwêvoël vehicles to carry canteen provisions

1 Kwêvoël vehicle with extra water

2 Kwêvoël vehicles with spares for vehicles

1 recovery vehicle.

3 Sep: 15 EF members' tracks were discovered, but they divided into smaller groups.

4 Sep: SA Infantry School members, 1,250 strong, were deployed in the Dova, Nehone, Mupa and Chiede areas to perform a high-density area-sweep as part of Operation Sefta (Dolfyn). A large number of waterholes were discovered in the area. Also 900 cattle were located.

8 Sep: Reports were made of a possible EF base which was present at a location 18km east of Mupa. A TM57 landmine was discovered at Ionde, which were 3 weeks old at a position approximately 40m from a landmine which was detonated earlier. A Povo reported that SWAPO members were 20km west of Mupa at the Mui River. It was decided to arrange a meeting while an ambush was laid.

14 Sep: Six EF members' tracks were found at the Dengoan Calemo River.

16 Sep: 40 EF members were present in the Vinticete area. An airstrike was planned against this group.

17 Sep: Contact was made with EF members but they escaped north. An EF transitional base was found at RV800450WN. Explosions were heard at Cuvelai and also a propeller-driven aircraft were detected.

19 Sep: Contact was made with 2 EF members.

20 Sep: EF shots were heard which were fired 8km north with 14.5mm guns and mortars.

21 Sep: EF members' tracks were discovered.

23 Sep: Seven EF members' track were discovered moving north. Two DISA (UNITA) members were attacked by eight SWAPO

members, probably a Recce group from SWAPO 8th Battalion, at a village. The DISA members fled but one's wife and child were abducted by SWAPO. Tracks led west. The soles of the SWAPO members' boots were removed to avoid their tracks being recognized. Two attacks were earlier launched on this village by SWAPO members during January and April 1983.

27 Sep: C/s 23, 32 Battalion had a contact. 20 EF members' tracks fled northeast. EF members had to discontinue their pursuit as they reached their northern restricted boundary at RV362700XN.

28 Sep: A 32 Battalion platoon was airlifted by a Puma from Ionde.

29 Sep: 100 ration packs were supplied to Ionde. Information was received that SWAPO will lay landmines across the border in Angola on the Santa Clara/Angina road. Further movement on the tar road was disallowed. Brig Joep Joubert left for Ongiva for an Ops meeting.

30 Sep: A planning meeting between Brig Joubert, Sector 10 Commander, Cmdt Preston-Thomas, SAAF Operations Commander and Capt Hougaard, 32 Battalion Operations Commander, was held to discuss a planned strike on a SWAPO base.

32 Battalion soldier with RPG. (Photo R. Griessel)

October 1983

1 Oct: Dr Cosnelt left Ionde and was replaced by Dr Grobler.

2 Oct: At Ops Dolfyn (Sevta) a strike force was formed, consisting of 2 companies 32 Battalion, one section 32 Battalion 81mm mortars, one

32 Battalion Recce wing, 2 Regiment AAA, six gunship helicopters, six Puma helicopters and six Impala fighter aircraft (on standby at Ondangwa). Possible EF targets were detected at 3090, 3080XQ, 2690XN and 4680XN. Cmdt Preston-Thomas arrived at Ongiva for operations planning. An EF cache was discovered.

3 Oct: A convoy with re-supplies arrived at Ionde from Ongiva. A HAA was established.

4 Oct: Gunships were dispatched to Ionde. Three EF members' tracks were found.

5 Oct: Four to seven EF members' tracks were found at the Mairiver. Stopper groups were deployed ahead of the tracks.

6 Oct: A Puma helicopter which left from Ionde to Ongiva did an emergency landing in Angola. One Puma was dispatched transporting a platoon from Ongiva to protect the area of the crash. A gunship was sent from Ongiva to repair the damaged aircraft. A FAPLA member was captured with a FAPLA identity document found in his possession.

7 Oct: An airborne assault was conducted in the Jaula area in Angola. One Coy (c/s10) Recce wing infiltrated the area, north of the target, deployed as a stopper group. The assault was conducted by a second Coy and an 81mm mortar section. Medical support was provided at Ionde Tactical HQ. An air-storm operation was launched at 11:00. 70 EF members retrieved from the area just 3 hours before H-Hour in the directions north and northwest. The OF dress code was camouflage; dayglow was displayed on bush hats. The overall commander of the operation at Ionde was Cmdt Preston-Thomas, Capt Hougaard, was the commander at the HAA. The radio frequencies for A72 handheld radios with air support were; channel 11 and with ground forces channel 8. After the operation was completed, the SADF forces withdrew from the area. An EF suspect was caught at Mybamho due to bruise marks visible on the sides of his body and his on feet. A Dakota landed at Ionde. Platoons mainly set ambushes and observation posts in the area. 100 EF members' tracks were found moving northeast. 14 EF members' tracks were found at RV 430790RN. A FAPLA member with a FAPLA ID document was captured.

8 Oct: An EF suspect was caught at RV 820180WN, known as Manual Mafidi.

10 Oct: The medical team at Ionde attended to the medical needs of Povos.

11 Oct: The final stage of the air-storm operation on 7 October was completed.

13 Oct: A Dakota was dispatched to Ionde. EF weapons were looted but orders were given not to use these weapons but to return them to HQ. Only registered weapons were allowed to be used at 32 Battalion.

15 Oct: 13 FAPLA suspects were captured.

16 Oct: EF members' presences were reported at Dova.

20 Oct: Request for following fuel resupply to be delivered at Ongiva by 5 Support Unit.: 7,000l x avtur, 10,000l x diesel and 10,000l x water.

22 Oct: Trooping from Ionde by aircraft: 4 Puma helicopters departed from Ongiva to Ionde, 2 Dakotas departed from Ondangwa to Ionde to move troops between Ionde and Ongiva. Pumas and Dakota aircraft then returned to Ondangwa with full loads. A request was made for the C-160 to land at Ongiva to reduce the flying time of the Pumas to 16 hours, and the Dakota to only six hours. The C-160 was not allowed to land at Ongiva due to safety reasons.

20 Oct: Trooping was conducted by road from Buffalo to Rundu and via Omauni.

21–23 Oct: The convoy travelled from Omauni through off-road terrain to Ionde.

25–27 Oct: The convoy returned from Ionde through off-road terrain to Omauni.

25 Oct: 32 Battalion Coys were deployed at Ionde Tactical HQ. The SAAF was utilizing the airstrip at Ionde on a regular basis. Ionde required the deployment of 14.5 mm AAA guns as well as 3,000 rounds of ammunition and 14.5mm sights. It had already been stated on 20 October that such requests for ammunition could not be met.

28 Oct: The convoy left from Omauni for Buffalo via Rundu.

November 1983

One Coy 1 Parabat Battalion handed the protection of Xangongo over to 8 SAI. On 20 November Puma helicopters flew Recce teams from Xangongo to a spot, 35km west of Chibembe as part of Operation Askari. (No further records for November 1983 could be found, as they were unfortunately destroyed.)

December 1983

1/2 Dec: 15 EF members' tracks indicated movement west. Also, vehicle movement was spotted in the area.

5 Dec: Rations and fuel were delivered to 32 Battalion Tactical HQ Ionde for preparation for Operation Askari: diesel: 9,000l, avtur: 42,000l and a tanker with 13,000l and 19 full drums, petrol: 4 full drums, avgas: 3 full drums. Fuel on the convoy: diesel: 47,000l plus 10 drums, avtur: 90,000l plus 60 full drums, 3,300 ration packs were at Ionde and 14,600 in the convoy

6 Dec: Very high rainfall was experienced in the area.

7 Dec: Info was received that SWAPO had withdrawn from the area aduring March 1983, and the Cubans in November 1983. At Caiundo EF 1 Battalion was present, and 1 Brigade was on the Caundo/Ionde road. A Political Commissar and schoolteachers were reported to be present at the town. Their military force's operational preparedness was reported to be very bad. It was reported that a trench system ran through the town. Three EF members were killed, and one OF was wounded during joint ground and air force attacks on the enemy.

9 Dec: Two UNITA members and 15 Povos were caught by SWAPO east of the Vingombe River. One Black Widow landmine was detonated, and one UNITA solder escaped. Two SWAPO bases were spotted at the junction of the Chiocha and Bale rivers. Negotiations started with UNITA regarding their role during these operations. D-Day for the attack was planned between 17 and 21 December 1983. The initial D-Day that was planned for 9 November was delayed to 9 December, due to Minister Pik Botha attending foreign meetings with prominent political leaders.

10 Dec: The final passing-out function at Rundu HQ for national servicemen at 32 Battalion took place.

10/11 Dec: Five PBs were searched and FAPLA and SWAPO brochures were discovered.

14 Dec: One EF member was caught and arrested.

16 Dec: Two Recce groups crossed at the junction of the Bale and the Cubango rivers, but they lost their equipment in the water. Heavy rain was experienced. The total strength of OF members was 617 persons. 32 Battalion: A, C, D and E Coys and an 81mm group were operating in the area.

17/18 Dec: 32 Battalion Recce group (C/s 81) was attacked by EF members. One EF member was killed and the attack failed. The bombardment of EF targets started by OF, but EF had earlier relocated to new positions. Heavy fire was heard from EF members. It was possibly a fire plan to scare off OF.

Operation Askari

The SADF consisted of Operation Javelin, Task Force Tango, 61 Mechanized Battalion, 102 Battalion, Task Force Delta, 4 Coys 32 Battalion, (at 140150XP), 81mm mortar group, 1 Coy 53 Battalion.

17 Dec: OF members opened fire on EF members at RV 3408 with 140mm, at RV 3608 with 127mm MVL, and at RV 4492 with 155mm rocket launchers for a period of 30 minutes. Task Force Delta and Task Force Victor crossed the river with 127mm MVL. More air support was required.

18/19 Dec: C and E Coys 32 Battalion were due to attack a suspected enemy base. 4 Puma helicopters were on standby. Gen Geldenhuys and his company were present at RV 660280XP and RV330330XP. Five EF members were killed without any OF losses. One EF member was captured. Requests were made for the deployment of C and E Coys 32 Battalion by Puma helicopter to be utilized as cut-off groups. UNITA was supported to lay ambushes.

18 Dec: Nine OF members were killed in action, and two OF members were wounded. One Buffalo vehicle was captured by EF members. A Mirage fighter aircraft bombarded a road that was used by EF members. Two Impala aircraft served as air protection for the Puma helicopters.

20 Dec: SADF and SAAF engaged in the Quiteve, Mulondo and Cahama areas. A force from Sector 20 was deployed 20km from Caiundo on the west bank of the river. FAPLA suffered high casualties when SAAF conducted an airstrike as part of a retaliatory offensive. Eight EF members were killed, three EF members were wounded. The Buffalo vehicle that was reported lost earlier has been recovered. One OF member was reported missing in action: Rfn Nkupebona.

21 Dec: Four 32 Battalion Coys laid ambushes during the night, and performed a reconnaissance of an enemy base. They distributed pamphlets among PBs.

22 Dec: EF targets were fired at. Impala fighter aircraft attacked targets at Mulondo.

24 Dec OF Electronic Warfare intercepted EF communication that reported that helicopters were spotted at Chalas and Mbale. Two EF members were captured.

27/28 Dec: 1 Recce wing and two platoons D Coy, 32 Battalion conducted a recovery and cleaning of the Puma helicopter crash site.

27 Dec: Impala fighter aircraft and Canberra bomber aircraft launched an airstrike on a SWAPO target in the Cuvelai area.

28 Dec: Op commenced with the building of a bridge over the Cuvelai River. An air attack was launched on EF to prevent EF launching of SA-8 missiles. OF members laid landmines on EF routes.

29 Dec: At 17:35 at Chama da Sacagsube, OF opened fire on Techemutete. Cmdt E. Viljoen, gave a briefing to Brig Joubert at Oshakati. The planned date for the OF attack was 26 December 1983 at RV 200185XP. A signal was transmitted to Brig Joubert, and Col Lord regarding the imminent launch of Operation Askari. They stated that they were experiencing low cloud cover. This made observation and air support for Task Team 2 impossible. Due to no support from artillery east of river, they deviated from their original plan. The plan was amended as follows: The Task Force to take over the western part of the high ground west of the river with one Coy, two gunships were available for support at the HAA. The artillery troop and a platoon west of the river delivered limited firepower on an AAA position, mortar stations as well as the 2nd Brigade HQ, and 2 Battalion HQ's east of the river. Two Puma helicopters and two gunships were on standby at the HAA. Two Pumas were on standby to conduct casevacs, and a Bosbok was on standby to become airborne after the weather cleared. As the weather cleared, commanders assessed the situation, but chances were slim that an attack would commence. If no attack commences, OF shall move south to cross the *shonas* before dark. Once reports were received from intercepting the EF communication by the Electronic Warfare team, the EF's response will be evaluated and a plan of action adjusted accordingly. Four Buccaneer bomber aircraft attacked the THTC SWAPO base outside Lubango. Firing commenced at the target referred to as *kwelvuur* (harassing fire). The high ground was occupied by OF members. One Ratel attack vehicle was destroyed by direct EF fire. One EF member was killed and 3 EF members were wounded. Three OF members were wounded by the accidental spontaneous ignition of a 127mm rocket launcher. OF launched

an aerial bombardment, but the EF did not show any response. Artillery fire commenced on the EF, but was inaccurate. After the Puma helicopter wreck was uplifted, a 32 Battalion member's body was discovered underneath the wreckage. Three vehicles from 61 Mech were destroyed by EF fire.

30 Dec: Instructions were issued to capture three SA-8 missiles as well as radio equipment to be transferred directly to the HQ. Radio settings should remain undisturbed. The bombardment of EF positions commenced.

31 Dec: An OF landmine was detonated by a goat in the road. EF caches were discovered containing food supplies. A search was conducted to locate the SA-8 missiles, reportedly present at an EF base.

January 1984

1 Jan: The EF members' morale was reported to be very low. Five EF members absconded. EF members reported to have expressed their concern over the safety of the Cuban solders in the area. Eight FAPLA members were wounded and one FAPLA member was killed. It was expected that the SAAF bombardment of EF installations will commence on 6 January 1984 with special bunker bombs. An attack was launched at first light north of the river on an EF target. It was reported that EF radar detected OF aircraft. This provided the EF members with early warning to seek cover in underground bunkers. Cuban advisers were reported to be hiding in underground bunkers at the EF HQ. Two EF vehicles were destroyed and five FAPLA members were wounded. The HAA was now situated at YN 550503.

2 Jan: An order was issued that EF targets should be identified for air attacks.

3 Jan: The actual assault on Cuvelai commenced with 10 Impala fighter aircraft and four Canberra bomber aircraft. The Task Force invaded a third of the area, but thereafter had to withdraw due to bad light. 15 EF vehicles were destroyed. A part of the EF Brigade HQ position was taken. One 32 Battalion member (Rfn T. Manganhes), was killed and one 7 SAI member was wounded. EF AAA directed their fire at OF positions. OF destroyed 60 EF vehicles in a carpark and another 15 vehicles were destroyed elsewhere. The Task Force delivered *kwelvuur* west of the river. A 120mm bombardment commenced on the Brigade HQ. The Task Force was situated east of the river. A part of the Brigade HQ was captured

with a large number of EF members killed inside their underground bunkers. EF members reported to be without any command, and a state of total chaos existed in their ranks.

4 Jan: Culelai was attacked by SADF ground forces. A Ratel 90 of 4 SAI was destroyed by an EF T-54 tank near Cuvelai. A report suggested that five OF members died. Rfn J.F. Pretorius, was the 6th person to have died in the Ratel, but his remains could not be identified. An OF ambulance detonated a landmine.

6 Jan: Task Force Delta performed a final sweep, clearing EF positions. One OF member detonated an anti-personnel landmine (Rfn A. Aurelio of 32 Battalion was killed in action on 3 January). Another OF member was wounded when an ambulance vehicle arrived and another landmine was detonated. EF T-54 tanks were reported to be 9km northwest of 32 Battalion positions. Impala fighter aircraft were called in but the airstrike was abandoned due to bad light. The HAA was moved again to another position. OF planned an attack on the EF installations to commence on 9 January 1984. The operation started with the bombardment of EF installations to weaken resistance. Three FAPLA members were captured. A conference was held at SA Army College to reflect on Operation Askari.

7 Jan: The airstrike on EF bases was reported to be only 50% effective. 20 SAAF aircraft made two airstrikes on the SWAPO Brigade HQ. Two direct hits, including one on the Brigade Commander's bunker were made. The Brigade Commander was reported to have been severely traumatized and suffered smoke inhalation. 20 EF members were killed due to sustaining severe burn wounds. One EF AAA station and one EF armoured vehicle were destroyed. Four FAPLA members were killed and two wounded. EF vehicles were relocated to Bambi. EF members withdrew from their base after the attack. An OF Ratel detonated a landmine. During the recovery of the Ratel, another landmine was detonated. Three EF members were wounded at an observation post. SAAF launched a bombardment at EF installations. The SADF succeeded in the capture of two SA-9 missiles from an EF base. This was indeed a very significant discovery, the first ever of its kind. Five T-54 EF tanks were destroyed. Three FAPLA members were captured. An OF Samil transport vehicle detonated a landmine.

8 Jan: An OF airstrike at EF installations

managed to destroy the EF fuel depot. Church services were held at the HAA. A request was made for four gunship helicopters. A specific request was made for Capt Anderson to pilot one, due to his experience. Four OF Bosbok aircraft were airborne to provide communication. The Task Force was deployed west of river but attracted very accurate EF fire and had to redeploy. An OF Kwêvoël transport vehicle detonated a landmine.

10 Jan: Contact was made with EF members. 15 EF members were killed, and two EF members were wounded. Two OF members died. They were probably Rfn I. Malonga, and Rfn J. Dala, of 32 Battalion. An 201 Battalion Buffalo vehicle detonated a landmine. Four OF members were wounded. Task Force Delta withdrew from any further participation of the operation.

11 Jan: Two TM57 landmines were discovered in the road. One was laid on top of the other. OF continued with river protection and clearing of the EF area.61 Mech withdrew from further participation in the operation. The remainder of OF withdrew from battle area.

15 Jan: Withdrawal of OF took place as follows: Task Force Echo Victor to withdraw to Ionde, 201 Battalion to withdraw to Ongiva, Task Force X-Ray to withdraw to Ongiva. Ten C130/C160 fixed wing aircraft to land at Ongiva airport to remove radar equipment.

15 April 1985: Operation Dikmelk

SA forces withdraw from Southern Angola. A military parade was staged north of the border at Santa Clara. FAPLA representatives were expected to attend these events.

APPENDIX II
32 BATTALION AND SWAPO CODES

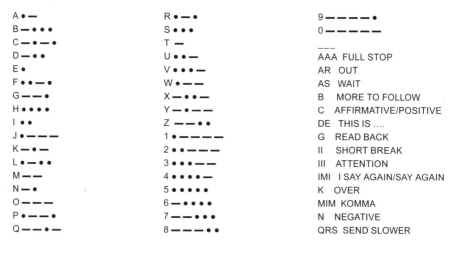

32 Battalion radio-code card.

Operation Snoek/Dolfyn frequencies and hopper settings.

Operation Snoek/Dolfyn 32 Battalion platoon call signs and general codes.

Supplies request for 32 Battalion platoons during operations.

Morse code

A ● —	R ● — ●	9 — — — — ●
B — ● ● ●	S ● ● ●	0 — — — — —
C — ● — ●	T —	___
D — ● ●	U ● ● —	AAA FULL STOP
E ●	V ● ● ● —	AR OUT
F ● ● — ●	W ● — —	AS WAIT
G — — ●	X — ● ● —	B MORE TO FOLLOW
H ● ● ● ●	Y — ● — —	C AFFIRMATIVE/POSITIVE
I ● ●	Z — — ● ●	DE THIS IS ….
J ● — — —	1 ● — — — —	G READ BACK
K — ● —	2 ● ● — — —	II SHORT BREAK
L ● — ● ●	3 ● ● ● — —	III ATTENTION
M — —	4 ● ● ● ● —	IMI I SAY AGAIN/SAY AGAIN
N — ●	5 ● ● ● ● ●	K OVER
O — — —	6 — ● ● ● ●	MIM KOMMA
P ● — — ●	7 — — ● ● ●	N NEGATIVE
Q — — ● —	8 — — — ● ●	QRS SEND SLOWER

QRU GOT NOTHING FOR YOU	AFFIRMATIVE	ZUJ STAND BY
Q-Q-Q EMERGENCY	XE CODE FOLLOWS	ZUN NOTHING HEARD
R ROGER/POSITIVE/	ZKJ CLOSE DOWN UNTILL...	QSA ANYTHING FOR ME?

SWAPO anti-aircraft codes

Previous no – Beans	Total – Drought
ZU-23 – Mango	Equipment/Aids Control – Drive
ZUG-1 – Apple	Mounts Control – Day
Streca – Tomato	Personnel Control – Night
L/Mechanism – Tea	A.A.D. – Morning
Gas Truck – Platoon	Sacrificed – Brave
Binocular – Sugar	Capture – Tired
T.Z.K – Coffee	Wounded – Salt
Compass – Petrol	Missing/lost – Cold
S/Barrel – Diesel	Defected – Ice
T.G.P – Fuel	Deserted – Warm
L/Machine – Rain	Withdrawn – Fire
M/Jacket – Drill	To Hospital – Lake
M-59 – Cat	Transferred – Rake
AK – Lion	Back from Hospital – Bite
T.T. Pistol – Elephant	Back from missing – Blind
Macarov – Tiger	Reinforced – Power
B.Z.T – OIO	Present no – Goat
O.F.Z – 444	Broken – Rice
B-32– 902	Ammo fire – Fuse
Ammunition Control – Door	Power supply source – Ready
Arms Control – Gate	Strela Launched – Went

SWAPO personnel codes

001	P/COS		008	8 BN
002	P/CAAD		009	STRIKING UNIT
003	P/AAD OFFICE		010	TYPHOON
004	RED SQUARE BN		011	PLAN CLINIC
005	ALPHA BN		012	OG
006	BRAVO BN		013	SG
007	MOSCOW BN		014	WG

APPENDIX III
SADF RADIO EQUIPMENT SUPPLIED TO 32 BATTALION

B22 HF manpack radio

Frequency range: 2-16 MHz
Output Power: 20W

TR15 HF radio

Frequency range: 2-16 MHz
Mass: 26 kg
Dimensions: 423 mm x 444mm x 18 mm
Output power: 100 w
Supply Voltage: 12-24V

A72 VHF AM radio

Frequency range: 130-136 MHz
Mass: 1.5 kg
Dimensions: 230mm x 175 mm x 60 mm
Output Power: 6W pep
Supply Voltage: 10-16V

A55 HF radio

Frequency range: 2-30 mhz with
28,000 channels at 1 kHz spacing
Output power: 6-20 watts
Mass: 7,9kg
In service: 1970s to mid-1990s
HF/SSB tranceiver

APPENDIX IV
SADF WEAPONS USED DURING THE ANGOLAN BUSH WAR

5.56 mm R4 Assault Rifle

1. Calibre: 5.56mm
2. Length: 1,005mm
3. Barrel length: 460mm
4. Weight: 4.3kg
5. Magazine capacity: 35-round detachable box magazine
6. Effective range: 300–500m sight adjustments
7. Operation: Gas operated
8. Ammunition : 5.56x45mm NATO
9. Muzzle velocity: 980m/s
10. Automatic rate: 600–750 rounds/min
11. In service: 1982

Former Minister of Defence, Magnus Malan, at the presentation of the first R4 automatic rifle.

7.62 mm R1 (FN FAL) Assault Rifle

The first R1 rifle to be incorporated in the SADF, presented by Minister Jim Fouché to the then Prime Minister of South Africa, H.F. Verwoerd, on 23 September 1964.

1. Calibre: 7.62mm
2. Length: 1,125mm
3. Barrel length: 533mm
4. Weight: 5.95kg
5. Magazine capacity: 20- or 30-round detachable box magazine
6. Effective range: 200–600 m sight adjustments
7. Operation: Gas-operated
8. Ammunition: 7.62x51mm NATO
9. Muzzle velocity: 840 m/s
10. Automatic rate: 650–700 rounds/min
11. In service: 1954

Ratel 90/60/20mm

Type: Support vehicle: wheeled, 6x6
Crew: 3+6 infantry; fewer infantry if
employed in the fire-support role, when
more 90mm ammunition is carried.
Armament primary: 1 x 90mm low-
pressure gun with 72 rounds
Armament secondary: 1 x 7.62mm
co-axial MG; 1 x 7.62mm GPMG at
commander's cupola; 1 x 7.62mm
GPMG on ring-mount at rear of vehicle

G5 Cannon

Type: 155mm gun/howitzer
Weight: 13.7 tonnes
Dimensions: length towing configuration,
barrel turned back 9.1m, height 2.3m
Crew: 8
Mobility: 10t gun tractor, towing speed
90km/h on roads and 50km/h on dirt
Self-propelled by 57kW auxiliary diesel
engine allowing speeds of 3–8km/h
Elevation: +75° to -3°
Traverse: 84° with elevation below 15°,
65° above 15°
Range: 3,000m minimum, 30,000m
maximum, standard round 39,000m with
base bleed
Rate of fire: 3 rounds/min for 15 minutes,
then 2 rounds/min for one hour

G6 Cannon

Engine: 410kW air-cooled diesel
Performance: Speed 90km/h on roads,
30–40km/h on dirt)
Gradient: 18°
Step: 50cm
Ford: 1m
Range: 600km
Side slope: 13.5°
Ditch: 1.5rn
Ordnance: 155mm tube identical to G5
but fitted with a fume extractor
Elevation: 5° to + 75°
Traverse: 80°
Range: 3,000m minimum, 30,000m
maximum

Type: 155mm self-propelled gun/howitzer
wheeled 6x6
Crew: 5
Weight: 37 tonnes (turret 9 tonnes)
Dimensions: length 9m, width 3.3m, height
3.25m

20mm Anti-Aircraft Gun

Type: 20mm (Nkm wz.38 FK) (1938/9)
Calibre: 20x136mm
Dimensions: length: 2,015mm; width: 202.5mm
Weight: 57.6kg
Barrel length: 1,476mm
Muzzle velocity: 856 m/s
Effective range: 5,000m
Feed system: Box/drum
At 400 metres can penetrate 23–15mm steel

Kwêvoël Mine-Protected Transport Vehicle

Type: Mine-protected logistical vehicle
Dimensions: length 10.87m, width 2.5m, height 3.13m
Weight: 12.9 tonnes with 9 tonnes of cargo
Ground clearance: 35.5cm
Engine: 200kW air-cooled V-10 diesel
Speed: 93 km/h
Distance: 700km

Buffel Mine-Protected Vehicle

Type: 4x4 APC
Crew: 1 + 10
Armament: two pintle-mounted 7.62mm GPMGs
Dimensions: length 5.1m, width 2.05m, height 2.955m
Weight 6.14 tonnes
Ground clearance: 42cm
Engine: 93.25 kW 6-cylinder water-cooled diesel

When fitted with a flat back the Buffel is referred to as a Moffel.

127mm Multiple Rocket Launcher

Type: 127mm self-propelled, 4x4, multiple rocket launcher
Crew :2 (+ 12 men in the 5t ammunition vehicle)
Weight: 6.44 tonnes
Dimensions: length 5.35m, width 2.3m, height 2.7m
Ordnance type: 24-tube 127mm rocket launcher
Range: 7,500m minimum (with large drag ring), 22,00 m maximum
Rate of fire: 1 round per second individually or if programmed, apples of between 2 and 24.

120mm Mortar

Type: 120mm mortar M1943 (USSR)
Calibre: 120mm
Length of tube: 1,854mm
Weight: 500kg
Rate of fire: 12–15 rpm
Maximum range: 5,700m
Minimum range: 460m
Crew: 6

81mm Mortar

Type: 81mm mortar (L16 British)
Calibre: 81mm
Length of tube: 1,280 mm
Weight: 35.3 kg
Rate of fire: 12–12 rpm
Maximum range: 5,650 m
Crew: 3

60mm Mortar

Type: 60mm mortar (M2)
Calibre: 60mm
Length of tube: 726mm
Total Weight: 19.5kg
Rate of fire: 18 rpm
Maximum range: 1,815m

APPENDIX V
SAAF MILITARY EQUIPMENT USED DURING 1983

Puma

Type: Medium transport helicopter
Country of Origin: France
First flights: Prototype and production: 1965
Delivered to SAAF: from 1969

Dimensions: length of fuselage 14.06m, rotor diameter 14.18m, height 4.18m
Weight: 7.4 tonnes
Power plant: 2 x 1,575hp Turbomeca Turmo IVC turboshafts
Maximum speed: 294km/h at sea level
Service ceiling: 4,800m
Hovering ceiling: 4,400m in ground effect, 4,250m out of ground effect
Range: 515km
Payload: 3.3 tonnes freight or 16 troops

Alouette III

Type: Light helicopter
Country of Origin: France

First flights: Prototype 1959, production 1962
Delivered to SAAF: 1962
Dimensions: length of fuselage 10.03m, rotor diameter 11m, height 3.09m
Weight: 2.1 tonnes
Power plant: 1 x 550hp Turbomeca Artouste IIIB turboshaft
Maximum speed: 210km/h at sea level
Service ceiling: 3,250m
Hovering ceiling: 1,700m in ground effect, 550m out of ground effect
Range: 100–500km
Payload: 820kg freight or 5 passengers

Mirage F1AZ and CZ

Type: Fighter, fighter-bomber
Country of origin: France
First Flights: prototype 1966, production 1973
Delivered to SAAF: from 1975

Dimensions: length 15m, span 8.4m, height 4.5m
Weight: 14.9 tonnes
Power plant: 5,035kg static thrust, Snecma Atar 09K50 turbojet, 7,166kg with afterburner
Maximum speed: Mach 2.2 (2,335km/h) at 12,000m, Mach 1.2 (1,472km/h) at sea level
Service ceiling: 18,500m
Radius action: 700–900km
Endurance: 3 hours, 45 minutes

Mirage IIICZ, EZ, RZ, R2Z, BZ, DZ and D2Z

Type: Fighter, fighter-bomber
Country of Origin: France
First flights: Prototype 1956, production IIICZ 1960
Delivered to SAAF: from 1963
Dimensions: length 13.85m, span 8.22m, height 4.2m
(IIICZ – others differ slightly)

Weight: 11.8 tonnes (CZ) 13.5 tonnes (EZ, RZ)
Power plant: 4,250kg static thrust Snecma Afar 09B turbojet, 6,000kg with afterburner (CZ); 4,280kg (BZ); 6,200kg 09C (EZ, DZ and RZ); 5,035kg and 7,166kg 09K (R2Z and D2Z)
Maximum speed: IIICZ Mach 2.1 (2,230km/h) at 1,1000m, Mach 1.22 (1,490km/h) at sea level IIIEZ -Mach 2.2 (2,336km/h) at 12,000m, Mach 1.1 (1,390km/h) at sea level

Impala Mk II

Type:Light attack aircraft
Country of origin: Italy, built under licence in South Africa
First flights: Prototype 1957, MB 326K on which the Mk II is based 1970

Delivered to SAAF: from 1974
Impala I trainers: from 1966
Dimensions: length 10.65m, span 10.15m, height 3.72m
Weight: 5.226 tonnes
Power plant: 1 x 1,547 kg static thrust Rolls Royce Viper Mk 540 turbojet
Maximum speed: Mach 0.82 (843km/h) at 6,100m
Service ceiling: 11,900m
Radius of action: 130–600km
Armament: 2 x 30mm cannon, up to 1,814kg of bombs or rocket pods on 6 underwing hard ports

Buccaneer S Mk 50

Type: Marine strike, strike aircraft
Country of origin: Britain
First flights: Prototype 1958, production 1962
Delivered to SAAF: 1965
Weight: 28.12 tonnes

Dimensions: length 19.33m, span 13.41m, height 4.95m
Power plant: 2 x 5,035kg static thrust Rolls Royce RB.168-1A Spey Mk 101 turbojets and 1 x 3,630kg thrust Bristol BS.605 wind chamber rocket motor for additional take-off power under 'hot and high' conditions
Maximum speed: Mach 0.85 (1,038km/h) at 60m, Mach 1.2 (1,472km/h) at sea level
Service ceiling: 15,200m
Radius Action: 805–965km, up to 3,700km with additional fuel

Canberra B(1)12

Type: Bomber, reconnaissance aircraft
Country of origin: Britain
First flights: Prototype 1949, production 1955
Delivered to SAAF: 1963

Dimensions: lenth 19.96m, span 19.51m, height 4.77m
Weight: 24.95 tonnes
Power plant: 2 x 3,357kg static thrust Rolls Royce Avon Mk 109 turbojets
Maximum speed: Mach 0.83 (901km/h) at 12,200 m
Mach 0.68 (821km/h) at sea level
Service ceiling: 14,630m
Radius action: 1,300km, range 6,100km

C-130 B Hercules

Type: Medium transport
Country of Origin: USA
First flights: Prototype 1954, production 1958
Delivered to SAAF: 1963

Dimensions: length 29.78m, span 40.25m, height 11.66m
Weight: 77.5 tonnes
Power plant: 4 x 3,017kW turbo-propeller engines
Maximum speed: 618km/h
Service ceiling: 9,150m
Radius action: 805–965km, range up to 3,700km with additional fuel

C-160 Transall

Type: Medium transport
Country of Origin: France
First Flights: prototype 1963; production 1965
Delivered to SAAF: 1969

Dimensions: length 32.4m, span 40m, height 11.65m
Weight: 54 tonnes
Power plant: 2 x 4,545kW turbo-propeller engines
Maximum speed: 513km/h at 5,000m
Service ceiling: 8,500m
Radius action: 805–965km, range up to 3,700km with additional fuel

DC-3 'Dakota'	
 Type: Transport Country of Origin: USA	First flights: Prototype 1935 Delivered to SAAF: from 1943 Dimensions: length 19.65m, span 28.96m, height 5.18m Weight: 13.15 tonnes Power plant: 2 x 1,200hp Pratt & Whitney R-1 830-92 or 90B radial engines Maximum speed: 368km/h at 2,590m Service ceiling: 7,300m Range: 2,430km Payload: 3.4 tonnes of freight

APPENDIX VI
SOVIET WEAPONS USED BY FAPLA, SWAPO, UNITA AND 32 BATTALION[2]

AK-47 ASSAULT RIFLE (USSR)	
	1. Calibre: 7.62mm 2. Operation: Gas, selective 3. Length: 870mm 4. Barrel length: 410mm 5. Magazine capacity: 30 rounds 6. Rate of fire: 600rpm 7. Range: up to 800m 8. Weight: 5kg 9. Ammunition: 7.62x39mm

SKS SELF-LOADING RIFLE (USSR)	
	1. Calibre: 7.62mm 2. Length: 1021mm 3. Barrel length: 500mm 4. Weight: 4kg 5. Magazine capacity: 10 rounds 6. Effective range: 400m 7. Operation: Gas, semi-automatic 8. Ammunition 7.62x39mm

7.62MM RPD LIGHT MACHINE GUN (USSR)

1. Calibre: 7.62mm
2. Operation: Gas, automatic, air cooled
3. Weight loaded: 8.8kg
4. Length: 1053mm
5. Sight: front: hooded post; rear: adjustable v-notch
6. Feeding device: 100-round metallic belt carried in drum
7. Effective range: 800m
8. Rate of fire: 150rpm
9. Ammunition: 7.624x39mm

7.62 MM DP LIGHT MACHINE GUN (USSR)

1. Calibre: 7.62mm
2. Operation: Gas, automatic, air cooled
3. Weight: 12kg with loaded magazine
4. Length: 1270mm
5. Barrel length: 610mm
6. Magazine: 47-round drum
7. Rate of fire: 500–600rpm
8. Range: 800m
9. Ammunition: 7.62x54R

M79 40MM GRENADE LAUNCHER (USA)

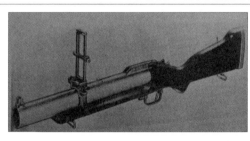

1. Calibre: 40mm
2. Length: 737mm
3. Length of barrel: 356mm
4. Weight: 2.76kg
5. Action: Break-open, single shot
6. Weignt of round: 227g
7. MV: 76m/sec
8. Maximum range: 400m
9. Maximum effective range: area targets 350m, point targets 150m
10. Ammunition: 33 varying shell types

RPG-7V ANTI-TANK GRENADE LAUNCHER (USSR)

1. Calibre: 40mm (tube), 85mm (projectile)
2. Weight: 5.5kg
3. Length: 95m
4. Effective range: 300–500m
5. MV: 120m/sec
6. Rate of fire: 4–6rpm
7. Ammunition: Rocket-assisted HEAT grenade
8. Armour-piercing capability: 3h-37cm/0°

M37 82MM MORTAR (USSR)

1. Calibre: 82mm
2. Length of tube: 1290mm
3. Weight: 58kg
4. Weight of bomb: 3.2kg
5. MV: 210m/sec
6. Range: 3,040m
7. Rate of fire: 25rpm
8. Ammunition: HE, Smoke

B10 82MM RECOILESS GUN (USSR)

1. Calibre: 82mm
2. Weight: 85.5kg
3. Length: 2,030m
4. MV: 320m/sec
5. Effective range, moving armour: 390m
6. Maximum range: 4,470m
7. Rate of fire: 5–6rpm
8. Ammunition: HEAT, HE
9. Armour-piercing capability: 20cm/0°

122MM SINGLE-SHOT LAUNCHER AND HE ROCKET (USSR)

1. Tube length: 2460mm
2. Weight: 21.8kg
3. Weight of tripod mount: 27.7kg
4. Short Rocket
5. Calibre: 122mm
6. Length: 1950mm
7. Weight: 46.3kg
8. Fuse: Point detonation
9. Maximum range: 10,973m

VLADIMIROV (KIV) 14.5MM HEAVY MACHINE GUN (USSR)

1. Calibre: 14.5mm
2. Length: 2,007mm
3. Barrel length: 1,348mm
4. Weight: 51kg
5. Rate of fire: cyclic 600rpm, practical 150rpm
6. MV: 1,000m/sec
7. Range: horizontal 2,000m, AA 1,400m, maximum 8,000m

ZFU-4 14.5MM ANTI-AIRCRAFT HEAVY MACHINE GUN (USSR)

1. Calibre: 14.5mm
2. Length of barrel: 1,348mm
3. Length of machine gun w/flash hider: 2,007mm
4. Weight: 1,810kg
5. Length: 4,630mm

6. Width: 1,859mm
7. Height: 2,286mm
8. Clearance: 458mm
9. Tyre size: 6.50x20
10. Height of axis: 1,020mm
11. Elevation: 90°
12. Depression: 8°
13. Traverse: 360°
14. Practical rate of fire per barrel: 150rpm
15. MV: 1,000m/sec
16. Maximum range: horizontal 8,000m, vertical 5,000m, AA 1,400m
17. Armour penetration 0°/500m: 32mm
18. Crew: 5

M1943 120MM MORTAR (USSR)

1. Calibre: 120mm
2. Length of tube in calibres: 15.4
3. Length of tube: 1,854mm

4. Total weight: 500kg
5. Length in travelling position: 2,260mm
6. Width in travelling position: 1,548mm
7. Height in travelling position: 1,206mm
8. Clearance: 370mm
9. Tyre size: 6.00x16
10. Maximum elevation: 80°
11. Minimum elevation: 45°
12. Traverse: 8°
13. Rate of fire: 12–15rpm
14. Maximum range: 5,700m
15. Minimum range: 460m
16. Crew: 6

T-34 MEDIUM TANK (USSR)

Weight: 32 tons
Length: 8,100mm
Height: 2,700mm
Width: 3,050mm
Engine model: VG-2-34
Horse-power: 500
Cylinders: V-12
Speed: 55km/h
Main armament: 85mm gun
Basic load: 50–60 rounds
Effective range: APHE 950m, HVAP 1,150m
Cruising range: 300km
Crew: 4

BM21 122MM ROCKET LAUNCHER (USSR)

10. Cooling: Water
11. Speed: 75km/h
12. Cruising range: 405km
13. Trench: 87.50m
14. Step: 65cm
15. Slope: 30°
16. Fording: 100cm

Launcher

1. Number of rounds: 40
2. Weight: 3,500kg
3. Elevation: 50°
4. Traverse: 240°
5. Time to reload: 10 minutes
6. Long Rocket
7. Calibre: 122mm
8. Length: 322.6cm
9. Weight: 77.5kg
10. Maximum Range: 20,500m

Vehicle

1. Weight: 11,500kg
2. Length: 735cm
3. Width: 269cm
4. Height: 285cm
5. Clearance: 41cm
6. Engine model: ZIL-375
7. Horsepower: 175
8. Cylinders: V-8
9. Fuel: Petrol

T-55 MEDIUM TANK (USSR)

13. Crew: 4
14. Speed: 48km/h
15. Cruising range: 400km
16. Ground pressure: 81kg/cm^2
17. Trench: 2,700mm
18. Step: 800mm
19. Slope: 30°
20. Tilt: 30°
21. Ford: I,400mm
22. Armour: glacis plate 100mm/60°; upper hull side 70mm/0°; mantlet 170mm basis

Vehicle

1. Weight: 36 tons
2. Length with gun forward: 9,000mm
3. Length without gun: 6,450mm
4. Width: 3,270mm
5. Height: 2,400mm
6. Track: 2,640mm
7. Clearance: 425mm
8. Engine model: V-54
9. Horse-power: 520
10. Cylinders: V-12
11. Fuel: Diesel
12. Cooling: Water

Armament

1. Main armament: 100mm gun D-10T
2. Basic load: 34 rounds
3. Elevation: 17°
4. Depression: 4°
5. MV: APHE 1,000m/s; HEAT 900m/s
6. Effective range: APHE 1,070m, HEAT 900m
7. Armour penetration: APHE 0°/1,000m 185mm; HEAT 0°/any range 380mm
8. Secondary armament: bow 7.62SGMT; coaxial : 7.62SG

BTR-152 (USSR)

Type: APC
Engine: 6 cylinders petrol (110hp)
Crew: 2 + 17 infantry
Main armament: 1 x 7.62mm MG gun with
1,250 rounds

GRAIL SA-7 MISSILE (USSR)

Total length: 127cm
Diameter: 15cm
Total weight: 10.6kg
Explosive charge: 1.8kg
Operation: Infra-red homing system
Speed: Mach 1.5 (1,700km/h)
Maximum horizontal range: 3,600m
Maximum vertical range: 2,700m
Effective range: 1,500m

M31 SA-9 MISSILE

Type: Surface-to-air missile
Country of origin: Soviet Union
Production variants 9M31, 9M31M
Specifications (9M31):
Weight: 32kg
Length: 1,803mm
Diameter: 120mm

Warhead: Frag-HE
Weight: 2.6 kg;
Detonation mechanism: RF proximity
Wingspan: 0.36m
Propellant: Single-stage solid propellant
rocket motor
Operational range 4,200m (also reported as
6.5km for 9M31, 8km for 9M31M)
Flight altitude: 3,500m, or higher
Speed: Mach 1.8
Guidance system: Photo contrast PbS
seeker (also reported as IR seeker of 1-3
umm and/or 1-5 µm wavelength)

GECKO SA-8 MISSILE

Type: Surface-to-air missile
Place of origin: Soviet Union
Production history: variants 9M33; 9M33M1;
9M33M2; 9M33M3; 9A33BM3
Specifications (9M33):

Weight: 170kg
Length: 3,158mm
Diameter: 209.6mm
Warhead: Frag-HE
  Weight: 16kg
  Detonation mechanism: Contact and
  proximity
  Propellant Solid propellant rocket motor
  Operational range: 15 kilometres (9.3 mi)
  Flight altitude: 12,000 meters (39,000 ft)
  Boost time: 2 sec boost, then 15 sec sustain
  Speed: 1,020 m/s
  Guidance system: RF CLOS
  Diameter: 209.6mm
  Steering system: dual-thrust rocket motor.
  Accuracy: 5m
  Launch platform: 9P35M2

MIG-21 (MIG-21UM LANCER B – ROMANIAN)

Type: Fighter aircraft
Country of origin: Soviet Union
First flights: production 1955–85
Dimensions: length 15.76m (with pilot tube),
span 7.154m, height 4.1m
Weight: 4,871kg
Power plant: Tumanskiy R11F-300, 37.27kN
(8,380lbf) thrust dry, 56.27kN (12,650lbf) with
afterburner each
Maximum speed: Mach 2.05 (2,125km/h)
Service ceiling: 19,000m
Radius action: 1,580km

MIG-23 (MIG-23MLD 'FLOGGER-K')

Type: Fighter-bomber aircraft
Country of origin: Soviet Union
First flights: production 1967–85
Dimensions: length 16.70m, span 13.97m,
height 4.82m
Weight: 9,595kg
Power plant: Khatchaturov R-35-300
afterburning turbojet, 83.6kN dry, 127kN
afterburning (18,850lbf/28,700lbf)
Maximum speed: Mach 2.32 (2,445km/h) at
altitude, Mach 1.14 (1,350km/h) at sea level
Service ceiling: 18,500m
Radius action: 1,150km with 6 AAMs combat,
2,820km ferry

POMZ-2 ANTI-PERSONNEL MINE (USSR), THE 'WIDOW-MAKER'

1. Diameter: 5.8cm
2. Height: 13.2cm
3. Fuse: MUV or VPF pull-fuse
4. Operating force: 1kg or more
5. Explosive: 1,08kg TNT
6. Total weight: 2kg

TMI-46 ANTI-TANK MINE (USSR)

1. Diameter: 29.7cm
2. Height: 7.3cm
3. Weight: 8.7kg
4. Fuse: Model MV-5 pressure
5. Operating force: 200kg
6. Explosive: Main charge 5.7kg TNT, booster 196g TNT

D74 122MM FIELD GUN (USSR)

6. Width: 235cm
7. Height: 274.5cm
8. Track: 203cm
9. Clearance: 400mm
10. Tyre size: 12.00x20
11. Height of axis of bore 0°: 166.8cm
12. Elevation: 45°
13. Depression: 5°
14. Traverse: 58°
15. Rate of fire: 6–7rpm
16. MV: 885m/sec
17. Maximum range: 24,000m
18. Armour penetration APHE: 185mm
19. Crew: 10
20. Ammunition: HE APHE

1. Calibre: 12.192m
2. Length of tube in calibres: 47cm
3. Length of tube: 645cm
4. Weight: 5,500kg
5. Length: 987.5cm

DH30 122MM HOWITZER

1. Calibre: 122 mm
2. Maximum range: 21,000m
3. Shell weight: 22kg

APPENDIX VII
ADDITIONAL PHOTOGRAPHIC MATERIAL

32 Battalion commanding officers at Buffalo. From left: Col Jan Breytenbach, Brig Gert Nel, Gen George Meiring, Col Deon Ferreira and Col Eddie Viljoen.

Marius Scheepers, Col Jan Breytenbach and Cmdt Willem Ratte, in 2008.

Colonel Eddie Viljoen, a 32 Battalion Commanding Officer.

Major Jan Hougaard, 32 Battalion Operations Commanding Officer for Operation Dolfyn, taken after Operation Super.

Brigadier-General Eddie Viljoen, the longest serving 32 Battalion CO, with Marius Scheepers. (Photo M. Scheepers)

32 Battalion commemorative tree trunk displaying names of 32 Battalion members who died in action, taken during a parade in Zeerust, 2008.

With a former head of the South African Defence Force, General Jannie Geldenhuys, in 2008.

With a former head of the South African Defence Force, General Constand Viljoen, in 2009.

With a former head of the South African Defence Force, General George Meiring, in 2009.

Inauguration of the Wall of Remembrance at the Voortrekker monument, Pretoria, 2009.

Ex-32 Battalion members and their families attending the inauguration of the Wall of Remembrance at the Voortrekker monument.

The author next to the 32 Battalion tree trunk during its inauguration at the Voortrekker monument, 2009.

32 Battalion tree trunk at the Voortrekker monument.

The entrance of Buffalo base during the author's 2003 visit.

Notes

[1] SANDF military archive original source documents
[2] Original war material confiscated from SWAPO

Glossary

241600B	24=day of month, 16=hours, 00= minutes, B=Bravo time
32 Bn	32 Battalion
61 Mech	61 Mechanized Battalion
AAA	anti-aircraft artillery (14.5mm, 20mm, 35mm)
AFCP	Air Force Command Post
ANC	African National Congress
AP	anti-personnel (mine)
APC	armoured personnel carrier
'ape cage'	observation post high up in a tree
Arty	Artillery
Bde	Brigade
Bn	Battalion
Bty	Battery
c/s	call sign
casevac	casualty (medical) evacuation
CF	Citizen Force
Coy	Company
CSIR	Council for Scientific and Industrial Research
D-Day	date of main assault
DISA	SADF code word for UNITA (*also* Silver Forces)
DZ	drop zone
EF	Enemy Forces
EW	electronic warfare
FAPLA	*Forças Armadas Populares para a Libertação de Angola* (Popular Armed Forces for the Liberation of Angola)
FNLA	*Frente Nacional para a Libertação de Angola* (National Front for the Liberation of Angola)
Gp	Group
HAA	Helicopter Administration Area
HAG	*see* HAA
H-Hour	time of main assault
HQ	headquarters
intrep	intelligence report
JMMK	Joint Military Monitoring *Komitee* (Commission)

kaplyn	cut-line, the border between South West Africa (Namibia) and Angola
KIA	killed in action
LAA	*see* AAA
LZ	landing zone
MAOT	Mobile Air Operations Team
minerep	landmine incident rapport
MK	*Umkhonto we Sizwe* (Spear of the Nation), the armed wing of the ANC
MP	Military Police
MPLA	*Movimento Popular para a Libertaçao de Angola* (Popular Movement for the Liberation of Angola)
MRL	multiple rocket launcher
NSM	national serviceman
OF	Own Forces
Parabats	1 Parachute Battalion unit
PB	*see Povo*
PF	Permanent Force
Pl	Platoon
PLAN	People's Liberation Army of Namibia, SWAPO's armed wing
Povo	local population / people
POW	prisoner of war
recce	reconnaissance
Recces	Reconnaissance Commando / Regiment
RF	Reaction Force
RGK	Regiment Groot Karoo
RMR	Regiment Mooi Rivier
RPG	rocket-propelled grenade
RPS	Regiment President Swart
RPV	remotely piloted vehicle
SAAF	South African Air Force
SADF	South African Defence Force (pre-1994)
SAI	South African Infantry (Battalion)
SANDF	South African National Defence Force (post 1994)
Sec	Section
Sector 10	Ovamboland
Sector 20	Kavango
shona	low-lying marshy area, or pond, dry in the winter months
Silver Forces	*see* DISA / UNITA
sitrep	situation report
SP	SADF classification for black troops
Sqn	Squadron

'States'	SADF slang for South Africa
SWAPO	South West Africa People's Organization
SWATF	South West African Territorial Force
Tac HQ	Tactical Headquarters
TB	tactical / temporary base
THTC	Tobias Hanyeko Training Camp (SWAPO)
tiffy / tiffie	SADF slang for a mechanic (from artificer)
UNITA	*União Nacional para a Independência Total de Angola* (National Union for the Total Independence of Angola)
USSR	Union of Soviet Socialist Republics
WIA	wounded in action

Bibliography

Bopela, Thula, *Umkhonto we Sizwe: Fighting for a Divided People* (Alberton: Galago, 2005)

Bothma, Louis Johannes, *Die Buffel Struikel: 'n Storie van 32 Battalion en sy Mense* (Bloemfontein: L.J. Bothma, 2007)

Bottoman, Wonga Welile, *The Making of an MK Cadre* (LiNc Publishers, 2010)

Breytenbach, Jan, *Eagle Strike: The Story of the Controversial Airborne Assault on Cassinga 1978* (Johannesburg: Manie Grove Publishing, 2008)

Breytenbach, Jan, *Forged in Battle* (Cape Town: Saayman & Weber, c. 1986)

Breytenbach, Jan, *The Buffalo Soldiers: The Story of South Africa's 32 Battalion, 1975-1993* (Alberton: Galago, 2002)

Breytenbach, Jan, *They Live by the Sword,* (Alberton: Lemur, 1990)

Bridgland, Fred, *The War for Africa: Twelve Months that Transformed a Continent* (Gibraltar: Ashanti, 1990)

Cocks, Chris, *Fireforce: One Man's War in the Rhodesian Light Infantry* (Johannesburg: 30° South, 2006)

Friedman, Philip, *Wall of Silence* (Wuppertal: Peter Hammer Verlag, 1995)

Groth, Siegfried, *Namibia, The Wall of Silence: The Dark Days of the Liberation Struggle* (Wuppertal: P. Hammer, 1995)

Heitman, Helmoed-Romer, *South African Armed Forces* (Cape Town: Buffalo Publications, 1990)

Lord, Dick, *From Fledgling to Eagle: The South African Air Force during the Border War* (Johannesburg: 30° South, 2008)

Nortjé, Piet, *32 Battalion: The Inside Story of South Africa's Elite Fighting Unit* (Cape Town: Zebra, 2003)

Steenkamp, Willem, *Suid-Afrika se Grensoorlog, 1966-1989* (Rivonia: Ashanti, 1990)

Stiff, Peter, *The Silent War: South African Recce Operations, 1969-1994* (Alberton: Galago, 1999)

van der Walt, Nico, *To the Bush and Back: A Story About the Last Phase of the South African Border War as Experienced by a Junior Officer of 32 Battalion* (Pretoria: N. van der walt, 2008)

van Wyk, At, *Honoris Crux* (Kaapstad: Saayman & Weber, c. 1985)

van Wyk, At, *Honoris Crux: Ons Dapperes II* (Kaapstad: Saayman & Weber, c. 1985)

Volker, Walter, *9C—Nine Charlie!: Army Signallers in the Field: The Story of the Men and Women of the South African Corps of Signals, and their Equipment* (Pretoria: Veritas Books, 2010)

Wall, Dudley, *Operation Askari 1983-1984 Southern Angola,* http://www.warinangola.com/Portals/31/Op%20Askari%20SWA.pdf (Accessed February 2012)

Wilsworth, Clive, *First In, Last Out: The South African Artillery in Action, 1975-1988* (Johannesburg: 30° South, 2010)

Index

Related titles published by Helion & Company and 30° South Publishers

Four Ball One Tracer: Commanding Executive Outcomes in Angola and Sierra Leone
Roelf van Heerden as told to Andrew Hudson
ISBN (UK)
978-1-907677-76-2
ISBN (SA)
978-1-920143-66-4

Mad Dog Killers: The Story of a Congo Mercenary
Ivan Smith
ISBN (UK)
978-1-907677-78-6
ISBN (SA)
978-1-920143-51-0

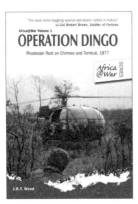

A@W Vol. 1 Operation Dingo: Rhodesian Raid on Chimoio and Tembué,1977
J. R. T. Wood
ISBN
978-1-907677-36-6

A@W Vol. 3 Battle for Cassinga: South Africa's Controversial Cross-Border Raid, Angola 1978
Mike McWilliams
ISBN
978-1-907677-39-7

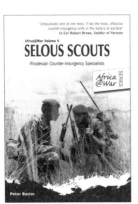

A@W Vol. 4 Selous Scouts: Rhodesian Counter-Insurgency Specialists
Peter Baxter
ISBN
978-1-907677-38-0

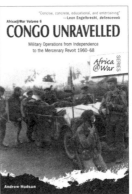

A@W Vol. 6 Congo Unravelled: Military Operations From Independence to The Mercenary Revolt, 1960-68
Andrew Hudson
ISBN (UK)
978-1-907677-63-2
ISBN (SA)
978-1-920143-65-7